Dangerous Tastes

The Story of Spices

PROSPERI ALPINI
MAROSTICENSIS
PHILOSOPHI MEDICI

Et in Gymnasio Patauino Medicamentorum simplicium
Professoris ordinarij, & horti medici Præfecti

DE RHAPONTICO

DISPVTATIO IN GYMNASIO PATAVINO HABITA.

In qua Rhapontici planta, quam hactenus nulli viderunt, me-
cidinæ studiosis nunc ob oculos ponitur, ipsiusque cogni-
tio accuratius expenditur, atque proponitur.

Ad
Perilluſtrem , & Excellentiſſimum D. D. BENEDICTVM
SYLVATICVM Patauinum,& in patrio Gym-
nasio Medic. Pract. Professorem.

PATAVII,
Apud Petrum Bertellium. M. DC. XII.
Ex Typographia Gaspari Criuellarij almæ Vniuerſitatis DD,
Artiſtarum impreſſoris.   Superiorum permiſſu.

DANGEROUS TASTES

The Story of Spices

Andrew Dalby

THE BRITISH MUSEUM PRESS

First published in 2000 by The British Museum Press
A division of The British Museum Company Ltd
46 Bloomsbury Street, London WC1B 3QQ

First published in paperback 2002
Reprinted 2002

A catalogue record for this book is available from the British Library

ISBN 0 7141 2771 X

Cover design by Peter Ward
Designed and typeset in Monotype Photina by Behram Kapadia
Printed in Great Britain by Ebenezer Baylis & Son Ltd

Frontispiece: Title page of Prosper Alpinus, *De rhapontico*, 'On rhubarb' (Padua, 1612), one of the earliest scientific monographs devoted to the medicinal properties of a single spice.

Contents

Preface

This book explores the story of spices and aromatics: the fascination that they have aroused in us, and the roads and seaways by which trade in spices has gradually grown. We observe the spice trade from its various origins in many parts of the world down to the point where modern trade networks begin to cross the globe. We see something of what spices have meant in human history: the pleasure they give, the health they bring, the greed they arouse and the warfare and barbarism that have sometimes resulted. It is a strange story, fascinating to all those who are interested in history, and food history in particular. There have been many histories of the modern spice trade, and several pioneering studies of spices and aromatics in the Classical West and the ancient East, but I believe this is the first book that begins at the beginning and focuses on the spread of human knowledge of spices worldwide.

Although this is not intended as a fully documented history, the sources used are carefully chosen. I hope that what is stated here of early written references to spices will be helpful to historians and archaeologists. I have tried, in the text and glossary, to be precise. For example, although botanists have known the distinct origins of the capsicum species for some decades, I believe this is the first book about spices that treats them separately, linking each with the cultural region in which it was domesticated and cultivated and with the early texts in which it is described.

This book contains several assertions of 'the first time' a certain spice is recorded in use in various parts of the world. These claims, sometimes disagreeing with what is stated in other books, are made on the best evidence I know. Of course they constitute a challenge. I expect that new earlier datings, from unnoticed or reinterpreted texts or from archaeology, will demonstrate that long-distance contact and trade are older than I have been able to show.

Meanwhile, this is a preliminary map of the spice roads. The aromatics now known across the world come from many different regions. Each region became a part of global culture and worldwide trade at a different time. This book explores each of them in turn, interweaving the general history with the story of the discovery and use of individual spices. About sixty of these are highlighted; many others are mentioned in passing, and all are listed and indexed in the glossary.

The information for this book has been largely gathered from ancient and medieval writings. Many of them are quoted directly, because it is important to see exactly what kind of evidence they provide. Whenever the quotations rely on a single already-published translation, I have acknowledged this in a note; but I have often worked directly with the original-language text. The quotations are as accurate as I can make them, but to save unnecessary words many of them have been silently abridged, and place names have often been converted to their modern forms.

It sometimes seems that there are as many spice names as there are speakers of English. This book has a separate glossary and index of spice names, giving many alternative terms and also the botanical name of the species from which each spice originates.

The historical weights and measures quoted in this book are on the following scales. The unit of volume is 1 pint (1.2 US pints, 0.55 litre); in the recipe for Aminaean wine (page 103) an amphora equals 48 pints (58 US pints, 26 litres). The usual unit of weight in this book is 1 lb. or pound (0.45 kg), which divides into 16 oz. or ounces; 1 ounce divides into 6 dr. or drams, and 1 dram divides into 3 scruples. When Columbus took on board 'half a ton' of the plants he thought were aloes (page 150), this was 1,120 lb. or 508 kg.

The historical prices quoted here are on the traditional scale in which 1 l., libra, livre or pound (in origin a pound of silver) was divided into 20 s., solidi, sous or shillings and the latter was divided into 12 d., denarii, deniers, dinars or pence. In ancient Roman currency, the denarius further divided into 4 sestertii. The Spanish colonial dollar or piece-of-eight, mentioned on page 145, was worth between 4 s. and 5 s. on this scale. 'Threescore crowns' (page 61) equalled 15 l.

Arabic and Indian words and names are generally given in the standard romanization, but, to smooth the path from author's to publisher's computer, long vowels are marked with the old-fashioned circumflex accent (^) instead of the modern macron (‾). Chinese appears here in Pinyin romanization.

In working on *Dangerous Tastes* I have read, in recent books and articles, that Alexander the Great introduced pepper to Greece; that Shen Nung, legendary founder of Chinese medicine, mentioned cassia in a herbal written in 2700 BC; that the plant source of *costus*, such a popular aroma in ancient Rome, is now unknown or extinct; that the plant source of the famous spice *silphium* still grows somewhere in the Maghreb and has been called *Ferula tingitana* by a reputable botanist. And I have been told by several twentieth-century British historians (but no others) that spices served in medieval times to 'mask the taste of putrid food'. All these statements are false: if you want to know the truth, read on!

I have also read of the ancient Spice Route, officially so named under UNESCO auspices. It crossed the sea from eastern Indonesia by way of Sri Lanka and southern India to the Arabian coast (which is true enough). It also ran north from eastern Indonesia by way of the Philippines to China, Korea and Japan (which is false, or at least unverified). But, as is explained below, this route from China to Indonesia by way of the Philippines really is of crucial importance in the prehistory of spices. It was along this route that ginger and sugar were transplanted, on the first stage of their worldwide expansion.

I have found existing books on and around spices indispensable. Some particular acknowledgements are made in the footnotes. I want to record here that I have frequently appealed to Alan Davidson's *Oxford companion to food*, E. H. Schafer's *The golden peaches of Samarkand* and *The vermilion bird*, Stephen Facciola's *Cornucopia*, Nigel Groom's *New perfume handbook*, the scientific work *Spices* by Purseglove and others, and *Martindale: the extra pharmacopoeia*; these and other useful books are listed in full on pages 162–4. I have enjoyed, and used, Charles Corn's recent *The scents of Eden* and Giles Milton's equally recent *Nathaniel's nutmeg*. And although I have sometimes cursed the fuzzy logic of Miller's *The spice trade of the Roman Empire*, still I have been very glad that his book existed.

I want to thank Anne Flavell at the Bodleian, and Jill Butterworth and Elizabeth Harrisson at Cambridge University Library, for their help. I hope my fellow members of a certain international organization will find that *Dangerous Tastes*, should it come to their attention, will serve to disturb one or two cobwebs on the shelf marked 'spices'.

The phoenix's nest

She collects the spices and aromas that the Assyrian
gathers, and the rich Arab; those that are harvested by the
Pygmy peoples and by India, and that grow in the soft
bosom of the Sabaean land.

ANONYMOUS LATIN POEM.

The story of spices

Human beings will always be searching for the exotic – for what we cannot get
at home. Trade by land and sea, difficult, slow, costly, dangerous as it has
always been, has brought the flavours and aromas of the other side of the
world to our food and festivity.

'The other side of the world' is literally true. Spices are among the earliest products
that have crossed the globe in trade networks. This book traces the early travels of
ginger, sugar, frankincense and myrrh, musk and ambergris, cinnamon, nutmeg and
cloves. In doing so it visits China, central Asia, Russia, Iran and Iraq, Indonesia,
Malaysia, India, Sri Lanka, Madagascar, Arabia, Egypt, west Africa and many
European countries. The explosion of new spice routes after Columbus brings more
regions into the story: Florida, Mexico, the Caribbean, Ecuador, Brazil and Peru.

Spices are aromatics, used in food, festivity and medicine: natural products, traditionally prepared for long storage and distant travel. The parallel story of herbs is not
told here. In that story the leading role is taken by gardeners, not traders, for the virtue
of herbs is at its peak when they are fresh and green. 'Spice', in this book, is defined by
distant origin and long-distance trade, as well as unique aroma (see 'What spices are',
page 16).

Spices have figured in legend and history for thousands of years. When Joseph was
sold by his brothers, the buyers were spice merchants on their way from Arabia to
Egypt (page 33); the incident is a turning point in the traditional history of Israel.

When the Queen of Sheba visited Solomon and tested his wisdom, his reward for success was a royal gift of the spices of Arabia (page 34); later writers were sure that this was the occasion when the balsam of Mecca was transplanted to Jerusalem. The hunger for spices has brought about some of the great events in our history, including the opening of the sea route around Africa by Vasco da Gama (page 101) and almost simultaneously the discovery by Christopher Columbus of a New World which, as he hastened to explain to his sponsors, was stocked with old and new spices (page 149).

But spices are truly a dangerous taste. The Assyrians fought and killed for the spice tribute of Arabia (page 101). The Romans, having butchered the desperate defenders of Jerusalem in the First Jewish Revolt (page 34), shipped living balsam trees to Rome to figure in the triumphal procession that marked their bloody victory.

Genoese and Venetians engaged in a long struggle for the spice trade of medieval Europe. The soldiers of the Fourth Crusade sacked Constantinople at the suggestion of Venice, and thus gave Venice control of the city's legendary spice trade (page 125). Genoese rule over Chios, giving them a monopoly of the trade in mastic, was one of the impulses for Columbus' voyage (page 150).

After the Discoveries, European states rivalled one another in greed and barbarity. The Portuguese lied and killed for control of Colombo and Malacca (page 43). The first English overseas possession, the tiny Indonesian island of Run, was wiped out by the Dutch (page 63), who reduced whole islands to poverty and exterminated the inhabitants of others in a doomed attempt to monopolize the trade in cloves and nutmeg. Spanish, French and British rulers of the Caribbean were equally ruthless; their vast plantations of sugar and other crops, using slave labour, led to economic collapse and misery (page 29). In the nineteenth century, threatened by a similar collapse of the price of opium, Britain fought two wars to force China to continue importing the opium of British India (page 135). China's pioneering attempt to eliminate opium addiction was set back by decades, and we still suffer the consequences.

As enthralling as the gold of El Dorado, the legendary cinnamon of La Canela (page 152) led Gonzalo Pizarro and his 2,000-strong expedition to exhaustion and death in the forests of Ecuador, in a two-year-long quest from which only 80 returned, naked and starving. Yet this hunt for American cinnamon led to an astonishing achievement: a breakaway party, under Francisco de Orellana, were the first Europeans ever to explore the whole course of the Amazon.

The mystery of spices

Two thousand years ago the Roman poet Vergil, in his verse outline of the agriculture business, knew that it was part of his task to describe '*Quid quaeque ferat regio et quid quaeque recusat*' ('the products that each country will bear and those that it refuses'). 'Each tree has its own homeland,' he explains. 'Only India bears the black ebony; the incense bush belongs to the Sabaeans alone. Then there is balsam, sweating from its aromatic wood...'[1]

Balsam of Mecca was not the best example of what Vergil had in mind. This spice originated, quite certainly, in southern Arabia. Later it was naturalized in Palestine; people often said that it had been brought there by the Queen of Sheba as a gift to King Solomon. So it was an exception to the usual rule. Although plenty of fruits and vegetables were transplanted across great distances by ancient gardeners, hardly any spices were. For millennia they kept their high price: it resulted partly from the cost of transport, partly from their rarity. There was generally only one place where they would grow, and Vergil was right: 'each tree has its own homeland.'

To arouse readers' wonder at the magical lifestyle of the phoenix, all that a poet needed to do was to list the spices from all over the world with which the Arabian bird builds her nest.

> She collects the spices and aromas that the Assyrian gathers, and the rich Arab; those that are harvested by the Pygmy peoples and by India, and that grow in the soft bosom of the Sabaean land. She collects cinnamon, the perfume of far-wafting amomum, balsams mixed with tejpat leaves; there is also a slip of gentle cassia and gum arabic, and the rich teardrops of frankincense. She adds the tender spikes of downy nard and the power of Panchaea's myrrh.[2]

To turn an imagined orchard into an imagined earthly Paradise, all that was needed was to plant a selection of spices among the fruit trees. Only poets could do this.

'My sister, my promised bride, is a walled garden; a garden within walls, a fountain as yet sealed,' writes a Hebrew love poet of the third century BC, whose work is known to us as the *Song of Songs*. Then he addresses the intended bride: 'Your scions shall be an orchard of fruit trees, and their fruit will be pomegranates. Yours are the rarest of spices: nard and saffron, *calamus* and cinnamon, and all the trees that bear incense; myrrh and aloes, and all the subtlest of aromas.'[3]

'There were two or three of every fruit-bearing tree,' begins Guillaume de Lorris in a dream sequence in the thirteenth-century French *Romance of the Rose*, 'except maybe the ugly ones. There were apple trees, I remember, heavily laden with pomegranates, a fruit so good for the sick; walnut trees whose fruits in season were like nutmegs, neither bitter nor bland.' Then, as if this incidental mention of nutmegs reminds him of the whole world of spices, he lets his imagination run riot. 'In that orchard grew many a spice: cloves, licorice, fresh grains of Paradise, zedoary, anise, cinnamon and every delectable spice that is good to taste after the meal.'[4]

Spices came in small quantities from very restricted locations. They also came, most of them, from the very edge of the known world. There were wonders and deadly dangers in these remote seas: European, Arab and Chinese observers agree. Cosmas, an adventurous Greek spice merchant of the sixth century, writes:

> One day, as we sailed rather far on along the African coast beyond Zanzibar, a place that is called the Mouth of the Ocean, we saw to our right a mass of birds

in flight, called albatrosses, at least twice as big as kites. The air was bad there, too. We were all afraid, and the crew and the merchants who had experienced this before said that we were close to Ocean. 'Turn back,' they said to the captain, 'or we shall be taken by the currents and fall towards the Ocean and we shall all be lost.' Where the Ocean meets the known sea it creates a monstrous wave, and there is an undertow from the sea towards the Ocean. We were terrified. Some of those birds called albatrosses flew with us a long way, high in the sky, as if to warn us that Ocean was still near.[5]

There are several such narratives of ancient and medieval travellers who had gone too close to the edge of the world. The Arab merchants, in the centuries after Cosmas' travels, pushed further towards the east: they found more spices and aromatics, but they also found new wonders and new dangers. The Arab geographer Ibn Khurdâdhbih writes:

Beyond Sarandîb is the island of Râmî where the rhinoceros lives: it is an animal bigger than the elephant but smaller than the buffalo. This island produces bamboo and brazilwood, whose roots are effective against deadly poisons. Sailors have in the past used this as medicine in cases of snakebite. In the forests there are people who go stark naked and whose language is a kind of inarticulate whistling. They avoid other peoples. Their hair is a reddish fur. They climb the trees with their hands without using their feet.

In this sea is an island of white people who can swim out to ships, even in stormy weather. They bring ambergris in their teeth and exchange it for iron.[6]

Sarandîb is Sri Lanka. We are crossing the Bay of Bengal, therefore; Râmî is probably Sumatra. The 'forest people' are not humans but *orang utan*, a name which really does mean 'forest people' in Malay. But the white people are the human inhabitants of the Nicobar Islands, and this is really how the Arab traders, in the ninth century, got their ambergris; we shall read another description that confirms it.

They dared to go beyond Sumatra, too, but not far beyond, for once more they were approaching the edge of the world. South-east of the coast of Indochina, wrote Mas'ûdî around 950,

is the realm of Maharaja, the king of the islands, who commands a limitless empire and an infinite army. The fastest vessel could not visit all his islands within two years. They produce all kinds of spices and aromatics. No king in all the world makes so much profit from his territories. These islands export camphor, aloeswood, cloves, sandalwood, areca nut, nutmeg, cardamom, cubebs and others that I cannot list. Towards the China Sea they border on an ocean whose extent and limits are unknown.[7]

This *Mahârâja* (a word that simply means 'great king' in Sanskrit) was also to be visited by Sindbad the sailor. Mas'ûdî bases his description of the semi-fictional realm on earlier, less literary reports by mariners who had really been in these parts. In doing so he succeeds in painting a picture in which everybody believed, not least the adventurous seamen themselves: a picture of the wondrous wealth of the spice islands on the doubtful eastern edge of the world.

This Eastern Sea – adds Dimashqî, who wrote in the fourteenth century – is sometimes called the Sea of Pitch, because it is dark and shadowy. Its shores lie at the eastern extremity of the world. Beyond, nothing is known. According to the Greek geographer Ptolemy and others, there are six islands in this sea, the isles of Sîlâ, rich in many minerals and precious stones. They are populous, and those who once reach them never want to leave, because of the pleasant climate, the sweet water, the beautiful women and the abundance of all good things.

> On the shores of this sea, towards the north, are three stone statues cut from the living rock, with terrifying faces. They stretch out their hands towards the sea, showing by their fearsome expressions that the voyager must go no further. At Cadiz and in the Fortunate Isles [the Canaries], at the gateway to the Outer Ocean of the West, there are similar statues that warn the voyager to venture no further upon the Green Sea.[8]

It was sometimes said that the statues had been erected by Alexander the Great himself.

These terrors were one day to be overcome. The great explorers of the fifteenth and sixteenth centuries at last crossed the 'edge of the world', and changed the world of spices for ever. In the 1560s Nicolás Monardes of Seville, in a lively and innovative survey of the new spices and drugs of the Americas, returns to Vergil's idea – the unique products of each region – and takes it a step further. Here are his examples of famous exotics, quoted in an Elizabethan translation by John Frampton:

> The philosopher doeth saie, that all Countries doeth not give Plantes and Fruites alike: for one Region yeldeth suche Fruites, Trees, and Plantes, as an other doeth not, we doe see that in Creta onely groweth the Diptamo, and the Incence onely in the Region of Saba, and the Almaciga onely in Ilande of Chio, and the Sinamom, Cloves, and Peper, and other spices onely in the Ilandes of the Maluca, and many other thynges you have in divers partes of the worlde, whiche was not knowen untill our tyme, and the people of old tyme did lacke them.

Precisely this – the exciting discoveries of previously unknown spices and aromatics in the age of the great explorations – formed the theme of Monardes' work. It happens to be especially well brought out in the English translation. Monardes was not very interested in titles, but Frampton or his publisher decided on a new and upbeat title for English publication, *Joyfull Newes out of the Newe Founde Worlde*.[9]

Nearly all of Monardes' examples, in the passage just quoted, will find their place in this book (but not Cretan dittany, which is a herb, not a spice). Here in his list is the incense of Sabaea once more; alongside it we recognize the 'almaciga' or mastic of Chios, and the cinnamon, cloves and pepper of the East. All these had been so costly in western Europe, and so essential as flavourings and medicines, that the search for direct access to them had been one of the chief impulses for the explorers.

Vasco da Gama opened the route to India for the Portuguese so that they need no longer rely on the Venetians and the Arabs for their spices. And it worked. In spite of the long voyage around Africa, in spite of the shipwrecks, the East India merchants of Portugal, Holland and England showed handsome profits.

Christopher Columbus, when it became clear that he had not discovered a fast route to the East Indies after all, but merely discovered the unexpected continent of America, offered two consolations to his patrons Ferdinand and Isabella, the Catholic monarchs of Spain: one, that there would certainly be gold; two, that he had already found new supplies of some of the costliest spices. We quote from his own papers later. Meanwhile, here is the adventurous Dr Chanca's report from the island of Hispaniola in 1494, written on one of Columbus' ships and addressed to the municipality of Seville: 'There are some trees which I think bear nutmegs but are not in fruit at present. I say "I think" because the smell and taste of the bark resembles nutmegs. I saw a root of ginger, which an Indian had tied round his neck. There is also aloes: it is not of a kind which has hitherto been seen in our country, but I am in no doubt that it has medicinal value. There is also very good mastic.' There were in reality no nutmegs, ginger, aloes or mastic in the West Indies; but the urge to find these products was very powerful.

Science accompanied trade – the revitalized science of the European Renaissance. It was now that Pierre Belon and Prosper Alpinus searched the shores of the eastern Mediterranean for the forgotten medicinal plants that they knew from Greek and Latin texts. It was possible now for the Portuguese physician García de Orta, working in Goa, to discover the real origins of spices about which so many legends had been told; to match names and descriptions from Greek, Latin, Arabic and Aramaic medical books; to gather new knowledge of their dietary and medical effects from Indian colleagues. His 'Conversations on the simples, drugs and medicinal products of India' provide some vivid quotations below. It was possible for Nicolás Monardes in Seville and his successors to experiment with the new spices of the New World – allspice, vanilla, chocolate; to test each species newly imported in bulk, or specially sent by correspondents in America; to compare them with the eastern products that they seemed to resemble and determine their real dietary value. In doing so, they asked some of the questions whose answers would eventually sound the death-knell of the age-old humoral theory. And new attempts were now made to transplant many species from their original unique homelands.

These were all the more likely to succeed because new colonial possessions provided suitably tropical habitats and climates. When the classical Greeks tried to transplant frankincense to Egypt, it failed. When Marco Polo planted brazilwood seeds in the lands near Venice, they did not germinate. But nowadays everyone has heard of Jamaica ginger. Nutmeg, too, does well in the West Indies now, and cinnamon is a staple of the economy of the Seychelles. Mastic, still produced only by the twelve mastic villages in southern Chios, is today an unusual case.

What spices are

If we concentrate for the moment on early history, it is easy to say what spices are. They are natural products from a single limited region that are in demand and fetch a high price, far beyond their place of origin, for their flavour and odour. These power-ful, pleasurable, sensual aromatics have been used in foods, drinks, scented oils and ~es, perfumes and cosmetics, drugs; in these various forms they have served human ... digestives, antiseptics, therapeutics, tonics, aphrodisiacs.

In most cultures ....es no sharp boundary existed between foods and drugs. The way to health was a correct diet and lifestyle, adjusted to one's constitution and to the climate. 'An apple a day keeps the doctor away' – and keeping the doctor away was much more advisable in those days than it is now. Spices and aromatics were different from other foods simply because they were more powerful; so, in traditional systems of medicine, they were particularly in demand as a good way of adjusting the diet. They were specially needed to correct serious illnesses (which were signs that the constitution was gravely out of order) and they were specially needed by the rich, who were tempted to live and eat unhealthily.

If evidence is wanted that foods, drugs and spices are traditionally part of a con-tinuum, we need only recall that a fair proportion of the stock of a traditional French épicerie (literally 'spicery') would match that of an old-fashioned US drugstore – and of a modern delicatessen (literally 'fine food'). And the traditional view retains validity. Foods, and spices in particular, actually do have good and bad effects on health. Several spices are still in the pharmacopoeia. In countries such as Britain and the USA, health food shops supply some of the traditional spices that are not to be found in supermarkets.

But modern medicine draws on a vast range of drugs, many of which are artificial and most of which have never been traded as spices. The modern food trade deals in fruits, vegetables, meat and fish that are transported all over the world in large quan-tities, often deep-frozen, to present themselves as whole and fresh to the eventual con-sumer; most of these well-travelled commodities have never been traded as spices either. Spices still have their role, but most of them are not particularly expensive any more. So, in the modern world, what are spices exactly?

This book is about the traditional spices. We concentrate on those that are still part of world trade, still serve as powerful flavourings, still lend their unique aromas to the spice markets of ancient cities: cinnamon and cloves, ginger and pepper, saffron and chilli. We deal with aromatics that are now little used in food but still belong to the spice trade and to traditional medicine: frankincense, myrrh, aloeswood, balsam of Mecca. We say a good deal, in the course of our exploration, about the products that used to be spices of world importance and are now almost forgotten: long pepper, cubebs, grains of Paradise. We meet some that are nowadays so widespread and common that no one thinks of them as spices any more: sugar, chocolate. We consider one or two that are lost: no one can ever know the wondrous flavour that they once imparted to food and festivity.

Silphium

That is how it is with silphium.

This legendary spice became known to the ancient Greeks, we are told, in 638 BC. Just seven years later Greek colonists founded Cyrene in a fertile valley on the north African coast within easy reach of the silphium country. From that date onwards, for six hundred years and more, Cyrene was a rich city, rich from the profits of the silphium trade.

The Greek scientist Theophrastus, in his *Study of Plants*, tells us what silphium looked like and how it was harvested. Theophrastus' information is based on enquiries made at Cyrene. His informant had not necessarily seen silphium growing, but the details must be roughly true because – as we now know – asafoetida, a very similar spice, is still obtained in almost this way.

> Silphium has a big thick root, a stem as long as giant fennel and just about as thick, and a leaf similar to celery. The valuable product is the resin. The silphium collectors tap in accordance with a sort of mining-concession: it is not permitted to cut at random, nor indeed to cut more than the ration, because the resin spoils and decays with age. If it is for export to Athens they put it in jars, mixing flour with it, and shake it. Under this treatment it develops a colour, and it remains stable during the voyage.
>
> It is found over a large region of the north African coast, but commonest along the eastern side of the Syrtes bay. The unusual thing is that it avoids cultivated land: it is retreating as the land is gradually brought under cultivation and farmed. Far from requiring husbandry, it is a quintessentially wild plant.[10]

How was silphium used? This is easy to answer. Greeks were always using it in cookery. They partnered it with vegetables. They loved its flavour and aroma in combination with meat: in sauces for roast meat, but particularly with their favourite rich, strong-tasting meat dishes such as tripe, udder and sow's womb. 'As you sip your wine,' wrote the early gourmet Archestratus, 'have served some such relish as this: tripe or boiled sow's womb marinated in cumin and sharp vinegar and silphium, and the tender tribe of birds, such as are in season.' Archestratus disapproved of silphium with fresh fish – 'Let no Syracusan and none of the Greeks of Italy come near you when you make this dish. They will spoil it by putting cheese over everything and dousing it with watery vinegar and pickled silphium;' yet strong flavours such as that of salted tuna were thought to suit silphium very well. And that unusual creature the sea-squirt (*Microcosmus sulcatus*) went well with silphium, as explained by the dietary writer Xenocrates: 'The sea-squirt is cut and rinsed and seasoned with Cyrenaic silphium and rue and brine and vinegar, or with fresh mint in vinegar and sweet wine.'[11]

Silphium was excellent for the digestion, so the ancient Greek medical texts tell us, though it was so powerful that it might upset those trying it for the first time. It is tempting to conclude that silphium did for ancient Greek cuisine something of what onion and garlic do for modern English or French food.

Romans liked silphium too. It was a costly spice, and if you wanted to buy good-quality silphium on the Roman spice market, you would have to look carefully. 'Its quality is shown in being reddish and translucent, myrrh-like and powerfully scented, not greenish, not rough in taste, not readily turning white,' writes Dioscorides in a first-century manual of pharmacology.[12] Roman physicians used silphium in eye-drops, in which it was mixed with gum ammoniac or with lentisk resin. They also appreciated its digestive qualities: 'Pepper, white if any, if not black, 3 oz.; celery seed 2 oz.; *laser* root, which Greeks call *silphium*, 1½ oz.; cheese 2 oz. Crush and sift them, mix with honey, keep in a new jar. When called for, mix just the quantity required with vinegar and fish sauce. If you have Syrian *laser* instead of *silphium*, better to increase by half an ounce.'[13]

But the Romans of the first century AD were the last people who ever tasted silphium. Why did it disappear? This is uncertain. The geographer Strabo, writing a century before the end, suggests that problems had arisen between the gatherers of silphium and the people of Cyrene who marketed it. 'It came close to dying out when the natives, in the course of some dispute, erupted and destroyed the roots of the plant. They are nomads.' Though Strabo did not yet realize it, this must have been the beginning of the final chapter. A hundred years after him, the encyclopaedist Pliny tells the sad story: 'For many years now silphium has not been seen in that region, since the agents who lease grazing land, scenting higher profits, overgraze it for sheep pasture. The single stem found within living memory was sent to the emperor Nero.'[14]

And what did the Greeks and Romans do, after Nero had consumed the last surviving stem of silphium? They had found a silphium substitute just in time, thanks to the expedition of Alexander the Great and his exploration of the Hindu Kush mountain range of Afghanistan. 'In these mountains nothing but terebinth trees and silphium grow,' a historian explains, and the geographer Strabo adds detail: 'Alexander crossed the mountains to Bactria by ways that were barren but for a little shrubby terebinth, so short of food that the soldiers had to eat their horses and so short of wood that they had to eat them raw; but with the raw meat their digestive was silphium, which grew there plentifully.'[15]

We shall return later to the story of this new silphium, known to us as asafoetida or hing, and to botanists as *Ferula assa-foetida*.

There have been claims, from time to time, that silphium has been rediscovered, somewhere near its original habitat in north Africa. No such claim has yet been proved. All that is required is a plant of the genus *Ferula*, or something very like it, producing a resin with a certain definite flavour and with certain nutritional and medicinal qualities. The appearance of the plant, the flavour of the resin and its dietary effects are all clearly described in the texts, and the plant is pictured on coins of Cyrene. But asafoetida as known today is very similar, botanically, agriculturally and as a finished product, to ancient silphium: so, if we rediscover silphium, it has to resemble asafoetida. And yet if silphium continued to grow anywhere on the north African coast through Roman times, it would be surprising that local people who knew its high value on the Roman market never found it and exploited it; and if there were ever any stands of silphium plants further inland, the increasing aridity of the Sahara would eventually have put an end to them.

Exports from Paradise

Graynes of Paradise: hoote and moyst they be.
JOHN RUSSELL, *Boke of Nurture.*

An Eastern crossroads

The islands of the Malay archipelago are dangerous and yet enticing. In almost every century, violent earthquakes and frequent volcanic eruptions have destroyed villages and cities. Malaria has been endemic. Threats to life abound in the jungle. Sea travel is far from safe. The hot, humid climate attacks most of the things that people make and build. Warfare has been frequent here. It still is: renewed Christian-Muslim conflict in the Spice Islands is reported as I write.

But meanwhile the heat and moisture combine to make these islands astonishingly fertile. Agriculture is productive and seafood is plentiful; the forests offer good hunting and a wealth of fruits and herbs. It is no surprise that Java, one of the islands of this archipelago, is among the most heavily populated places on earth.

The smaller islands, fertile though most of them are, do not offer the range of produce and resources that humans have come to demand. Even tens of thousands of years ago, and even through the times when sea level has fluctuated and some now-separate islands were joined, travelling by sea has been the best solution when people have wanted to meet, to migrate and to exchange the staples and the luxuries of life. Out of all the regions of the world this is the one where sea trade first became a daily habit and a daily necessity.

Among the myriad landfalls of the archipelago are the Moluccas, the Spice Islands. In local markets their wonderful products are just one commodity among many. But already, two thousand years ago, the cloves of Ternate and Tidore were passing from hand to hand along complex trade routes and were regularly travelling the many thousands of miles that led eventually to India, east Africa and Europe. Already the greed for exotic spices, from fabulous southern and eastern islands, was growing. It would lead to the great explorations, to war and colonization, to slavery and genocide.

Far earlier than two thousand years ago, the islands where cloves and nutmeg grow were already at a crossroads in the history of aromatics. Two more of the world's great spices – ginger and cane sugar – were transplanted, by way of these very seas, to new habitats. In the course of their migrations they turned gradually from local delicacies into commodities of world trade.

So, for better and for worse, the distant Spice Islands have shaped the course of history, Milton's 'isles of *Ternate* and *Tidore*, whence merchants bring thir spicie drugs'.[1] If we are to explore the spice trade from its beginnings, we must begin precisely here.

Ginger

By the fourth millennium BC – six thousand years ago – the 'Austronesians' were beginning to spread southwards across the Malay archipelago, starting from the coast of south-eastern China and from mountainous Taiwan (Formosa, 'the beautiful', as Europeans later named it). No written history, and no surviving oral tradition, tells of this epic series of migrations. Eventually they reached as far as Madagascar on the western edge of the Indian Ocean and even distant Easter Island in the eastern Pacific.

We know of the migration by linguistic detective work. This vast region extends 5,000 miles (8,000 km) north to south and 6,500 miles (10,500 km) west to east. Practically all the languages spoken here, from Atayal of Taiwan to Maori of New Zealand, from Malagasy of Madagascar to Rapanui of Easter Island, belong to a single language family that linguists now call Austronesian. In other words, they can all be traced to one ancestral language, long since disappeared, once spoken in southern China, conventionally called proto-Austronesian. The people who have spoken these languages can be labelled 'Austronesians'.

Among the typical flora of southern China and Indochina are the wild gingers and their relatives – showy plants with typically large white or yellow flowers, spicy, aromatic, very important in traditional medicine. These include galanga, zedoary and zerumbet, discussed later. For the present, we concentrate on ginger itself, because there are two good clues that ginger is a very ancient spice, perhaps the most ancient of all.

The botanical clue is that, unlike its relatives, ginger is propagated only by splitting the root, never from seed – a sign that it has grown for so long under human control that it has lost one of the essential characteristics of the wild plant from which it derives. This happens to be true of several major cultivated plants, but of scarcely any spices.

The linguistic clue is that a name for ginger can be traced back from its modern forms in many of the Austronesian languages to the early Austronesian speech of the Philippines. This means that in all their long migrations from the Philippines onwards the speakers of Austronesian languages never lost their familiarity with ginger. Yet the florae of each island group are different, and ginger could not be native to them all. There is only one good answer to the puzzle: the Austronesian speakers carried ginger with them on their voyages.

In the boats that humans built in those ancient times there was no room for luxuries. Ginger, then, must have been recognized as a necessity of life. The speakers of early Austronesian languages were so familiar with the value of this plant – a spice, herb and medicine – that they knew they would need it *en route*. As a matter of fact we know that more recent navigators of the Indian Ocean did exactly the same: 'they plant potherbs, vegetables and ginger in wooden troughs,' says the fourteenth-century Arabic traveller Ibn Baṭūṭâ of the Chinese mariners he encountered in southern India.[2]

Finding that it did not already grow where they planned to settle, the Austronesian-speaking migrants planted ginger in their gardens on each new island. Thus it spread from southern China to the Philippines and the Spice Islands – and, from that crossroads, onwards both east and west, to New Guinea and to Java, to Sumatra and the Malay peninsula on either side of the Straits of Malacca. Eventually it spread much further still.

English children are likely to enjoy the biscuits popularly known as 'ginger nuts' and ginger beer long before they first encounter ginger wine and preserved ginger; until quite recently, it would have been longer still before they were likely to see the fresh root and experience the effect of ginger in Thai and Cantonese cookery. Many will never taste the stem or the flower. To most English-speaking readers of this book, ginger, while an attractive flavouring, has been a luxury rather than a necessity of life.

Why, then, did ginger spread so far and so early? Why was it in demand?

The traditional medicine of the Greeks and Romans, two thousand years ago, begins our exploration of the written history of ginger. To physicians and pharmacists of the early Roman Empire, like Dioscorides, ginger (*zingiberi*) came as an exotic eastern plant – but not from so very far off as we might expect. 'Zingiberi is a different plant from pepper,' he writes, 'grown mostly in Eritrea and Arabia, where they use it fresh, as we use leeks, boiling it for soup and including it in stews. It is a small tuber, like galanga: whitish, peppery in flavour and aromatic. You must choose roots that are not worm-eaten. Some producers pickle it, to preserve it, and export it in jars to Italy: it is very nice to eat like this, pickle and all.' So we learn from Dioscorides that already the adventurous sailors of the Indian Ocean had planted ginger in Eritrea and east Africa, 5,000 miles (8,000 km) from its native habitat. It still grows there today. And from Dioscorides' next sentence we learn when and why Greek dieticians prescribed ginger to their patients: 'Its effect is warming, digestive, gently laxative, appetizing; it helps in cases of cataract, and it is an ingredient in antidotes against poison.'[3]

Latin sources fill out the picture. Ginger was one of the ingredients in the famous *Mithridaticum*, the antidote against all poisons regularly taken by King Mithridates of Pontus (the recipe is quoted later in this book). Pliny, first-century author of the

Natural History, agrees with Dioscorides that ginger was farmed in north-east Africa. He adds that a pound of ginger cost six *denarii* in the first century AD – three days' wages for a working man – making it a little cheaper than pepper, and one of the cheapest of the exotic spices that came to Rome. The Roman recipe book *Apicius* seems to tell us that ginger was used rather sparingly in the Roman kitchen; but it was needed in digestives, in which its heating power would help to counteract other foods such as the chilling lettuce.

> Take lettuce with *oxyporum*, vinegar and a little fish sauce. This will help diges-
> tion, prevent wind, and make the lettuce wholesome.
>   *Oxyporum* is made as follows: 2 oz. cumin, 1 oz. ginger, 1 oz. fresh rue,
> 12 scruples juicy dates, 1 oz. pepper, 9 oz. honey; the cumin may be Ethiopian,
> Syrian or Libyan. Pound the cumin, then moisten with vinegar. Let it dry, and
> bind all with honey. When needed, mix half a spoonful with vinegar and a
> little fish sauce. Or, as a digestive after the meal, take half a spoonful neat.[4]

With its piquant flavour and health-giving effects, ginger was both a necessity and a pleasure. In the *Qur'ân*, the sacred text of Islam, we can read of ginger (*zanjabîl*) as one of the two aromatics of the next world.

> The righteous shall drink of a cup tempered at the Camphor Fountain. God will
> reward them for their steadfastness with robes of silk and the delights of
> Paradise. Reclining there upon soft couches, they shall feel neither the scorch-
> ing heat nor the biting cold. Trees will spread their shade around them, and
> fruits will hang in clusters over them. They shall be served with silver dishes,
> and beakers as large as goblets, silver goblets which they themselves shall mea-
> sure; and brimming cups from the Fountain of Ginger.[5]

In this carefully planned Paradise camphor guards against the scorching heat; ginger is the spice that keeps out the biting cold. Later Arabic and Persian dieticians regarded ginger as 'hot in the third degree', their highest category, and prescribed it in cases of impotence. Their long-distance trade links allowed them to make the first comparative tasting, and so to distinguish between Chinese ginger – the original stock, the most expensive, and in their view still the best – and Zanzibar ginger, descended from the roots that had long ago been transplanted to Madagascar, the Comores and the east African coast.

While this long migration had taken ginger southwards and westwards, it was nat-urally still prized in its homeland. Ginger has long been an indispensable ingredient in the cookery of the south of China – Cantonese cuisine as we know it now. To the north, where Chinese civilization and medicine developed, ginger was already well known by about 160 BC (the date at which it is first found in excavations of Han tombs) and was certainly available some time earlier.

Five hundred years after that, when Ji Han compiled his *Nanfang caomu zhuang* or 'Plants of the South', ginger was so well known to his fellow-northerners that he does not trouble to describe it. It was slightly exotic – it would not survive northern winters – and not quite an everyday flavouring, as it was in the south. It was important, none the less, in diet and medicine. Ginger was a heating agent: it combated cold diseases and favoured sexual potency and fertility. Ji Han does mention one of the so-called wild gingers, *Alpinia chinensis*, which is sometimes grown in gardens in Guangxi and Vietnam. 'To drink water in which this wild ginger has been boiled,' he writes, is 'very effective in treating cold.' Other 'wild gingers' were cultivated and also belong to the tradition of Chinese medicine. *Zingiber mioga*, mioga ginger, has edible shoots and flowers. *Alpinia kumatake*, kao-liang ginger, was dispatched northwards in the annual tribute offerings from the island of Hainan. Like ground ginger, it was regarded as specially effective against the 'cold' disease cholera.

Nearly a thousand years after Ji Han, Marco Polo travelled through the ginger country of south-western China. To him, though not to his predecessor, ginger was a rare and exotic spice. After twenty days of mountain roads Marco Polo emerged into a wide valley on the northern edge of Sichuan and observed that 'this province produces such a vast quantity of ginger that it is exported throughout the whole of Cathay, bringing great profit.' Meanwhile a medieval Chinese trader noted that dried ginger peel – the most powerful part of the root, with a special place in Chinese medicine – was an article of trade in its own right and was imported to China from Cambodia, a sign that in those days Cambodia was also one of the places where ginger was conserved.[6]

In medieval Europe ginger was costly and much in demand. Its heat was proverbial. 'He's of the colour of the nutmeg,' says the Duke of Orleans, appraising the Dauphin's horse, in Shakespeare's *Henry V*. 'And of the heat of the ginger,' the Dauphin counters.[7]

Like the Romans, the fifteeenth-century English needed to be told how to choose their ginger and how to deal with it. John Russell, in his *Boke of Nurture*, explains:

> *Se that youre gynger be welle y-pared, or hit to powder ye bete,*
> *And that hit be hard, withowt worme, bytynge, and good hete.*
> *For good gynger Colombyne is best to drynke and ete;*
> *Gynger Valadyne and Maydelyne ar not so holsom in mete.*[8]

The three grades of medieval ginger – Colombine, Valadine and Maikine – are named in many sources. Most medieval writers probably did not know what the names meant. As a matter of fact Maikine ginger was named after Mecca. It is not clear why: this may have been the place where east African ginger was marketed. Colombine was named after *Quilon* or Kollam on the west coast of India. The word Valadine meant originally 'local' – local to the city of Calicut on the same coast. The 'Householder of Paris', an anonymous author of 1393, took a different view from John Russell about two of the grades: 'Note that there are three differences between Mecca ginger and Colombine ginger. Mecca ginger has a darker brown rind, it is easier to chop with a knife, and it is whiter inside than the Colombine. It is better, and always more expensive.'⁹

As with so many other spices, the great discoveries of the 1490s and after begin a new chapter in the history of ginger. In the early sixteenth century the young Francisco de Mendoza, son of the Viceroy of New Spain, transplanted the spice to the West Indies and tropical America. Here real green ginger, the young root, chopped into salads, was tasted for the first time by Europeans. West Indian ginger – Jamaica ginger in particular – is nowadays a high-quality constituent of the worldwide ginger trade.

In addition, scientists were able, for the first time, to clarify the eastern origins of the plant. The basic work was done by García de Orta, whose *Coloquios dos simples e drogas he cousas medicinais da India*, 'Conversations on the simples, drugs and medicinal products of India', were printed at Goa in 1563. In the course of this lively, fictional dialogue García clears up several misconceptions. 'Begging Dioscorides' pardon', he rightly insists that ginger had never grown in Arabia and never could; he agrees, on the other hand, that it certainly did grow in east Africa and Madagascar. It was grown in many districts of India – García guessed wrongly that it must also grow wild there – and it was familiar in every part of the country, as shown by the fact that Indian languages had a range of different words for fresh green ginger and for the dried and ground spice. The 'sweetest' or mildest kind came from around Bassein on the west coast of India, and the women there made a conserve of it with plenty of sugar.

'What about the preserved ginger you gave me the other day? Where was that made?' asks García's Portuguese guest Ruano.

'That was home made,' García replies. 'Now you're going to try another jar, even better, which was sent me from Bengal. Go and fetch it, girl, let him have a taste.'

Ruano politely disputes that Bengali preserved ginger is better than the kind his host had made at home, though, as García explains, Bengal is where the best sugar in India is grown, and that contributes to the flavour of the conserve.¹⁰ In more recent times some have been prepared to swear by Burmese preserved ginger as made in the ancient city of Moulmein. 'I have never tasted ginger preserve to equal that made by the old families of Moulmein,' said the cookery writer 'Olivia' in the 1930s, and since she herself came from one of these families she published her family recipe, Ida's Ginger Preserve. It demands equal quantities (five viss, about 16 lb or 7 kg) of ginger and of 'no. 1 white crystallized sugar'.

You must secure the real mammoth shoots, tender and stringless, that only seem to grow to perfection at Moulmein. Nowhere else have I been able to procure these large tubers, so succulent and 'meaty', yet capable of being sliced like butter. Select the tender tubers only. Scrape peel evenly off and prick with fine needles all over. Soak in water for two days, changing the water ever four hours; on the third day, boil, and continue to change the water and to boil afresh until most of the pungency has been boiled out. Then drain it overnight. On the fourth day, make a thin syrup with half the sugar and 7½ large cups water, and leave the ginger in this syrup for 24 hours. Strain, boil the syrup and replace the ginger in it overnight. On the sixth day boil and clear the syrup with white of egg and eggshell, adding the rest of the sugar and 7½ cups water. Strain the syrup, replace the ginger in it, simmer for 3 or 4 hours until the ginger is transparent and when lifted out of the syrup appears shiny and clear. Bottle. Ginger preserve, like wine, attains mellow perfection only after a year's storage in large wide-mouthed Pegu jars, with an abundance of rich amber-coloured syrup to well cover the sprouts.[11]

With some justification, ginger still retains its place in traditional medicine. It is now known all over the world, but still in very different forms. In some northern countries you will find only ground ginger. In others the root is in demand, but it is the older, mature root that is usually seen, woody and strong-flavoured. In tropical markets both old roots and fresh young ones are to be found. Young ginger root is pale yellow, with a very thin skin, and with pinkish shoots from which the green stalks grow. It is much tenderer and juicier than the mature root, can be eaten raw, is easily grated or pounded to extract the juice, and pickled young ginger remains very popular in China and Japan. Finally, those who grow ginger can enjoy the fresh flavour of the stalks and flowers. In modern Japan, as in ancient Rome, the pickled stalk is a delicacy: it is used in Japan as an edible garnish for grilled fish.

Sugar

The end of García de Orta's conversation on ginger brings us to sugar, a commodity so familiar and so cheap now that we no longer count it as a spice at all. In medieval Europe, on the other hand, sugar was an exotic spice just like cinnamon and ginger.

The sugar cane *Saccharum officinarum*, botanists believe, is a species that originated in human cultivation. Its natural ancestor is most probably *S. sinense*, of southern China. Once more it is linguistic detective work that suggests how the development must have occurred. The word for 'sugar' can be traced back to proto-Austronesian, spoken somewhere in southern China before the migrations began. The same single word – reconstructed as *tebus* – has descendants, all meaning 'cane sugar', in the languages of Taiwan and the Philippines and in very many of the other modern Austronesian languages. Malay *tebu* and Fijian *dovu* both derive from it. As with ginger, to explain the fact we have to postulate that the sugar cane in its original form was known to the speakers of proto-Austronesian and that they planted it in their new settlements. It was in the course of this spread, possibly in the Philippines some five thousand years ago, that the improvement of the crop began to take place. From that event onwards it was the new 'noble' species *Saccharum officinarum* that spread north, east and west: northwards back to China; east to New Guinea and the Pacific islands; west to western Indonesia and to India.

In its original form cane sugar is a sweet liquid. Only those who have drunk it from the freshly crushed cane, or sucked it by chewing segments of the stem, know how refreshing it is. In this form it is not a spice at all: it can have no part in long-distance trade. There are four forms, of increasing convenience, in which sugar has been prepared for trade: as syrup, as loaves, as granulated crystals and as crystals of refined 'white' sugar.

Sugar syrup could be made easily enough by leaving raw sugar to evaporate for several days in the sun. It was a costly luxury, imported from the south where sugar canes grew, already known to the Chinese of the second century BC and quite familiar to the Chinese court in the early centuries AD. The poet Sima Xiangru, with his early mention of 'sugar liquor', may have meant syrup or perhaps a sugar wine. The eventual end product of the evaporation is loaf sugar ('stone honey' to the Chinese) and this, too, was manufactured in southern China and known in the north.[12] Medieval China enjoyed sweets made from cane sugar boiled in milk, some of them shaped into figurines such as lions. Making these for the Chinese market was a speciality, apparently, both of Sichuan and of distant Persia.

By 200 BC the wonderful sweet liquor was known in the West too. This was when the famous Greek geographer Eratosthenes, in his survey of the world, mentioned a strange plant that grew in India, 'a big reed, sweet both by nature and by the sun's heat'.[13] We may guess that he had heard of the sugar cane as a result of Alexander the Great's exploration of the Indus valley.

The discovery of granulated sugar – that is, of how to persuade sugar to form regular small crystals – was certainly made in India, and a Greek source gives us a terminus before which this great discovery must have been made. Around the time of Christ, Dioscorides devotes a short paragraph to sugar. Naturally enough, he treats it as a special kind of honey, the best-known and most effective sweetener in the Roman world; and this is where we first hear the Greek and Latin name for sugar – which, naturally again, is borrowed from Pali (*sakkharâ*) or a related Indian dialect. Dioscorides' description shows us that a new highly useful form of sugar is now in existence: 'There is also a substance called *sakkharon*, a sort of crystallized honey, in India and Arabia. It is found in reeds; it is not unlike salt in its texture, and can be crunched between the teeth like salt. It is laxative, good to drink dissolved in water, beneficial in bladder disorders and for the kidneys; in eyedrops it helps with cataract.'[14]

Until the sugar cane gradually spread westwards in medieval times, this remained the profile of sugar in the Western diet: a product resembling honey in flavour, but so much more expensive that it was seldom used in food. It was reserved for medicinal use and could be prescribed only for the rich, which is ironic when we remember our mothers' assumption that sugar, the common sweetener, was bad for us, while honey, relatively expensive, was almost 'medicinal' and would do us good.

India – already to the Greeks and Romans – was the land of sugar. It was really so. Several varieties of *Saccharum officinarum* flourished there; so did some native *Saccharum* species, and they also produced sweet saps of varying flavour. *Carakasaṃhitā,* one of the two ancient Indian medical manuals, lists the four kinds of sugar cane from which wine could be made, and it has a great deal more to say on sugar in the diet. The juice of the sugar cane is appetizing, digestive and helps with constipation and with bowel diseases. If one chews the fresh cane and sucks the juice, it is additionally very nutritive and 'increases the semen'. If fermented as a light wine, it 'produces a feeling of cheerfulness and light intoxication'. We can quote an out-sider's view: 'They make wine out of sugar,' Marco Polo was to report; 'it's very good and it quickly makes you drunk.'[15]

For a long time India was the only world source of crystallized sugar. Some sort of 'sand sugar' – this obviously means granulated sugar – may have been made in Vietnam or southern China by the fifth century, but the quality was poor. On the other hand, importing bulk granulated sugar from Iran to China by the Silk Road was dread-fully expensive. It was in AD 647, on welcoming a friendly embassy from the kingdom of Magadha in northern India – one of the results of the Indian journey of the Chinese Buddhist monk Xuanzang – that the Chinese emperor determined to solve the sugar problem by asking for technical assistance. The helpful Magadhans were happy to accept a Chinese researcher's visit and to give him full instructions. On his return, sup-plies of sugar cane from southern China were obtained, and the resulting colour and taste of the new Chinese granulated sugar were far better than anything imported by way of the Silk Road. A further great advance was sugar refining. White sugar, from which the impurities have been removed, so that only sucrose remains, was called 'sugar frost' in medieval China, and the process may possibly have been invented in the eighth century by a Chinese monk, Tsou, who lived on Umbrella Mountain in central Sichuan

In Marco Polo's time India was still best known for its *śakarkaṇḍ* (French *sucre candi,* English *sugar candy*), the solidified loaf sugar that the Chinese had called 'stone honey'. 'Sugre candy is best of alle, as I telle thee,' said John Russell in the fifteenth century. After some puzzlement when they first encountered it in bulk, European traders soon reached the conclusion that the granulated and refined sugar of south-eastern China – the hinterland of Fuzhou – was even better than sugar candy. It was already being exported to south-east Asia and the Malay archipelago, even though these places grew sugar cane more abundantly than China itself did. And so in the six-teenth century it was China, not India, that became a large-scale exporter of refined sugar to Europe by way of European trading ships. 'There is a lot of excellent sugar in China, and large quantities are exported by the Portuguese both to Japan and to India.'[16]

In medieval times the growing of sugar had gradually spread westwards. By the year 1000 it had reached the Middle East and the coast of east Africa. Around 1500, sugar plantations were begun in the new colonies, notably in the Canaries and the

West Indies. Thus, from the sixteenth century onwards, we can read first-hand descriptions by Europeans of how to grow the cane and how to refine the cane sugar. The first crop, *planta*, came two years after initial planting. The canes were then burned off to ground level and the roots produced a second crop, *zoca*, two years later. The process could be repeated several times, till eventually the yield would begin to decline. Several grades of sugar and molasses could be extracted after a succession of refining processes.

Investment in the planting and manufacture of sugar continued unchecked until, in the seventeenth century, the world market collapsed. The price of sugar dropped like a stone. In the West Indies, around 1700, there were far too many sugar plantations and far too much sugar being produced. It had been allowed to become the agricultural staple of the whole region. Not only was it sold, very cheaply, in crystal form; not only was it drunk, as fresh juice, or fermented as wine; but it was also a currency. In the French possessions, freed slaves who sheltered runaway slaves were fined 300 lb of sugar for each day. For others the fine was 10 pounds in money – an indication of the very low price of sugar.

This low price was a good reason to experiment with sugar confectionery, which had already become complicated, varied, multi-flavoured and much loved in seventeenth-century Europe. The making of rum was another use for sugar, or rather for the refuse and by-products of the sugar industry. Rum is the popular spirit in the West Indies and it is also widely enjoyed in Britain, France and Spain, the countries that used to rule the Caribbean.

The price of sugar has never fully recovered from the seventeenth-century collapse. But nowadays most of the sugar used in our food, from either sugar cane or sugar beet, is so highly refined that the two cannot easily be told apart, and nothing is preserved of the original spiciness of sugar. Unrefined 'Demerara sugar' and other less-refined cane sugars are now beginning to be something special, chosen both for their flavour and their naturalness. Just possibly cane sugar is set to become a spice once again.

Sandalwood

Two of the great aromatics of southern Asia are aloeswood and sandalwood. As cosmetics, in classical Indian medical thinking, they complement one another. Sandalwood paste is applied to alleviate burning of the skin, and you will see children, and others with sensitive skin, liberally smeared with it under the hot tropical sun. Aloeswood protects against the cold. Both have their own unmistakable, exotic aroma. We explore the history of aloeswood as a south-east Asian aromatic (page 68).[17]

The more important of the two in India, sandalwood (*Santalum album*) has been less known in the West. It is is the heartwood and root of a parasitic tree, one that grows on the roots of other trees, and as such was rather easy for people to transplant.

Just as with ginger and sugar, this must have happened in very early times.

The closest relatives of this unusual tree – the bush plum, native peach and Australian sandalwood – grow in northern Australia. *Santalum album* itself is native to the islands of Indonesia, among which Timor and Sumba are two where a good deal of sandalwood is produced. But somehow sandalwood was well known in India, and was being grown there, some centuries at least before there were any frequent trading voyages from the Malay archipelago across the Bay of Bengal. Sandalwood is not often used in food and is not especially prominent in medical prescriptions. Its remarkable, attractive aroma and its cosmetic uses are the only properties by which it can have attracted human attention. Early in the first millennium BC – nearly three thousand years ago – sandalwood was perhaps already used as an incense, in worshipping the gods, as a perfume to enhance sexual attraction and as a cosmetic to block the sun. Whatever the reason or combination of reasons for its importance, they must have been strong enough for it to be allocated precious space on an early coasting vessel from the Malay archipelago and to be carefully planted at journey's end in southern India.

From here sandalwood took its place as one of India's most versatile products: a decorative timber, a medicinal powder, a fine aroma and a colour. Some preferred the yellow grade, some the brown. It is mentioned in early texts from northern India where evidently it was known, and not only known but familiar, much admired and often used in the last centuries BC. 'You have cut through their root as if they were a sandalwood tree!' exclaims a disputant in the great Indian epic *Mahâbhârata*.[18] Again, in the *Questions of King Milinda* – a debate between the Indo-Greek king Menander and the Buddhist philosopher Nâgasena, set in the second century BC but written somewhat later – sandalwood provides a striking image.

> A piece of brown sandalwood, however fine, may have a section that is rotten and without aroma. This does not disgrace the piece of sandalwood: the part that is healthy and sweet still fills the air all around with its perfume. In the same way, someone who renounces the world under our religion, but then goes back on his promises, may be lost to the religion. This does not disgrace the religion, because the remaining brothers still fill the world of gods and men with the perfume of their good conduct.[19]

The southern mountains that divide Tamilnadu from Kerala were its favoured habitat in India, and these mountains could be called poetically *Candanagiri* or 'sandalwood hills'. An imaginary southern journey in search of the lost goddess Sîtâ is sketched in Vâlmîki's *Râmâyaṇa*, a poem of the early centuries AD. The itinerary passes the pure waters of the river Kaveri, the bright mountain Mâlaya, the river Tâmraparni abounding in crocodiles, and 'lovely forests of sandalwood covering the islands in its waters as they flow to the sea, as if they were a young bride coming to meet her lover'. The unreal but aromatic image of the sandalwood forest suggests a young woman in love, one whose body would be redolent of sandalwood perfume.[20] In Tamil, the language of classical poetry in southern India, we hear (in the second century AD and before) of hills fragrant with sandalwood, and of a city enriched with 'sacks of black pepper in carts, sandalwood and aloeswood born in the western hills'. And from the Chinese Buddhist pilgrim Fa Xian, who was in Sri Lanka in the early fifth century, we know that 'sandalwood, aloeswood and other fragrant woods' were placed atop the funeral pyre on which a king's body was to be cremated.[21] It was used so liberally that the Greek traveller Cosmas, writing in the sixth century, may be right that sandalwood, though long since naturalized in India, was also imported to Sri Lanka from the further East.

He calls it *tzándana*, a precise rendering in Greek letters of the Sanskrit and Pali *candana*. Unknown in the West before the fall of the Roman Empire, sandalwood slowly became a little more familiar in later centuries: it was *sandana* to the early Byzantine physician Aetius, *sandal* to the tenth-century Persian Muwaffiq ibn 'Alî, *sandali* in thirteenth-century French and *sandal* in fifteenth-century English. But until the sixteenth century very little of it reached Europe.

The twelfth-century Chinese author Zhao Rugua traces sandalwood to Sumatra and two other islands of the Malay archipelago, possibly Sumba and Timor; also to western India and Zanzibar. 'The natives fell the tree and let it dry underground,' he explains. 'Its aroma is pure and strong; in burning it surpasses all other incenses. The best quality comes from old trees, with thin bark and a full complement of fragrance. The root is called "incense head".'[22] The maturing underground is traditional: during these two months white ants are said to eat away the non-aromatic bark and exterior wood, refusing to touch the coloured and highly aromatic heartwood.

Yellow (or 'white') and brown kinds of sandalwood were distinguished by Chinese and Arab merchants. Yellow was often said to be the best, and this, in the nineteenth century, was the sort produced in Timor, 'in small logs; [it] is chiefly exported to China, where it is largely used to burn in the temples and in the houses of the wealthy,' writes Alfred Russell Wallace in *The Malay Archipelago*. At the same period Japan offered a market for some of the Indian sandalwood. There is also a red sandalwood, or 'red sanders', but that, as we shall see, is something quite different.

A Western crossroads

While ginger and sugar were beginning their lengthy journey along the trade routes, the aromatics of southern Arabia were also attracting attention beyond the arid country where they grow. We know of the beginnings of this trade not by exploring the prehistory of languages but by searching through early texts from the ancient civilizations of the Near East. From these we know that the aromas of frankincense and myrrh, with others not so easily identified, were ubiquitous in Mesopotamia and Egypt, in festivity and worship, 3,500 years ago and more.

Among the oldest records of the spice trade of Arabia that are precisely datable are the royal inscriptions of Assyrian kings. The so-called 'Annals of Tiglathpileser III', who was King of Assyria from 744 to 727 BC, record his disputes with Samsi, an Arabian queen, and with other states in the Arabian peninsula, well to the south of his own territory. He boasts:

> As for Samsi, Queen of Arabia, I took from her 1,100 prisoners, 30,000 camels, 20,000 oxen, 5,000 measures of spices of all kinds, and she fled for her life, like a wild ass, to the waterless town of Bazu. The people of Mas'a, Tema, Saba', Haiappa, Badana, Hatti, and the tribe of Idiba'leans from far away to the west, knew of my power and bowed to my rule. As one, they brought me tribute: male and female camels and all kinds of spices.[23]

His famous successor Sargon II (reigned 721–705) in turn received 'all kinds of aromatics' as presents from Queen Samsi. The succeeding Assyrian monarchs, Sennacherib and Esarhaddon, continued to demand aromatics, in increasing quantity, as tribute from Arabia. And it was only a century after their time that the compiler of the book of *Kings*, who was putting together a national history for the Jewish community in exile in Babylon, inserted the visit of the Queen of Sheba in his patriotic romance of the glories of King Solomon.

> She came to test him with difficult questions. She brought immense riches to Jerusalem with her, camels laden with spices, great quantities of gold, and precious stones. On coming to Solomon, she opened her mind freely to him; and Solomon had an answer for all her questions, not one of them was too obscure for the king to expound. And she presented the king with a hundred and twenty talents of gold and great quantities of spices and precious stones; no such wealth of spices ever came again as those given to king Solomon by the queen of Sheba.[24]

It is only natural, since the brutal Tiglathpileser III had gained spices from an Arabian queen by force, that the wise Solomon should have done exactly the same by the power of his intellect.

One of the Arabian kingdoms whose tribute Tiglathpileser claims to have received is Saba'. The lady who was astonished by Solomon's wisdom was Queen of Sheba. These names form a real historical link. They tell us that the spices that came to Assyria and Babylonia from the eighth century onwards originated from precisely the same source from which frankincense, myrrh and other aromatics travelled to the lands of the Roman Empire many hundreds of years later. For there was a real kingdom in southern Arabia, known to Greeks and Romans as Sabaea, the source of many spices: its capital was not far from modern San'a. A description of it was pieced together by Agatharchides, geographer to the Ptolemies of Egypt, in the second century BC.

PLATE I

Quelling revolt in the Dutch East Indies: from the revealing history by François Valentyn, *Oud en nieuw Oost-Indien* (1724).

PLATE 2

Nicolás Monardes, tireless investigator of New World aromatics. Portrait from the title page of his second edition (Seville, 1569).

Georg Eberhard Rumphius, German scientist who systematized the flora of Indonesia. Frontispiece from his six-volume masterpiece, *Het Amboinsch Kruid-boek* 'The Ambon herbal' (1741–50).

OPPOSITE PAGE
(*Top left*) Ginger was already well known in central America in the mid 16th century when Francisco Hernandez compiled his *Rerum medicarum Novae Hispaniae thesaurus* (1648–51).

(*Top right*) Sandalwood: illustration from the 'Ambon herbal' of G. E. Rumphius (1741–50).

(*Below left*) Balsam of Mecca: from a rare copy of Prosper Alpinus' pamphlet *Dialogus de Balsamo* 'A conversation on balsam' (Venice, 1591).

(*Below right*) Tejpat or malobathrum: an ancient aromatic rediscovered, from Carolus Clusius, *Exoticorum libri decem* 'Ten books of exotica' (1605). Clusius uses the Sanskrit name *tamalapatra* in his caption.

PLATE 3

Sandalum album. Tenerense.

PLATE 4

Ternate (Indonesia), island of cloves, with its threatening volcano, and Dutch and Ternatean vessels lying offshore. A plan of the European fortress is added (*top left*). From François Valentyn, *Oud en nieuw Oost-Indien* 'The East Indies then and now' (1724).

PLATE 5

Cloves, the cause of almost endless warfare, from G. E. Rumphius' 'Ambon herbal' (1741–50).

An English silver nutmeg grater, *c.* 1680.

PLATE 6

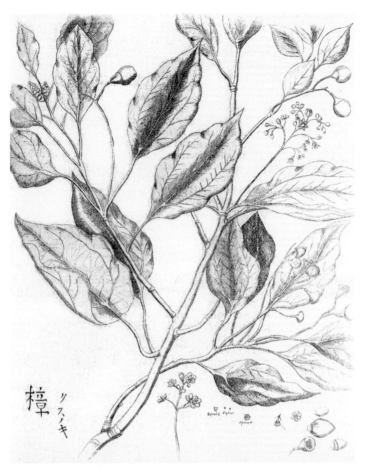

Chinese camphor: a very early illustration of *Cinnamomum camphora*, from Engelbert Kaempfer's report of his scientific travels across Asia, *Amoenitatum exoticarum fasciculi V* 'Five studies of exotic wonders' (1712).

The coat of arms of the East India Company, on a cup and saucer dated 1728. The motto, 'They grow in harmony', was ideal for a joint trading company.

PLATE 7

The island of Naira (Indonesia), source of nutmeg and scene of English-Dutch rivalry, from François Valentyn, *Oud en nieuw Oost-Indien* (1724). The names 'Nassau' and 'Belgica', once attached to colonial settlements on these islands, did not stick.

Jan Pieterszoon Coen, ruthless governor of the Dutch East Indies, from François Valentyn, *Oud en nieuw Oost-Indien* (1724).

PLATE 8

Jacques Specx, Coen's successor, from François Valentyn, *Oud en nieuw Oost-Indien* (1724).

'Samboepo', later Macassar and nowadays Ujungpandang. This hub of the trade in opium and spices, on the coast of Sulawesi (Indonesia), was once an English possession. From François Valentyn, *Oud en nieuw Oost-Indien* (1724).

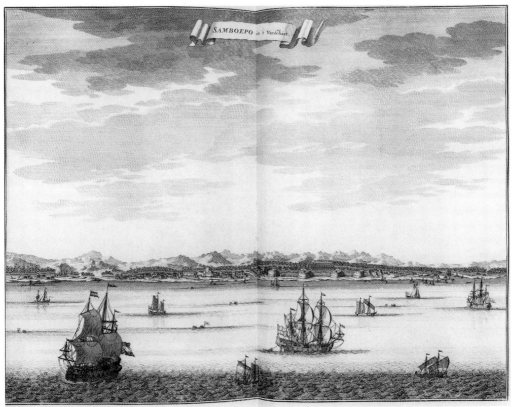

SAMBOEPO in 't Verschiet.

Further on are the Sabaeans, the most populous people of Arabia. Their country is called 'Arabia the Blessed': a natural sweet aroma pervades the whole country, because almost all the plants that excel in fragrance grow there pell-mell. Along the coast grows the balsam tree, and cassia, and another unusual plant which when fresh is pleasurable and most attractive to the eye. Inland are thick forests with big trees yielding frankincense and myrrh, alongside date, *kalamos*, cinnamon and all other such aromatics. One can never recognize any single spice because of the overwhelming power of the mingled fragrance given off by all of them together. The aroma strikes and stirs the senses of every visitor: it seems divine, beyond the power of words. Those coasting by, even at some distance off, have their share of the pleasure, because in summer, when there is an offshore breeze, the aromas exhaled by the myrrh and other such trees will carry that far: these are not the products known to us, dried and stored and stale with age, but fresh living plants at the peak of their vigour. Those who experience this wondrous aroma can describe it only as the ambrosia of myth.[25]

It has been suggested that the unusual, fragrant flowering plant observed by Agatharchides' informants in southern Arabia was sambac (*Jasminum sambac*). This beautiful jasmine species certainly originates somewhere not too far from Arabia, and it is nowadays grown commercially in Yemen.

Wealthy and inaccessible, Sabaea profited not only from its own home-grown spices but also from others that had crossed the Indian Ocean – including, as we shall see, the cassia that Agatharchides thought was native. All of them, home-grown and imported, were sent on northwards by camel caravan, crossing the vast Arabian desert on their way to the cities of Mesopotamia, to the ports of the eastern Mediterranean, and by way of Palestine to Egypt.

Recorded in writing possibly as early as the tenth century BC – if so, earlier than any of the Assyrian records cited above – is the story of Joseph 'the dreamer', sold by his brothers to a passing caravan of Ishmaelite or Arab traders, who were on their way from Gilead to Egypt. 'Their camels were loaded with *nachoth*, *tseri* and *loth*,' states the writer of *Genesis*, selecting three ancient words that were not too easy for later readers. 'Their camels groaned under incenses, resins and essences,' state the Greek translators; we may decide that this, slightly vague as it is, makes as convincing a cargo as the 'gum tragacanth, balsam and ladanum' of modern English translators.[26]

Balsam of Mecca

Balsam, at any rate, deserves to be in that list. Just as much as frankincense and myrrh, balsam typifies the spices of southern Arabia. This legendary aromatic is the resin of the tree *Commiphora opobalsamum*. Properly called 'balsam of Mecca', it owes an alternative English name, 'balm of Gilead', to the faint possibility that it once travelled from Arabia by way of Gilead to Egypt on that famous caravan journey.[27]

Balsam does actually originate in southern Arabia and still grows there. However, it was successfully transplanted to Jerusalem and Jericho in very ancient times. It was even said that the seedlings were brought by the Queen of Sheba on her visit to Solomon. This story, although it is not in the Biblical narratives of Solomon, is still a very early one, faithfully repeated by later authors who no longer knew where Sheba was, or that it was the real homeland of the balsam tree. And the balsam plantations of Palestine are truly old: as old, at least, as the Jewish prophet Ezekiel. Writing at the beginning of the 'exile to Babylon', in the early sixth century BC, Ezekiel (quoted below) looks back to the independent Jewish kingdoms, and lists balsam among their exports to the great trading city of Tyre.[28]

Much closer to the lands of the Mediterranean than Sabaea, the balsam groves of Palestine would soon become famous. Many Greek and Roman writers believed that 'the valley of Syria' (the valley of the Jordan and the Dead Sea depression) was the actual origin and the only possible habitat of this valuable plant. 'They say that there are only two royal parks in which it grows, one of about 2 hectares, the other much smaller, and that it is not found wild anywhere. From the larger park are obtained [annually] twelve jars, 1½ litres each, of the resin; from the other, no more than 2. The pure balsam resin sells for twice its weight in silver,' writes the Greek botanist Theophrastus.[29]

The rebellious Jews, as they faced defeat by Roman troops under the future emperor Titus, tried to destroy these admirable and valuable trees, to prevent their own source of wealth falling to their conquerors. The Romans mercilessly slaughtered the rebels but managed to save the balsam trees, taking a few of them all the way to Rome to figure in Titus' triumphal procession. 'The balsam tree is now a Roman subject,' concludes Pliny; 'it pays tribute just like the people who tend it.'[30] More prolific than in Theophrastus' times, it now covered whole hillsides in Palestine: the growers had gradually perfected the method of propagating the tree and increasing its yield. It probably brought Roman speculators more profits than the Jews had ever gained from it in their years of independence.

It was not only the resin that was marketed. The seed, the seed husk and also the wood of the balsam tree were valued in Rome for their aromatic qualities. But the resin, *opobalsamum*, was the choicest and most expensive of all and was said to be 'very sweet in taste'. It was an ingredient in the hair unguents that were used by Roman men: 'a fashionable man combs his curled hair neatly and always smells of balsam and cinnamon,' wrote the poet Martial disapprovingly, and with his sensitive nose he recognized the evanescent scent of balsam still lingering in empty ointment jars.[31]

Balsam was also employed in costly medicines. 'The free-run resin is the best,' writes Dioscorides, 'strong in aroma, clean, without sharpness, easily dissolving, smooth, astringent and rather biting to the tongue.' Its effects, he continued, were very powerful. It was extremely 'hot'. Taken in drinks it was digestive and diuretic, and helped with asthma. It was often called for as a constituent of pain-killers, ointments and poison antidotes.[32]

Balsam of Mecca continued to be an important spice, in demand all over the world, through medieval times. This description from a ninth-century Chinese text is an indication of how far it travelled:

> The plant *apocan* comes from the country *Fulin* [Syria]. The tree is over 10 feet high. Its bark is green and white in colour. The blossoms are fine, two being opposite each other. The flowers resemble those of rapeseed, being of a pure yellow. The seeds are like pepper. By cutting the branches one obtains an oily resin which serves as a remedy for ringworm and is useful for all diseases. This oil is much prized: it is worth its weight in gold.[33]

So the Chinese were prepared to pay even more for their balsam than were the classical Greeks.

By this time, alongside 'balsam of Mecca' there was a new cultivated form of the product, the 'balm of Mathara' from al-Maṭarîyah just north of Cairo. The Irish pilgrim Symon Semeonis, on his way to the Holy Land, saw the balsam trees at al-Maṭarīyah in 1324. We know from a contemporary author how this balsam was gathered: in summer the tree was shorn of its leaves and incisions were made in the trunk. This had to be done with great care so as not to damage the wood. The resin was collected, during the heat, in jars that were sunk into the ground. Then they were taken up and exposed to the sun. The oil floating on the surface was cleaned of dirt. This was the true, pure balsam, and it comprised only one-tenth of the quantity of resin that had flowed out of the tree.[34]

In the sixteenth century balsam was still a major commodity, and the Italian scientist Prosper Alpinus devoted a whole book to it. This work takes the form of a debate between three doctors – the Egyptian Arab Abdela, the Jew Abdachin and the Italian Alpin – on balsam and its value to man. Do we still have the true balsam described in the Greek and Roman texts? Some recent authors had doubted it, but Alpin insists that we do; the two trees still remaining in Egypt (both, incidentally, dead by 1615) were really of the same species that Theophrastus and Pliny valued so highly; more important, so were the still-surviving plantations in Palestine.[35]

In modern times balsam of Mecca is no longer used in aromatizing wine, and scarcely at all in perfumes, in which it was once so popular.

The beginnings of world trade

We have located the oldest centres of the spice trade in the East and the West. How old are the long-distance routes that join the two regions to one another and to the rest of the Old World?

Every scrap of evidence encourages us to believe that they are very old indeed. The exiled Jewish prophet Ezekiel has been cited for the detail that Palestine exported balsam through the Phoenician city of Tyre. Here are some of Ezekiel's memories of Tyre:

> Judah and Israel dealt with you, offering wheat from Minnith, wax, honey, oil and balsam, as your imports. Damascus was a source of your commerce, offering from its abundance the wine of Helbon. Dan and Javan, from Uzal onwards, supplied you with wrought iron, cassia and *calamus* in exchange for your goods. Dealers from Sheba and Raamah dealt with you, offering spices of the first quality. When your wares were unloaded from the sea you met the needs of many nations.[36]

Here, once more, are the spices of Sheba, on their way northwards to the Mediterranean ports by camel caravan. But there is something else to notice: the mention of cinnamon. Curiously, just about the same time that Ezekiel remembered his observation of the spice trade of Tyre, we find another text that tells us the destination of some of the cinnamon that passed through Tyre: a Greek poem by Sappho of Lesbos. 'Myrrh, cassia and frankincense rose in smoke,' writes Sappho in the sixth century BC, imagining a wedding in the antique city of Troy; 'all the old women wailed, and all the men raised a fine cry. They blessed the far-shooting master of the lyre, and they sang the praises of the godlike couple Hector and Andromache.'[37]

Cinnamon

These two authors – Sappho and Ezekiel – give us two very early occurrences of cinnamon or cassia in Mediterranean texts. In addition there is an early archaeological find of cinnamon at the sanctuary of Hera on the Greek island of Samos, a find dated to the seventh century BC; and Herodotus, who wrote in the fifth century, tells us that *kasie* was used in embalming in Egypt. The forty-fifth psalm, probably at least as old as these sources of information, contains another significant reference. In it an unknown poet addresses a royal bride: 'Your robes are redolent of myrrh, aloeswood and *kasi'a*; harps entertain you in halls of ivory; princesses are among your waiting-women.'[38]

We can be clear, then, that cinnamon reached the Mediterranean by the seventh century BC and was in regular use by the sixth. Earlier still? That depends on the translation of the Egyptian word *ty-šps*, found in texts of the early second millennium BC as the name of a spice imported by the Egyptians from Punt at the mouth of the Red Sea. It is 'cinnamon' to some Egyptologists, 'camphor' to others: if either camp is right, a south-east Asian spice was regularly reaching Mediterranean lands a thousand years earlier than other evidence so far suggests. A less adventurous suggestion is the east African tree *Ocotea usambarensis*, which has some medicinal uses and is a relative of the canela tree that ensnared Gonzalo Pizarro into a cinnamon hunt three millennia later. All three guesses could well be wrong.

Cinnamon was a true exotic. It travelled to the West over very great distances, and in early times there were many wild guesses and possibly some deliberate mystification about its origin. The earliest Greek historian, Herodotus, is able to tell a remarkable story of how cassia and cinnamon were obtained:

> The Arabians cover their bodies and faces, all but their eyes, with ox-hides and other skins before going out to collect *kasie*. It grows in a shallow lake. The lake and all the country round are infested by winged creatures like bats, which screech horribly and are very fierce. They have to be kept from attacking the men's eyes while they are cutting the cassia.
>
> The process of collecting the cinnamon is even stranger. In what country it grows is quite unknown. The Arabians say that the dry sticks, which we call *kinamomon*, are brought to Arabia by large birds, which carry them to their nests, made of mud, on mountain precipices which no man can climb. The method invented to get the cinnamon sticks is this. People cut up the bodies of dead oxen into very large joints, and leave them on the ground near the nests. They then scatter, and the birds fly down and carry off the meat to their nests, which are too weak to bear the weight and fall to the ground. The men come and pick up the cinnamon. Acquired in this way, it is exported to other countries.[39]

Herodotus' story is totally untrue, though it is good reading. He already makes a distinction between cinnamon and cassia; in fact he describes them as two completely different products. But he and his fellow authors are so badly informed about the origin of the two that we now have no idea what difference there actually was between 'cinnamon' and 'cassia' in the ancient West. In this book I use the word 'cinnamon' to cover both, while letting early authors choose their words for themselves.

Theophrastus, who wrote more than a century after Herodotus, also supposes that cinnamon comes from Arabia – somewhere near Sabaea, in fact. Agatharchides, whose description of Sabaea is quoted above, has the same idea. Strabo, in his long geographical survey of the ancient world, written around the time of Christ, mentions cinnamon several times. More than once he dares to suggest that it originates much further away than Arabia, but whether in southern India or somewhere on the far side of the Indian Ocean he does not make clear.

Pliny's *Natural History* has a remarkable story to tell – as fantastic as Herodotus' in its way, but rather more convincing. He begins with a sneer – quite justified on this occasion – at Herodotus and Agatharchides.

> Those old tales were invented by the Arabians to raise the price of their goods. There is an accompanying story that under the reflected rays of the sun at midday an indescribable sort of collective odour is given off from the whole of the peninsula, which is due to the harmoniously blended exhalation of all those aromas, and that the first news of Arabia received by the fleets of Alexander the

Great were these odours, wafted far out to sea.

All these stories are nonsense. In fact *cinnamomum*, which is the same thing as *cinnamum*, grows in 'Ethiopia', which is linked by intermarriage with the Cave dwellers. These buy it from their neighbours and bring it over vast seas on rafts which have no rudders to steer them, no oars to push them, no sails to propel them, indeed no motive power at all but man alone and his courage. What is more, they take to sea in winter, around the solstice, which is when the east winds blow their hardest. These winds drive them on the proper course across the bays. When they have rounded the Cape, a west-north-west wind will land them in the harbour called Ocilia, so that is the trading place they prefer. They say that their traders take almost five years there and back, and that many die. On the return journey they take glassware and bronze ware, clothing, brooches, bracelets and necklaces: so here is one more trade route that exists chiefly because women follow fashion.[40]

There is a great deal of accurate reporting here. The particular harbour on the Yemeni coast that Pliny names really was exactly the place where you would first pause after crossing the Indian Ocean with the monsoon. Greek and Latin writers usually call it 'Acila' or 'Ocelis'; it is now Ghureira Bay, just north of Cape Bab-el-Mandeb. But there is also a horrible source of confusion in Pliny's words. The 'Cave dwellers', *Trogodytae*, lived on the coast of north-eastern Africa, so, after buying cinnamon from their neighbours, what ocean did they have to cross to deliver it to Roman traders? The answer is that to Pliny, as to the Greek geographer Ptolemy, the coastal people on the distant Far Eastern shore of the Indian Ocean were also called 'Cave dwellers'. Pliny (unlike Ptolemy) for symmetry's sake calls the inland people, on that side, 'Ethiopians', just as the inland people in Africa were called Ethiopians. In other words, Pliny knew that cinnamon came from south-eastern Asia and crossed the whole breadth of the Indian Ocean on its way to the West, but he confused the geographical names so effectively that no later writer saw what he was getting at.

He had it right. The *cinnamomum* and *casia* of the ancient Mediterranean had crossed the two vast bays of the Indian Ocean, and quite possibly had done so on monsoon sailings across the open sea rather than on coasting vessels.

There are actually two historic sources of the spice. One is Sri Lanka and southern India, where the bark of the tree *Cinnamomum zeylanicum* furnishes the grade now considered finest (and always called 'cinnamon'). The other is northern south-east Asia and southern China. Here several other species of the genus *Cinnamomum* produce bark rolls and chippings which may be called 'cinnamon', 'cassia' or various other specific names. Among these *C. loureirii* is 'Saigon cinnamon' and is also the source of nikkel oil, used in perfumery; *C. cassia* is 'Chinese cinnamon'.

This south-east Asian and Chinese cinnamon was certainly well known in the Far East in ancient times. To judge by early Chinese poetry, it was one of the most evocative of aromas in northern China, certainly known by the early second century BC; and thus it was one of the most valued imports from the south. In those regions, wrote Ji Han, large forests consisting entirely of evergreen *C. cassia* trees were to be found in the high mountains. These trees were also cultivated in orchards or plantations in what is now northern Vietnam.[41] *Cinnamomum* trees grow in the forests surrounding the Burmese plains, which in these ancient times were the realm of the Pyu.

We have to admit that we have no idea from which of these sources the prized product began its long ocean journey to become the *cinnamomum* and *casia* of Greece and Rome. Neither Pliny's description nor Ptolemy's geographical coordinates allow us to decide (though both tell us that it was somewhere on the mainland); and we have no other source. The first Western author who specifically describes cinnamon as a Chinese product is perhaps the Arabic geographer Ibn Khurdâdhbih, in the ninth century. As to whether any of the cinnamon of Sri Lanka and southern India entered as yet into long-distance trade, ancient sources say nothing at all, and modern historians read this silence in two opposite ways. Some hold, since the first clear reference to cinnamon of Sri Lanka comes only in the tenth century, that it must have been unknown and unexploited earlier. Others, noting that ancient Indian texts have a simple local word for cinnamon, *tvac*, quite different from their name for Chinese cinnamon, *dârcînî*, tend to assume that there happens to be no early mention of its local origin simply because there is no early information at all on the products or trade of Sri Lanka.

Cinnamon, in the ancient West, was an aroma of divine worship and of sensual luxury. 'Take the choicest spices,' God says to Moses in a (possibly fifth-century BC) instruction that will be quoted in full later (page 136): cinnamon and cassia are to form part of this selection. 'I have sprinkled my bed with myrrh, with aloeswood and with cinnamon,' declares an adulteress in a Hebrew parable, possibly of about the same date; 'come, let us drink deep of love until the morning, and abandon ourselves to delight.'[42]

Cinnamon remained much sought after, very expensive and utterly mysterious in the medieval West. The sixth-century Greek merchant Cosmas, though he had sailed the Indian Ocean, still repeats the nonsense that cinnamon came from *Trogodytica*, that is from Eritrea or Somalia. A Byzantine dietician, Simeon Seth, asserts in the eleventh century that the best cinnamon came from Mosul in Iraq (from which, at least, we learn that the spice was brought overland in those days from the Persian Gulf ports by way of Mosul to the eastern Mediterranean). The Arabic *Summary of Marvels*, written about the same time, lists cinnamon as an export of the mythical land of the Wâqwâq bird, located 'east of China. Gold abounds there to such an extent that the people make reins and dog-leads of pure gold, and wear shirts made of cloth of gold. They export aloeswood, musk, ebony and cinnamon.'[43]

It is in about the tenth century that we begin to find a few Western sources that discuss where cinnamon comes from and get rather closer to the truth. We may begin with a puzzled glance at the reported travels of Abû Dulaf Mis'ar, poet of Bukhara in central Asia. His 'observations', apparently noted down about 940, are retailed by the later Arabic author Yâqût. Abû Dulaf speaks of a city, Jâjullâ, apparently in south-western India, whose inhabitants were vegetarians. They were 'the only Indians to stand against Alexander' and were careful observers of the heavens, with a particular regard for the 'Heart of the Lion', the star known to us as Regulus. Cinnamon was gathered in Jâjullâ, the adventurous poet reported, and from here it was exported to the rest of the world. The cinnamon tree was common property: the plantations had no individual owner.[44]

We might well suppose this to be all invention – an invention in which the geography of cinnamon production happens to be roughly correct. At almost the same time a seaman from the Persian Gulf was able to make a much more matter-of-fact report, one suggesting that to those who had really looked into the matter there was no longer any need for mystery. Of the island of Sarandîb or Sri Lanka he writes: 'The bark of its trees gives an excellent cinnamon, the famous Sarandîb cinnamon.'[45]

At last, in the fourteenth century, the observant envoy Ibn Baṭûṭâ, after a mention of cinnamon in the southern Indian forests, gives a fuller description of the cinnamon of Sri Lanka.

Puttalam, the capital, is a small and pretty town, surrounded by a wall and palisades. The whole of the coast near here is covered with the trunks of cinnamon trees brought down by the rivers. They are collected in mounds on the sea shore. People from Coromandel and Malabar take them away without paying for them, but they give the sultan cloth and such like in exchange.

It is one day and one night's voyage from Coromandel to Ceylon. The island has also plenty of brazilwood and *hindî* aloeswood.[46]

Slightly surprisingly, what Ibn Baṭûṭâ says of the trade in cinnamon supports the poet Abû Dulaf Mis'ar: people from southern India came and got it from Sri Lanka by barter, and it was they who dealt with traders from elsewhere.

Early in the sixteenth century the Portuguese took control of the export of cinnamon from Sri Lanka, and foreign observers for the first time were able to remark the organization of the cinnamon harvest. The harvesters, according to Gaspar Correia, worked for an agent who was compelled to supply a fixed number of bundles of cinnamon sticks to the king each year. Royal clerks kept account of deliveries and paid a specified sum per hundred bundles. Another Portuguese author, Duarte Barbosa, adds detail. 'The king requires the cinnamon to be cut in small sticks, and the harvest to be gathered only at certain months of each year. The king himself sells it to the merchants who go to Sri Lanka for it, because no one else is authorized to deal in it.' The king kept a warehouse in Colombo entirely for the trade in cinnamon.[47]

At the same time as Ibn Baṭûṭâ was writing of the cinnamon of Sri Lanka, another fourteenth-century Arabic author provides details on the cinnamon and cassia of south-east Asia.

The isle of Champâ is 1,600 miles long and almost equally wide. The best kinds of aloeswood and of various other spices are found there. Cassia, coconut and cinnamon trees grow there too. The fruits of the cassia resemble those of the palm, but the tree is not so long-lived. When it flowers one cuts the flowers before they open and places them in oil till it has taken up their aroma: this is the so-called 'cassia oil'. When the flowers have opened they dry up and fall, and the aroma is lost. There is nothing like the scent of cassia; the oil has the power to refresh and calm the agitated blood. The spirit of cassia is also in common use.[48]

Champâ, incidentally, even more famous for its aloeswood than for its cassia buds, is no island. It is the medieval Muslim kingdom of Champâ in what is now southern Vietnam. The mysterious geography of cinnamon and cassia had not yet been sorted out.

About the same date again, in far-off England, John Russell was among the earliest writers in modern times to instruct his readers to distinguish between cinnamon and cassia. He calls the latter 'canelle', the same name that is used in modern French.

> Looke that your stikkes of synamome be thynn, bretille, and fayre in colewre,
> And in youre mowthe fresche, hoot, and swete: that is best and sure,
> For canelle is not so good in this craft and cure.
> Synamome is hoot and dry in his worchynge while he wille dure.[49]

Nowadays, writers in Britain and the USA still draw this same firm line between cinnamon and cassia. But the average spice buyer rarely has the luxury of choice.

Tejpat

On the subject of varieties of cinnamon, consideration must be given to one other aromatic plant, now obscure, that once provided a spice highly valued many thousands of miles from its place of origin. The leaves of *Cinnamomum tamala* (called 'tejpat' in Indian English), still appreciated in southern Asia, are the *malobathrum* of Roman poets. By contrast with cinnamon, we know where Rome's *malobathrum* came from with fair precision.

Every year there turns up at the [south-eastern] border of China a certain people, short in body and very flat-faced, called Sesatae. They come with their women and children, carrying great packs very like mats of green leaves, and settle at a certain place on the border between them and the Chinese and hold a festival for several days, spreading out the mats for themselves, and then take off for their own homes in the interior. Those who know about this custom of theirs go to the place at that particular time and collect the mats of leaves. Taking out the fibres from the reeds and lightly doubling over the leaves to make them into ball shapes, they string them on the fibres from the reeds. There are three grades: big-ball *malabathron* from the larger leaf, middle-ball from the less large, small-ball from the smaller; this is the origin of our three grades of *malabathron*. Then they are carried down to India by the people who make them.

What lies beyond this area, because of extremes of storm, bitter cold, and difficult terrain and also because of some divine power of the gods, remains undiscovered.[50]

This careful description comes to us from a most unusual Greek author, one who has never been caught out telling an untruth, or in asserting more than he knows. This anonymous merchant – that is surely what he must have been – wrote in Greek *Periplus Maris Erythraei*, a 'Sailing Guide to the Indian Ocean', in the first century AD, and here, at the end of his work, describes the most distant trading network that he knows of, a network that brought cinnamon leaves or *malabathron* to a port at the mouth of the Ganges. It came there, after what must already have been a difficult journey, from the mountains of Sichuan or north-western Yunnan.

Malobathrum syrium, to Roman poets, was one of those costly aromas that could be picked out in the scent of perfumed oils, typically applied to the brow or the hair. It may have been named *syrium* because it had once reached the Mediterranean by way of Syria; and not many realized that it actually came from much further off. Until modern times, no one at all understood that the puzzling name *malobathrum* came straight from Sanskrit – *tamalapattra* or 'the dark leaf', a name used occasionally of tejpat leaf, though that is not its usual meaning. García de Orta, perceptive as usual, was right to identify *malobathrum* with tejpat.

Tejpat leaves were processed into oil, apparently in Egypt, for use in perfumes. Pliny prices the oil at 60 *denarii* the pound. The whole dried leaf was also known in Rome. It was used in ritual, in medicine and also in cookery, generally under the simple name *folium* (the leaf) or in full *folium Indicum* (Indian leaf). Tejpat leaf or oil is called for now and then in the Roman recipes of *Apicius*; it is an optional ingredient in '*Cumin sauce for oysters and shellfish*: Pepper, lovage, parsley, dried mint, bay leaf, tejpat oil, fairly generous cumin, honey, vinegar and fish sauce; or pepper, lovage, parsley, dried mint, fairly generous cumin, honey, vinegar, fish sauce.'[51]

Two ancient spice routes

The two historic routes by which spices and other costly produce passed between East and West were the Indian Ocean sailings and the Silk Road.

We have now seen something of the early spices that crossed the Indian Ocean. Originating in southern China, ginger had been transplanted to the Malay archipelago and from there to east Africa, and it was available in the Mediterranean by the first century BC. Cinnamon and cassia had been transmitted from the further East to the West; they had reached the Mediterranean, hauntingly aromatic and fearfully expensive, by the seventh century BC if not before.

We can name some major events in the history of this Indian Ocean route.

Some time before 100 BC a Greek mariner, Hippalus, observed that at the right season you could rely on the steady monsoon winds to deliver you safely from shore to shore without the need for coasting. Possibly Arab and Indian mariners already knew this, but for the trade between India and Ptolemaic Egypt, and later Rome, it was a crucial step forward.[52] Following this great discovery, the *Periplus* or 'Sailing Guide' written in the first century AD advises mariners in what month they are to set off from Egypt to reach their Indian destinations safely, and in what month they are to return.

Perhaps in the seventh century sailors speaking an Austronesian language settled the great island of Madagascar and left not only their language but also their typical double-outrigger boats as lasting evidence of their presence. It is thought that they were already familiar with the whole coast from the Straits of Malacca to east Africa, and earlier Austronesian settlements have been postulated – in southern India and even in the Persian Gulf.

About 750 AD a Chinese priest observed, 'on the river of Guangzhou [Canton] there are innumerable vessels belonging to Hindus, Persians and Malays.'[53]

At the end of the fourteenth century an exiled Sumatran warlord founded the seaport of Malacca on the coast of the Malay peninsula. The site was masterfully chosen: it commands the narrowest point of the straits that separate Sumatra from the Peninsula, now the 'Straits of Malacca'. The sea route between the Indian Ocean and the South China Sea passes this way, and the owner of Malacca had the opportunity to control the route and to share in its profits – a privilege now usurped by the city state of Singapore, not many miles further south.

In 1497–8 Vasco da Gama succeeded – where the Carthaginian prince Hanno and the Greek adventurer Eudoxus had long ago failed – in opening a route around southern Africa, thus making direct contact between Europe and the Indian Ocean seaways. Less than twenty years later the Portuguese had seized Malacca.

Although it is possible to write its annals, it is not possible to give a date when the old Indian Ocean route was first opened. Its history is essentially anarchic. Even before cinnamon and ginger such staple plants as sesame travelled between India and east Africa. Chinese, Malays, Indians, Persians, Arabs, Egyptians, Greeks, Jews, Armenians – all are on record, along with many other peoples, as conducting trade in these waters, and if one community ceased to be active, another was sure to take its place.

Vasco da Gama's was only the most famous of many government-supported missions that have undertaken to explore or control this route. As far back as the second century BC interpreters and buyers were sent south from China to buy pearls, beryls, precious stones and other exotics of the Southern Sea, taking with them gold and silk to exchange. They had to change from one foreign ship to another in the course of their mission, which is thought to have attained Kancipura in India. In the other direction an embassy reached the Chinese court in AD 166 that had come from the direction of Indochina bringing ivory, rhinoceros horns and tortoise shells and claiming to represent 'Andun of Daqin', the Roman emperor Antoninus Pius. The first official Arab mission reached China in AD 651, at about the same period when – moving in the opposite direction – the Austronesian speakers began to settle on Madagascar.

Undoubtedly the Ocean sailings repaid the efforts of seaman and merchant in generous measure. Not very long after the settlement of Madagascar, at a period when the Indian Ocean navigation was shared among several nations, the Arab geographer Ibn Khurdâdhbih made a list of its most valuable commodities. He does not have all their origins correctly identified, as will become clear, but he says enough to demonstrate why, year after year, men went on sailing this route.

> Now as to the products of the Eastern Sea. China produces white silk, coloured silk, damask silk, musk, aloeswood, saddles, marten furs, porcelain, cinnamon and galanga. India produces various kinds of aloeswood, sandalwood, camphor, camphor water, nutmeg, cloves, cardamom, cubeb, coconuts, vegetable cloths, velvet cotton cloths and elephants. Sri Lanka produces all kinds of rubies and other such stones. Kerala produces pepper. The southern islands produce brazilwood. Sind offers putchuk, rattan and bamboo.[54]

The journey was a dangerous one. 'Many died,' as Pliny briefly observed. The Persian seaman Buzurg ibn Shahriyar in his little manual *The Marvels of India* gives plenty of examples of the disasters of the voyage – of the ships that go down with all hands, far out at sea or within sight of harbour; of the ships that strike rocks or are pierced by a narwhal's horn; of the shipwrecked crews from which only a single man survives; of the rich cargoes, sole purpose of the whole undertaking, reluctantly jettisoned in a vain attempt to keep the vessel afloat.

However, there was an alternative. You could cut the distance to China almost in half, observes Cosmas, if, instead of going by sea across the Indian Ocean, you took the land route by way of Iran, 'and this is why there is so much silk in Iran'.[55] As he implies, the land route to China was used for many centuries for the export of Chinese silk. We know it as the Silk Road.

Like the Indian Ocean route, the Silk Road was, to a certain extent, anarchic: it was possible for merchandise to start out at one end of the route, East or West, and to arrive at the other end having changed hands several times, its origin, in the course of this transmission, obscured or forgotten. But we know exactly when the Silk Road was opened and brought to general attention. This was the work of the bold and pertinacious Chinese general Zhang Qian. At the command of the emperor, Zhang Qian set out in about 139 BC from the Chinese capital towards the north-west in an attempt to reach the distant realm of the Indo-Scythians and forge an alliance with them against a dangerous mutual enemy, the Huns. He was away from home almost as long as

Odysseus. After crossing the vast Gobi Desert he was captured by the Huns, was kept under house arrest, was given a wife and had a son by her. After ten years, less closely watched than at first, he managed to escape – with his new family – and continue his mission. He reached the Indo-Scythian kingdom, then established in Sogdiana (modern Tajikistan), and explored the great city of Samarkand and its markets. He spent a whole year there, making enquiries about the geography and trade of western Asia. On his return journey he was detained by the Huns for a further year, finally making a second getaway when the Hun nation was thrown temporarily into turmoil at their king's violent death in 126.

Zhang Qian was honoured by his emperor, on his return, with the position of palace counsellor. Yes, it was true that after his thirteen years of effort the planned alliance between China and the Indo-Scythians had come to nothing. 'In the end he was never able to interest them in his proposals. They considered the Chinese too far away to bother with.' But he had made initial contact with all the major states of central Asia, most of them previously quite unknown to the Chinese. Soon afterwards the Huns providentially withdrew from the Chinese borders, and a new expedition in 123, again led by the expert Zhang Qian, established permanent communication and diplomatic contacts along what we now know as the Silk Road.

In terms of world history the results of Zhang Qian's expedition were truly awesome. In spite of the fearful difficulties that he himself had faced on his first journey, within a few years Chinese envoys, traders and even pilgrims were regularly taking the long and hard route that he had explored across the Gobi Desert to reach the cities of central Asia.

The grape vine and the manufacture of wine, observed by Zhang Qian in Bactria, were, as an immediate result of his journey, introduced to China. Silk, China's unique luxury textile, till then almost unknown in Iran and further west, was soon a regular article of trade, though the secret of its manufacture was guarded for many centuries more.

One of the pilgrims who followed the Silk Road in later years was the Chinese Buddhist monk Xuanzang. He set off for India by this route in AD 630, returning home about ten years later burdened with no fewer than 657 volumes of the Buddhist scriptures. Among the terrors that he had to face was the 300-mile (480-km) desert crossing called the 'River of Sand', where one sees neither birds nor quadrupeds, nor water, nor pasture; where the night is illuminated by strange lights kindled by evil spirits, and the daylight reveals only featureless plains stretching to the horizon. Xuanzang's aims were strictly religious: yet his eventual arrival in the Indian kingdom of Magadha marked the opening of a diplomatic exchange that was important in the history of spices, as already noted.[56]

The Silk Road was not the first or the only land route out of China to the West. Zhang Qian, on reaching Samarkand, reported that he 'saw there a stick of Qiong bamboo and some Shu cloth. When I asked the people how they came by these things, they replied: "Our traders buy them in the markets of India."'[57] Evidently they had reached India from southern China by way of Yunnan and northern Burma. This unofficial trade route, of unknown age, has remained open ever since – though often at some risk – until modern times.

The Silk Road carried many more trade goods than silk alone. But the journey by camel caravan took months, and only the most valuable of products were likely to repay the enormous cost of transport. So it was that the opening of this route enabled several spices and aromatics, otherwise known only locally, to enter world trade. They include such unexpected items as rhubarb, licorice and musk.

Musk

In 1590 an anonymous Portuguese trader wrote:

> The kingdom of China overflows with valuable spices and aromatics. One notes in particular its cinnamon, though this is not the equal of the cinnamon of Ceylon; its camphor, too, and its musk, which is of the first quality. Musk is named after an animal like a beaver from whose sexual parts, when bruised and rotted, comes a most delicate and fragrant smell much liked by the Portuguese. They export a great deal of this product to India and to Japan.[58]

Musk was unknown to earlier Greeks and Romans. It first reached the Roman Empire in St Jerome's time (around AD 400). Jerome, the first Westerner to mention it, considered this, like other strong perfumes, 'well suited to lovers and hedonists'.[59] Needless to say, the saint disapproved. Later Romans were vaguely aware that the best musk came from Tibet ('a city called *Toubata*, some way east of Khwarezm', according to Simeon Seth),[60] though there was also some musk imported by way of the Indian Ocean route. Cosmas, in the sixth century, knows of musk from his Indian trading voyages, and he knows that the musk deer (*Moschus moschiferus*) had to be killed to obtain it; he even draws a picture of the musk deer at the mercy of a huntsman.

Even Cosmas gives no sign of knowing exactly where the musk deer lived. Most Westerners, then and later, had little idea of the real origin of this aromatic. In a play by Ben Jonson (1572–1637) perfumes come under discussion, and a character remarks: 'Jove! what a coil these musk-worms take, to purchase another's delight! for themselves, who bear the odours, have ever the least sense of them.'[61] The 'musk-worm' that he imagines taking the punishment is a musky-smelling insect – but no competitor to the musk deer that is the real source of the aromatic.

Somewhat later than Cosmas, Arabic authors are able to explain the business in more detail than he did. 'The best musk is that of Tibet. Then comes that of Sogdiana, and after that the Chinese. The best Chinese musk comes from Khânfû, a great city, a port of trade to which the Muslim ships come,' writes Ya'qûbî in the late ninth century.[62] Musk was evidently bought by Arab merchants both at Samarkand and at the Chinese ports – in other words, at the two ends of the Silk Road. In the twelfth century Abûl Fazl Ja'far tells us more.

> Of all drugs musk is the one that is most subject to adulteration and falsification. If it is in a bottle, check that the seal is that of a dealer whom you trust; then open it, and confirm that the colour is bright red, the aroma powerful but pleasant; then taste it: the taste should be rather bitter, but not excessively so. If presented with the musk sac, examine the outside before opening it. Lead and iron are often added, or the musk may be taken out, mixed with extract of walnut, and replaced: you will notice this by the bad smell. Musk will spoil from the effects of water and of light: it is therefore always put into a container which is carefully wrapped in waxed cloth.[63]

'Of a dark purplish colour,' says the *Encyclopaedia Britannica*, 'dry, smooth and unctuous to the touch. A grain of musk will distinctly scent millions of cubic feet of air without any appreciable loss of weight, and its scent is not only more penetrating but also more persistent than that of any other known substance.'

Its evident power persuaded early doctors to prescribe it frequently. 'It is hot and dry in the third degree,' warns the Persian pharmacist Muwaffiq ibn 'Alî in the tenth century, 'producing headache in hot constitutions; hence it is effective against cold diseases of the head. It strengthens heart and body, and when inhaled with saffron and camphor it alleviates headaches caused by cold and moist humours.'[64] But beside various medical uses musk has long served as a perfume. In medieval Cambodia, for example, although clothes were kept to a minimum – Zhou Daguan along with other Chinese traders used to lounge by the river on their day off to watch the nude bathing – the wearing of perfumes was *de rigueur*: 'both men and women wear perfumes of musk, sandalwood and other scents,' writes this observant traveller.[65]

In the fourteenth century the Chinese artist Ni Zan noted down in his cookery book a sweet recipe in which musk – surely only a very little – was called for: '*Stuffed lotus roots*. Use the best real starch flour, add honey and musk, and fill the holes in lotus roots, pouring from the bigger end. Wrap in oil paper and tie. Cook; slice; serve hot.'[66]

The principal use of musk is still in perfumery, not only for its own enthralling aroma but also as an ingredient in compound perfumes, in which it helps to fix and to strengthen the other scents that make up the mixture.

The spices of African trade

As they explored the west African coast, in preparation for striking out across the Indian Ocean, Portuguese (and later English) sailors found themselves already in a position to buy cheaply spices that had till now been expensive, or quite unobtainable, in Europe.

Unknown beyond their region of origin before that time were the Guinea peppers: Ashanti pepper or African cubebs, the fruit of *Piper clusii*, growing in what is now Ghana; and Benin pepper, the fruit of *Piper guineense*, whose homeland was the old kingdom of Benin in southern Nigeria. These had their brief European heyday at the end of the sixteenth century. Benin pepper, in fact, was the goal of the first English voyage to the Guinea coast, guided by Antonio Pinteado, in 1553. The voyage was a disaster. The captain and his Portuguese guide quarrelled continually, and both succumbed to disease; the surviving crew mutinied and left for home without waiting for the merchants, who were still negotiating for pepper at Benin City. The eventual fate of the unlucky merchants has never been known. Forty years later Benin pepper was available in Europe, but it never dislodged Indian black pepper from the market.

The beautifully named grains of Paradise, by contrast, were already well known: we have read of them already in the dreamy orchard of the *Roman de la Rose*. They were a species of cardamom, and were were so much prized in the medieval West that they fully repaid the high cost of transport by camel caravan across the vast Sahara. 'Graynes of Paradise: hoote [hot] and moyst they be', wrote John Russell in the fifteenth century, using the classification system of the physicians. Richard Eden, a sixteenth-century English sailor, veteran of the same voyage to Benin and of another the next year, found that these coveted grains of Paradise were offered for sale to mariners on the Guinea coast, in what is now Liberia. He writes of 'the great river of Sesto [Cess], where they might for their merchandizes have laden their ships with the graines of that countrey, which is a very hote fruit, and much like unto a fig as it groweth on the tree. For as the figs are full of small seeds, so is the said fruit full of graines, which are loose within the cod, having in the mids thereof a hole on every side. This kind of spice is much used in cold countries.' On his second journey he notices something more. 'They growe not past a foote and a halfe, or two foote from the ground, and are as red as blood when they are gathered. The graines themselves are called of the Phisicions *Grana Paradisi*.'[67]

The Spice Islands

>...the isles
> Of Ternate and Tidore, whence merchants bring
> Thir spicie drugs.
>
> MILTON, *Paradise Lost.*

Ternate and Tidore

After our bird's eye view of the most ancient spice routes, and of some of their most evocative products, we now begin to explore the world of spices more systematically. We start, naturally enough, at the Eastern crossroads where sugar and ginger were the first commodities to turn from local foods into delicacies that the whole world wanted to enjoy.

The Malay archipelago was not uninhabited when the Austronesians began their migration. A few of the aboriginal negrito peoples subsist even now as hunter-gatherers in the remoter highlands. But as they reached the Moluccas – perhaps three thousand years ago – the Austronesian settlers found themselves, probably for the first time, in serious competition with an already established coastal culture. We know this because the inhabitants of the spice islands of Ternate and Tidore, along with those of neighbouring Halmahera, speak not Austronesian but 'Papuan' languages. In all probability they have continued to do so since before the migrations. Somehow, and uniquely, the people of these two islands were able to maintain themselves, their language and their culture, even as the tide of Austronesian advance washed around them. They must have been extremely well adapted to their environment, and crucial to the regional economy, to have held on in this way against powerful forces for change.

There is only one likely explanation. The cloves of Ternate and Tidore must have been already in demand, at least in neighbouring islands; their growers had become powerful and prosperous – and proficient sailors, too – because they supplied the demand. They were at the centre of a very early trading network. However, cloves became available elsewhere in the world rather later.

Cloves

It is possible to give a fairly precise date, because Roman, Chinese and Indian sources are in approximate agreement here: it was around the time of Christ, just two thousand years ago. From that date onwards, early texts from far-distant countries can tell us what cloves are, and why people need them. 'One who wants clean, fresh, fragrant breath must keep nutmeg and cloves in the mouth,' advises the early Indian *Carakasaṃhitā*, and a Chinese text of the second century agrees.[1] A second Indian source recommends including cloves (*lavaṅga*) in compound medicines for cough, hiccups, vomiting and inflammations of the mouth and throat.

It was clearly in the first century AD that cloves (the unripe buds of *Syzygium aromaticum*) became known to the Romans. Pliny described them as 'resembling a grain of pepper, but larger and more fragile. They say that it grows on the Indian lotus tree. It is imported here for its aroma.'[2] In the sixth century Cosmas knew that cloves came from somewhere in the further East but were to be found on sale in the markets of Sri Lanka. No other writer of the Roman Empire, early or late, ever found out more about cloves than that, though several texts advise on the use of cloves in diet and medicine. 'It is of the nature of a flower of some tree, woody, black, almost as thick as a finger; reputed aromatic, sour, bitterish, hot and dry in the third degree; excellent in relishes and in other prescriptions,' writes the fifth-century Greek physician, Paul of Aegina.[3]

To these early peoples – Chinese, Indians, Greeks and Romans – cloves were something of a mystery, both because of their very distant origin and because of their shape, which Paul attempts to describe in the passage just quoted. The 'nail spice', the 'chicken-tongue spice' are the usual Chinese names for cloves, and the comparison with nails recurs in many other languages – for example, in French *clou de girofle*, literally 'nail of clove', the immediate origin of the English term *clove*.

In China an official pharmacologist of the seventh century, Su Gong, specifically recommended to courtiers that they keep cloves in their mouths whenever they had some matter to lay before the emperor, to avoid the slightest possibility of bad breath. Supplies of this spice came to Beijing from Guangzhou, to Guangzhou from Vietnam, and that, the early Chinese believed, was where it grew. Ji Han, in the fourth century, had regarded cloves as the flowers of the aloeswood tree, a typical product of Indochina; Su Gong, too, thought that they came from Annam. In tracing them (albeit vaguely) to the 'Eastern Sea' the Sichuanese pharmacist and poet Li Xun, writing in the tenth century, was quite unusually accurate.[4]

Even among Arabic writers, although Arabs sailed the Indian Ocean from end to end, the origin of cloves was outside common knowledge. Around the year 1000 Ibrâhîm ibn Wâṣif-Shâh makes a daring attempt to fix this exotic product into a geographical framework.

Also somewhere near India is the island containing the Valley of Cloves. No merchants or sailors have ever been to the valley or have ever seen the kind of tree that produces cloves: its fruit, they say, is sold by genies. The sailors arrive at the island, place their items of merchandise on the shore, and return to their ship. Next morning, they find, beside each item, a quantity of cloves.

One man claimed to have begun to explore the island. He saw people who were yellow in colour, beardless, dressed like women, with long hair, but they hid as he came near. After waiting a little while, the merchants came back to the shore where they had left their merchandise, but this time they found no cloves, and they realized that this had happened because of the man who had seen the islanders. After some years' absence, the merchants tried again and were able to revert to the original system of trading.

The cloves are said to be pleasant to the taste when they are fresh. The islanders feed on them, and they never fall ill or grow old. It is also said that they dress in the leaves of a tree that grows only in that island and is unknown to other people.[5]

This is one of many stories of trade at the edge of civilization, the particular kind of trade that is known to historians of money as 'silent barter'. We have already come across one such tale, explaining how cassia leaves or *malabathron* were obtained in the mountains of south-western China. There is another, concerning the trade in frank-incense and myrrh at the Temple of the Sun in southern Arabia (page 114). Ibn Wâsif-Shâh himself draws attention to yet another instance, of the Arab merchants who used to travel inland from Sofala to trade for the gold of Zimbabwe. In the case of cloves the story persists even as the geography becomes more accurate. A generation later the geographer Bîrûnî gives a similar version, as an aside, while discussing Sri Lanka. Unlike Ibn Wâsif-Shâh, Bîrûnî is prepared to imagine that the other party in the silent barter consists of humans rather than genies.

The name Laṅka reminds me of something else, the cloves whose name is lawang because they come from a country called Laṅga. All the sailors agree that ships that are sent to this country take as merchandise old Maghrebî dinars, cloth, salt, and other ordinary trade goods. The merchandise is placed beside the sea on leather mats marked with the owner's name. Then the merchants retire to their ships. Next day they find cloves on the mats as payment. The quantity varies depending on whether the local harvest has been good or bad. Some say the other party in the trade are genies; others say that they are a savage people.[6]

In every early source the island of cloves has a different name – and it never resembles Ternate or Tidore.

By the twelfth century the early stories of trading with genies are gradually being forgotten. The Chinese business author Zhao Rugua correctly lists cloves, along with sandalwood, as a product of the islands to the east of Java, though he thinks that cloves grow on Java too. Both he and Marco Polo write of the bulk trade in cloves at the southern Indian ports. It is to an Arabic author roughly contemporary with these two, Idrîsî, that we can look for an early precise description of this spice. *Salâhaṭ* seems to be one of the islands east of Java, or Java itself.

> The island of Salâhaṭ produces much sandalwood, nard and cloves. The clove tree bears a flower which opens in a calyx exactly like that of the coconut tree. After the leaves fall, the calyx is gathered. In its raw state it is bitter and awkwardly-shaped, but it is handled with all care, so that it will remain undamaged in transport. It is dried in the open air, and then sold to foreign merchants, who take it to all the countries of the earth.[7]

The use of cloves in medicine has already been mentioned. They continued to be an important culinary spice in medieval times. Although the Roman recipes of *Apicius* do not mention them, the 'illustrious Vinidarius', in a little cookery book from the end of the Roman Empire, lists cloves among the spices that 'must always be on hand in the kitchen'.[8] He finds support in the almost contemporary dietary manual of Anthimus, a Greek physician who served a Gothic king in sixth-century Gaul. Anthimus includes cloves in the beef casserole recipe that follows, and also in a sauce for hare which is quoted later.

> When the beef is boiled, put in the casserole about half a cup of sharp vinegar, some leeks and a little pennyroyal, some celery and fennel, and allow to cook for one hour. Then add half as much honey as you had vinegar, or make it sweeter than that if you like. Cook over a low heat, stirring the pot frequently so that the sauce is well mixed with the meat. Then grind 50 peppercorns, half a *solidus* each of putchuk and spikenard, one *tremissis* of cloves. Carefully grind all these spices together in an earthenware mortar, adding a little wine. When well ground, add them to the pot and stir well. Allow time for them to lose some of their individual force and to blend their flavours into the sauce before it is taken off the fire. If, besides honey, you have must or concentrated must available, you may choose any of the three to add as sweetener.[9]

It is in Indonesia, around their native island, that the majority of the cloves of the world are used nowadays, in the popular kretek cigarettes, which are a mixture of about 60 per cent tobacco and 40 per cent cloves, blended with other spices. Many cloves are also used in southern Asia packed into a betel leaf for chewing. Cloves are a cooking spice in India; in Europe they are more used in pickles and with preserves, though the most typical occurrence of cloves in English cuisine is surely as the traditional flavouring of apple pie.

Nutmeg and mace

Cloves and nutmeg were the most exotic of all the costly ingredients in the 'royal perfume' of the Parthian court, in early Iran. This is just about the earliest textual evidence of the use of either spice anywhere in the world. In many later texts, likewise, they go together.

This is totally appropriate. Nutmeg, the aromatic fruit of the tree *Myristica fragrans*, also originates from certain small islands in the eastern part of the Malay archipelago – in this case the Banda islands. It is not one spice but three: the true 'nutmeg' or kernel of the dried seed, the kernel's deep red fibrous covering or 'mace', and the whole outer fruit, harvested when ripe. In the sixteenth century García de Orta writes:

> It is the loveliest sight in the world to see the nutmeg trees laden with their ripe golden fruit, which splits to reveal the red mace within. The outer fruit is very good conserved with sugar. It has a fine taste and an even better aroma. It is believed to be very good for the brain, for the nerves, and for disorders of the womb. It comes to us here in Goa from Banda in jars in vinegar, and some people eat it like that, as a side salad, but most of what we get here is made into a conserve with sugar.[10]

Nowadays, in Indonesia, the fruit flesh is mixed with palm sugar and sun-dried to make a pleasant and nourishing sweet. This form of the spice was once well known in Europe. An Elizabethan nutritionist advises nutmeg as a healthy dietary supplement for students, especially the conserved or 'candied' nutmeg which was stocked by chemists: 'if they can get nutmigges condit, which must be had of the apothecaries, that they would have alwaies by them halfe a pounde or more to take at their pleasure.'[11] Far earlier, this was also the first form of nutmeg that reached China. In the fourth century Ji Han writes of an aromatic 'resembling the brush tips of pens, but about three quarters of an inch in length,' and continues: 'The tree flowers in the second month; its flowers have a colour like the lotus. Fruit develops and ripens in the fifth or sixth month. The taste is pungent and, when mixed with the five spices, fragrant. It can also be salted or dried. In AD 203 the governor of Tongking presented Wu Ti of Wei with nutmeg conserves.'[12]

If 'nutmeg' is the correct translation here – some think otherwise – we have to suppose that nutmegs afterwards ceased to reach the Middle Kingdom, because when they reappear in Chinese texts, in the eighth century, they have a different name, meaning literally 'fleshy cardamom'.

As with cloves, several Chinese authors insist – quite wrongly – that nutmegs grew in Indochina. Their mistake serves as good evidence that nutmegs reached China not by any direct route, coasting the Philippines and Taiwan, but by way of Java and Tongking. Tongking was, for centuries, the most southerly Chinese province and the place of entry for many exotic products from further south. Even Zhao Rugua, as late as the thirteenth century, knows very little about nutmeg, though at least he knows that it comes from the Malay archipelago. '"Fleshy cardamom",' he writes, 'comes to us from the wild tribes in the interior of two islands to the east of Java. The tree attains a height of over a hundred feet. Its trunk, boughs and foliage appear to form a large shady roof, large enough to shelter forty or fifty men. When the blossoms open in spring they are taken off and dried: this is what we know as mace.'[13]

To summarize: on the Chinese market nutmeg may have made a brief appearance in the third and fourth centuries, but reappeared in the eighth under a different name. Nutmeg is first recorded in Western markets at around the same time.

There was a red bark called *macir*, first described by Dioscorides in the first century AD. 'I cannot discover what kind of tree it comes from,' Pliny writes. 'The principal use of this bark is to take it, boiled in honey, as a cure for dysentery.' García de Orta investigated and decided, rightly, that this could not be true mace: its properties, described by Pliny and others, are quite different; it came from India, not the further East; and no one mentioned a nutmeg that came with it.[14] Whatever it is, *macir* occurs from time to time in Latin and Greek medical texts until it is supplanted, around the sixth century, by another and better red bark, *macis*, soon accompanied by a new companion spice, *nux muscata* or 'musky nut'. Here, at long last, we evidently have true mace and nutmeg. Nutmeg occurs in Greek texts of the ninth century, in French texts in the twelfth, in English texts in the fourteenth. 'The best *noix muguettes* are the ones that are heaviest and hardest to cut,' a thirteenth-century Paris householder instructs his wife.[15] And here is nutmeg in Chaucer's description of the fantasy forest through which Sir Thopas rides:

> Ther springen herbes grete and smale,
> The lycorys and cetewale,
> And many a clowe-gilofre;
> and notemugge to put in ale,
> Whether it be moyste or stale,
> Or for to lye in cofre.[16]

For those who do not know the medieval tasting terms evoked by Chaucer's mention of 'nutmeg to put in ale', here they are. The best ale may be described as 'moist', in other words young; perhaps 'corny', meaning that it has a taste of the malted barley; perhaps 'stale', which means old, strong and clear; perhaps 'nappy', with a good head. Chaucer's 'moist' and 'stale' are opposites, more or less, but they are both favourable terms, because whatever the precise qualities of the ale, you certainly will not waste expensive nutmeg on it unless it is a very good brew.

Nutmeg has many other uses beside its wondrous contribution to the flavour of medieval ale. Byzantine Greek monks who followed the Rule of St Theodore Studites were permitted to sprinkle nutmeg on the pease pudding that formed their typical fast-day dinner. Nutmeg purifies the senses and lessens evil humours, according to the medieval nun Hildegard of Bingen. Chaucer, in the text just quoted, reminds us that nutmeg was placed in *cofres* or clothes chests to fumigate and aromatize them.

Hence nutmeg was among the spices that the European explorers were most anxious to find, and we have already read Dr Chanca's hopeful speculation (in his letter from Cuba, on Columbus' expedition in 1494) that 'there are some trees which I think bear nutmegs but are not in fruit at present'. It was not so; but European nations would compete to possess the real nutmeg plantations when they discovered them, they would fight for the monopoly of the trade, and they did eventually succeed in breaking that monopoly and (whether they wanted to do this or not) in flooding the market and smashing the price. Although Dr Chanca was wrong in 1494, nutmegs are now a major crop of Grenada, Guadaloupe and Martinique and can be found all over the West Indies.

In real terms nutmeg nowadays fetches a small fraction of its earlier price. 'I hope you like nutmeg?' asks an aspiring host in a late eighteenth-century sketch by the French author Boileau. 'We've put nutmeg in *everything*!'[17] He was too late: nutmeg had just that moment ceased to be an expensive luxury. Candied nutmeg fruit is now forgotten in the West. Today dried nutmeg and mace rival one another in cookery – mace as the rarer and more expensive aromatic, more delicate according to some; nutmeg as the leading name. It stands alone, not mixing especially well with other spices. The English identify nutmeg with desserts: where Romans found pepper sprinkled atop an egg custard, we find nutmeg.

Cubebs

The fruit of *Piper cubeba* is a spice that is now little known in Europe. This relative of the black pepper tree is 'a climbing plant that blossoms in spring and fruits in the summer. It has a white flower and black fruits, which are dried in the sun before being packed for sale. It is native to Java,' writes Zhao Rugua in the thirteenth century.[18] Unknown in ancient times, cubebs had a certain popularity in medieval Europe and in China too.

In Europe they were almost forgotten in the seventeenth and eighteenth centuries, but they had a second vogue in the nineteenth 'owing to the medicinal power of the article having become known to our medical officers during the British occupation of Java', according to Yule and Burnell in *Hobson-Jobson*. To put it another way, quoting Martindale's *Extra pharmacopoeia*, oil of cubeb was 'formerly used as a urinary antiseptic'. To put it still another way, as these worthy sources modestly fail to do, oil of cubeb used regularly to be prescribed for the venereal disease gonorrhoea. Its relative kava (*Piper methysticum*), best known as the source of the native alcoholic beverage of the Pacific islands, had a similar vogue.

Nowadays cubebs are cultivated in the West Indies, though not for the little, pepper-like, tailed fruits, which are the traditional spice. What is still wanted today is oil of cubeb, much used as a commercial flavouring and in perfumery.

The Portuguese adventure

The coming of Islam to the Malay archipelago, in the thirteenth century, had no effect on the trade in cloves, nutmeg and other spices – except to strengthen it. Tidore and Ternate were converted, as were most of their neighbours. Their rulers henceforth took the title of sultan, and were more active than ever before in trade and regional politics. The ruler of Malacca was converted in the late fifteenth century. Having meanwhile concluded an alliance with the Chinese emperor, Malacca had little need to fear local rivalries, and was rapidly growing into the greatest market city in south-east Asia. It was the transshipment port where the spices of the archipelago met the vessels of the Indian Ocean route.

The results of the Portuguese explorations, by contrast, were far-reaching. Their arrival in India in 1498 had been rapidly followed by further voyage. They were forever pushing eastwards in their quest for the sources of spices. A Portuguese expedition first reached Malacca in 1509. Its initial aim was to establish itself at the legendary trading port. From there the party was instructed to press on into unknown waters and to locate, if humanly possible, the still-fabulous Spice Islands. The future circumnavigator 'Magellan', Fernão de Magalhães, was a member of this Portuguese party, whose mission ended in chaos and undignified retreat.

Two years later the Portuguese were back in force. The viceroy and admiral Alfonso de Albuquerque came to conquer, and conquer he did. The Portuguese were to hold Malacca for 130 years as their base for the exploration of the archipelago. In that very first year of 1511 three ships set out for the Spice Islands, and they were the first European vessels to reach Banda. There they loaded gloriously rich cargoes of local nutmeg, along with cloves ferried in from nearby Ternate and Tidore. From one of the three vessels, shipwrecked as it began its return journey, the adventurer António de Serrão swam ashore to establish himself as first minister to the Sultan of Ternate, and to patch together a brief alliance between Portugal and the sultanate. 'To this day,' writes Charles Corn in *Scents of Eden*, 'Portuguese helmets are worn by Moluccans in elaborate ceremonies' that preserve a memory of Serrão's brief success.[19]

The short-lived Portuguese ascendancy in the Malay archipelago found its most sonorous chronicler in the sixteenth-century poet Luis de Camões. As he approaches the grandiose finale of the *Lusiads*, the epic of Vasco da Gama and his legacy, Camões gives a bird's eye view of the rich islands of the Far East, with repeated glances at the spices and aromatics that had been the explorers' original goal, while other natural wonders, such as the lilac-coloured nutmeg pigeon, also find their place in his catalogue.

> *Olha cá pelos mares do Oriente*
> *As infinitas ilhas espalhadas...*

Cast your eyes over the numberless scattered islands in these eastern seas. Find Tidore and Ternate – identify its burning peak throwing out waves of fire – and there you will see the fiery clove trees, bought at the cost of Portuguese blood. Look at the isles of Banda, enamelled with the bright colour of their russet fruit; the brightly coloured birds, their offspring, take a tribute of the green unripe nuts. And look at Borneo, where there are ever tears – tears of those trees whose sap, coagulated and dried, is called camphor. It is this that gives the island its fame.[20]

Camphor

This brings us to camphor, often overlooked nowadays except, perhaps, for a vaguely remembered link with an odour of fumigation. Camphor was once among the most sought-after of aromatics.

There are two main sources of this unmistakable aroma. 'Chinese camphor' or 'Japanese camphor' is produced from the timber of the tree *Cinnamomum camphora*. But its quality is relatively poor. Even in China, its country of origin, this product fetches only a small fraction of the price of the 'camphor of Baros' or 'Borneo camphor', which comes from the tree *Dryobalanops aromatica*, a native of Borneo and of Sumatra.

The town of Baros (*Fansur* to Marco Polo and in other early sources), from which this camphor gets its traditional name, is in western Sumatra. 'On your left, two days from Kilah [Malaya], is the island of Bâlûs,' writes the Arab geographer Ibn Khurdâdhbih: he means Baros, and the whole of Sumatra. 'It is inhabited by cannibals. It produces excellent camphor, bananas, coconuts, sugar canes and rice.' In describing Borneo, a little earlier in his survey, he had given some details of the trade:

> To get camphor they make an incision at the top of the tree. From this the water of camphor escapes in sufficient quantity to fill several jars. Once it has been collected another incision is made lower down, about the middle of the tree, from which the pieces of camphor fall. It is the gum of the tree, but it is found in the wood itself. Once the operation has been performed, the tree becomes useless and dries out.[21]

'The trees are found on the slope of a mountain overlooking the sea,' adds the poet of Bukhara, Abû Dulaf Mis'ar. As often, he is right. Paul Wheatley, in his *Geographical notes on some commodities involved in Sung maritime trade*, describes camphor as 'locally abundant and gregarious...but always on well-drained sites between two hundred and twelve hundred feet above sea level. It often seems best developed on steep ridges.'[22]

In the twelfth century a Chinese author knew that camphor collecting was a seasonal and communal activity. 'When the natives of Borneo go into the hills to gather camphor they go in troops of several dozen. They wear special clothes made of tree bark, and take supplies of sago for food.' The fourteenth-century Arabic author Dimashqî cites 'Ahmad, the Egyptian bookseller' for some more picturesque details. The camphor collector has to drop his hatchet and run for his life immediately after making the incision, for fear that the fresh camphor will begin to flow and splash his face, which would be fatal. And some say that there are poisonous male and female snakes living all around the trees, and no one can go near them at all except at one short period each year, just after the snakes' mating season, because after giving free rein to their passions the snakes go down to the sea to cool off. The snakes may be imaginary, but the 'special clothing' is not: it matches descriptions in J. G. Frazer's *The golden bough* of the magical practices that accompany camphor collecting and the special secret language that must be used in the course of the camphor expedition. All is intended to detach the collectors, for the time being, from their human milieu and to bring them closer to that of the trees. The bark clothing helps, and so does the sago, for (as Marco Polo explains in his description of Fansur) it is 'a flour made from trees'.[23]

Arab sources, wild though their stories may be, are unanimous that the camphor they loved so much came from south-east Asia or the islands beyond – even Sindbad the sailor visited the island of camphor. This seems to tell us that it was Borneo camphor, not Chinese camphor from the mainland, that was the first to reach the Arab countries and the West. When did it arrive? The word *kaphourá* occurs in the manuscripts of at least one Roman recipe for medicinal ointment, in a medical textbook of the fifth century by Paul of Aegina. The latter's 'massage oil' recipe includes the words 'add camphor if it is available' as if it were something especially difficult to get. The old theory that Paul of Aegina could not possibly have known camphor, and that the word must have been inserted in the text by later readers, will not hold: camphor has been identified in an Egyptian mummy of the first century BC.[24] We know independently that camphor was well known in India in the early centuries AD; indeed, the early collection of tales *Kathâsaritsâgara*, 'Ocean of Story', names an imaginary southern country *Karpûradvîpa* or 'land of camphor' to remind us of how exotic and famous camphor already was.[25] The Greek name for camphor and the Indian names (Pali *kappûra*) are almost identical: they are loanwords, originating in an Austronesian language, an early form of Batak or Malay.

Even in China, where Chinese camphor was easily available, the camphor of Baros was an early and a valuable import, often known as 'dragon's brain spice'. In the twelfth century, as no doubt long before, it was one of the main products not only of north-western Sumatra but also of the northern coast of Borneo, the region that we now call Sarawak. Zhao Rugua describes for us the formalities at the arrival and departure of a Chinese trading ship at a port on this coast.

When the ship's people have moored and gone on shore, it is customary, before they begin to negotiate, for the traders to offer to the king daily gifts of Chinese food and liquors: hence when vessels go to Borneo they must take with them one or two good cooks. On the day when the ship is about to sail for home, the king also gives out wine and has a buffalo killed by way of a farewell feast, and makes return gifts of camphor and foreign cotton cloth, corresponding to the value of the presents received from the ship's people.[26]

In Chinese medicine camphor cured diseases of the eye and drove out noxious winds from other parts of the body. Indians used it as an ingredient in poison antidotes. To Romans it was a constituent of healing ointments. Most traditional pharmacopoeias have counted camphor as 'cold', which is why, as we have seen, the Muslim paradise is furnished both with a fountain of ginger and a fountain of camphor.

We hardly think of camphor as a spice, but the well-named 'clear wind rice', a snow-white concoction including rice, milk and camphor, was chilled in ice and served to the Chinese boy emperor Jing Zong (825–7) on the hottest days of summer. The camphor was surely chosen not only for its colour but also for its cooling effect, and the imperial cooks were not alone in viewing it as possessing these properties.

Camphor is known in many cultures as the aroma of death, for it is traditionally used in preserving a corpse. We have already heard of its presence in a late Egyptian mummy; Chinese and Indian sources tell the same story, while among the Bataks of Sumatra, naturally enough, the bodies of kings were preserved in camphor until the arrival of the appropriate moment for burial. It is this connection of camphor with death that lies behind this last example of the wild Arab stories of the 'Camphor Islands', a fearsome tale of cannibalism, first told around AD 1000 and several times repeated.

It is said that in the Camphor Islands are people who eat men, then take their heads, place camphor and aromatics in them, hang them in their houses and worship them. When they have to decide some course of action, they take one of these heads, venerate it, prostrate themselves before it and ask it what they need to know. It advises them on the good or bad outcome of their proposed course of action.[27]

Camphor has plenty of other, more cheerful, associations. The young Jing Zong, evidently a camphor-lover, thought of the game of shooting his 'concubines' with paper darts scented with musk and the costly camphor of Baros. There were others, too, for whom camphor was an aroma of pleasure. Jing Zong's predecessor Xuan Zong (712–56) gave his own favourite concubine ten amulets moulded from camphor, a royal gift indeed – and she in turn gave several of them to her illicit lover, the swashbuckling An Lushan.[28]

The camphor of Baros is still today an extremely costly product which sells only on the Chinese market. Chinese camphor, on the other hand, is much used in the West – never as a food additive, but often in medicine and in perfumery. The tree is now grown in India, Madagascar, Argentina, California and several other parts of the world, and a synthetic camphor is also made.

Gum benzoin

One of the less-known products of the Malay archipelago, gum benzoin began to reach China in the ninth century, and the Middle East somewhat later. This resin is produced by two trees of the genus *Styrax* native to Indochina, Sumatra and Java. A wound in the bark fills with a yellow fluid that hardens into sticky tears, reddish brown on the outside, perhaps milky white inside: 'the kind that is milky inside when broken is the best,' according to Zhao Rugua.

On the medieval Chinese market gum benzoin took the place of gum guggul, which in ancient times had come to China from Iran by way of the Silk Road and was called *anxixiang*, 'Parthian aromatic'. And so gum benzoin is called 'Parthian aromatic' in China, though its origin is half a world away. The confusion may have helped Arab and Persian merchants, who carried both, to mix cheaper gum guggul with costlier gum benzoin and to keep their customers in ignorance. Wherever it came from, the smoke of 'Parthian aromatic' was believed to drive a demon or an incubus from the body.

It was at some later time that Arabs and Europeans began to hear about gum benzoin. When they learnt to know its aroma at first hand is uncertain. 'It is hot and dry in the second degree,' said the Arabic scientist Averroes, 'giving a healing and comforting aroma to the "moist" and weak stomach; it perfumes the breath, strengthens the limbs and [like so many of the spices we encounter in this survey] enhances sexual intercourse.' But García de Orta, from whose summary this is quoted, has his doubts whether Averroes really meant gum benzoin. It certainly was familiar to Ibn Baṭûṭâ, the intrepid diplomat and traveller of the fourteenth century, who saw and described the tree in Sumatra: 'The Java incense tree is small, certainly growing no taller than a man. Its branches are reminiscent of the cardoon or the artichoke, and its leaves are small and thin. The incense is a resinous substance from the branches of the tree. Most of them grow in the Muslim part of Sumatra.'[29]

'What am I to believe?' asks the interlocutor in García's dialogue. 'An Italian author tells me that Alexander the Great's people found it in the mountains of central Asia – and he also tells me that his own compatriot, Ludovico di Varthema, found gum benzoin in the far-off island of Sumatra.'

García de Orta has the habit of being right. Gum benzoin cannot come from central Asia, he asserts: if it did, why would Arabs and Persians come to India to buy it? Varthema seems to tell the truth, he continues, and seems to have travelled to Sumatra and to the islands beyond in some Arab vessel before we Portuguese had ever got that far. Varthema is right, García concludes: we do get fine gum benzoin from Sumatra and we call it *benjuy de boninas*, 'daisy benzoin', though the very best comes mostly from Thailand, and we call that *benjuy amendoado*, 'almond benzoin', because it is made up partly of white, almond-like tears. What the Arabs call it is *lubân Jâwî*, 'incense of Java', and it is from that Arabic phrase that the Portuguese *benjuy* and the English 'benzoin' derive.

It is a tall and beautiful tree, with numerous well-shaped branches and a fine crown. The lower trunk is thick, dense and hard to cut. Some of these trees grow in the jungle near Malacca, in damp places. They wound the trees so that the gum will flow from them, and this is benzoin. The base leaf is smaller than that of the lemon tree, and not so green. The tip leaf is like a willow leaf, a little wider, not so long. It cost me money to find all this out. When you go into the jungle around Malacca, apart from being hard going, it is dangerous: there are tigers.[30]

Gum benzoin was much used by the early Chinese in compound perfumes. This is Zhao Rugua again: 'Its aroma is very stable, making it suitable for combining with other perfumes, and it is much used in this way by people who carry sachets of ambergris and other more evanescent aromas. Foreigners also include it in massage oils.' Its use as a vehicle for perfumes shows up in a text from the other end of the world, the play *Cynthia's Revels* by Ben Jonson, written in 1600.

AMORPHUS: Is the perfume rich in this jerkin?
PERFUMER: Taste! Smell! I assure you, sir, pure beniamin, the only spirited scent that ever awaked a Neapolitan nostril. You would wish yourself all nose for the love on't. I frotted a jerkin, for a new-revenued gentleman, yielded me threescore crowns but this morning, and the same titillation.

The perfumer's phrase 'pure benjamin' does not mean that gum benzoin is the only ingredient. There follows a discussion and a list of them all – musk, civet, amber, turmeric along with thirteen others that came out of Ben Jonson's Latin books – but, as the perfumer says, 'it is the sorting, and the dividing, and the mixing, and the tempering, and the searching, and the decocting' that make for success. The result is praised, by Amorphus and his friends, as 'most worthy a true voluptuary;' for courtship is in view, and in the England of 1600 men were still ready enough to discuss with one another the perfumes that they wore on such occasions.[31]

Sumatra benzoin, García de Orta's *benjuy de boninas*, comes from *Styrax benzoin* trees of Sumatra and Java and is still used as a vehicle for perfumes. It is one of the ingredients in Friars' Balsam, an inhalation for catarrh. Better than Sumatra benzoin from the point of view of modern perfumers is the Siam benzoin or Siam balsam that originates from Thailand: this is García's *benjuy amendoado*, the benzoin-with-a-hint-of-vanilla of species *Styrax tonkinense*.

The European centuries

In their arrival at the longed-for Spice Islands the Portuguese had actually been forestalled. The first European to visit the Moluccas, a few years before António de Serrão, had been the Italian Ludovico di Varthema. He reported on the 'rough and inhospitable islands of Banda' with their nutmegs and their 'rascally and beastly' inhabitants.[32] His narrative was relatively little known, and the Portuguese traders who followed Serrão were not anxious to broadcast their commercial secrets. The islands were truly placed on European maps only after they had been visited – this time on behalf of Spain – in the course of the circumnavigation led by Magellan in 1521. The ships reached the Moluccas shortly after Magellan's own death in the Philippines.

That was the beginning of four centuries of European claims and counter-claims to the islands themselves and to the clove and nutmeg monopoly. English interest in 'the Spicery' was soon aroused by the Tudor merchant Robert Thorne, who reported at length to King Henry VIII on what was then a two-way dispute between Portugal and Spain over the right to rule the islands. 'There is no doubt but that the Islands are fertile of Cloves, Nutmegs, Mace, and Cinnamom,' Thorne wrote, urging his monarch to join the spice race.[33]

Thorne was ahead of his time; but, two generations later, England briefly did exactly that. In 1579, in the course of his circumnavigation of the world with the *Golden Hind*, Sir Francis Drake called at the nutmeg island of Ternate. He was heartily welcomed by a sultan by now very tired of Portuguese and Spanish rivalries. When he returned to England, his flagship was laden with the spices of the Moluccas. In 1592 the booty of the big Spanish ship *Madre de Dios*, auctioned at Dartmouth, was valued at £500,000, including 425 tons of pepper, 45 tons of cloves, 35 tons of cinnamon, alongside cochineal, mace, nutmeg, gum benzoin, musk and ambergris. In 1598–1600 Richard Hakluyt published the definitive version of his *Principal naviga-tions, voyages, traffiques and discoveries of the English nation made by sea or overland...at any time within the compasse of these 1600 yeares*, gathering hundreds of documents, published or unpublished. He included Drake's log and also gave to Thorne's paper, at long last, the publicity it deserved. The East India Company was founded in the very same year, on 31 December 1600, as 'The Company of Merchants of London trading into the East Indies'. Its royal charter asserted free trade, a timely protest against the carving-up of the globe between Spain and Portugal. Almost the first practical result came in 1602, when the company's first-ever fleet visited Aceh in northern Sumatra – and even took possession of Run, the most isolated of the Banda islands, the sources of cloves. Known in English as 'Pulorun' from the Malay phrase *pulau Run*, 'island of Run', this bleak little outpost became the first English overseas possession.

Run was all very well; but the English, like the Portuguese in the previous century, had been forestalled. The Dutch East India Company, the *Vereenigde Oostindische Compagnie*, had already taken control of the centre of the island group – Great Banda and Naira – and in the years to come they held on to their ascendancy. In spite of the dogged efforts of John Jourdain and Nathaniel Courthope, defenders of this early English colony, the Dutch seized Run in 1621. The English, in an eventual treaty settlement, were awarded a consolation prize: they lost Run but gained the Dutch fort of New Amsterdam, now New York.

In the East Indies the Dutch rapidly increased in power. Having begun in 1606 with the capture of Ambon, roughly equidistant between the clove and nutmeg island groups, they soon dominated almost the whole archipelago that we now call Indonesia. By the time that they had captured Run they were sure of their monopoly in cloves and nutmeg. They occupied Jakarta (and renamed it Batavia after the tribe that occupied Holland in Roman times) in 1618. They even captured Malacca from the Portuguese in 1641. They seized the profitable English trading post of Ujungpandang, founded by John Jourdain and a centre of the opium trade, in 1667.

Under Dutch rule death and deportation cleared the Banda islands of English and of local people. On Run, unlucky enough to have been the focus of English resistance, every adult male was killed and every nutmeg tree destroyed. A new immigrant population was drafted in to farm the nutmeg trees of the other islands, though indigent Dutch settlers proved unsuitable for running nutmeg plantations. Meanwhile cloves were newly planted on the securely held island of Ambon, and, once they were producing, the clove trees on Ternate and Tidore, sole source of local income, were destroyed. The cruel policy of planned plantings and sudden mass uprootings of clove and nutmeg trees, by which the *compagnie* aimed to maintain a high price on the European market without regard to local economies, led to bankruptcies, starvation and rebellion.

The founder of Dutch policy was the governor Jan Pieterszoon Coen. Responsible for many thousands of deaths and for many decades of poverty in the potentially rich Moluccas, he is (unreliably) said to have died of terror at his forthcoming meeting with his successor, Jacques Specx. Coen had had Specx's daughter Zara publicly whipped for fornication, and her lover beheaded.

Dutch planters were not driven out by the successive natural catastrophes of the seventeenth century, the many eruptions of Gunung Api in the Banda islands, the typhoons and tidal waves that wreaked havoc with human settlements and with nutmeg groves. The *compagnie* was destined to maintain its sway in the East Indies for more than three centuries.[34] The long series of European invasions would end only with Indonesia's independence, in the aftermath of one more invasion, in some ways the most barbaric, but the briefest – the Japanese occupation during the Second World War.

The aromatic shore

Vês, corre a costa que Champá se chama
Cuja mata é do pau cheiroso ornada.

Look! here runs the shore called Champa,
Whose forest is ennobled by the aromatic wood.

Luís de Camões, The Lusiads.

The Golden Chersonese

So far the Malay archipelago, clustering around the coast of south-east Asia, has been in the limelight. The continent, too, is a source of exotic scents and spices. *Chryse*, the 'Golden Land' of Greek and Roman records, corresponds with the broad peninsula that we now call Indochina (extending from southern Burma across Thailand, Laos and Cambodia to Vietnam) and the much narrower southern extension known to us as the Malay peninsula. In this region, farming – the cultivation of crops – goes back many thousands of years: some believe that rice was first domesticated in south-east Asia. It was also a land rich in spices, gold, silver and precious stones, as we can gather from this rapid eastward glance in an Indian epic of the early centuries AD.

> Ravana saw lovely forests of sandalwood, thousands of aromatic trees whose roots were full of scented sap; plantations of excellent aloeswood trees, ambrette trees, areca nut trees, flowers of gorka and vines of pepper; heaps of pearls lying on the sea shore, conch-shells and coral, mountains of gold and silver, rushing rivers of crystal water; cities filled with grain and with treasure, their squares crowded with women as lovely as pearls, their streets thronged with horses, elephants and chariots.[1]

Vessels plying between southern China and the India Ocean have generally passed the Straits of Malacca and the southern point of the Malay peninsula, where Singapore

PLATE 9

The sugar warehouses at Batavia (Jakarta, Indonesia), from François Valentyn, *Oud en nieuw Oost-Indien* (1724).

PLATE 10

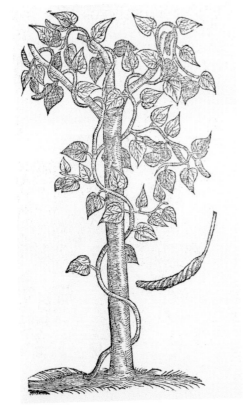

(*Above left*) Aloeswood, from G. E. Rumphius' 'Ambon herbal' (1741–50).

(*Above right*) Chinese pepper: a very early depiction of a spice unknown to earlier Westerners, from G. E. Rumphius' 'Ambon herbal' (1741–50).

(*Left*) Betel leaves: the climbing plant *Piper betle* is an aromatic relative of black and long peppers. From Carolus Clusius, *Exoticorum libri decem* (1605).

PLATE II

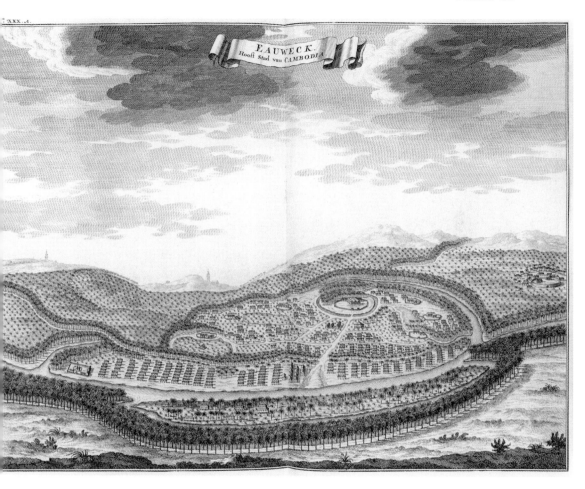

The 18th-century capital of Cambodia, source of the finest aloeswood. From François Valentyn, *Oud en nieuw Oost-Indien* (1724).

The true cinnamon of Sri Lanka, *Cinnamomum zeylanicum*, from an early 19th-century Indian botanical painting for the East India Company.

PLATE 12

'A fine fleet of great ships ...' (see p. 101). A fleet lying off the Persian port of Bandar Abbas, from Engelbert Kaempfer's 'Five studies of exotic wonders' (1712).

Asafoetida or hing: the earliest drawing of the plant, from Engelbert Kaempfer's 'Five studies of exotic wonders' (1712).

PLATE 13

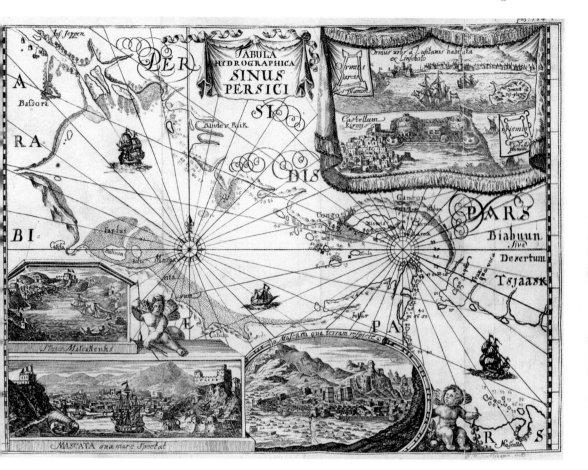

The Persian Gulf, a major spice route for thousands of years. Vignettes depict the ancient ports of Musqat and Ormuz. From Engelbert Kaempfer's 'Five studies of exotic wonders' (1712).

PLATE 14

Engelbert Kaempfer's greatest scoop: the first scientific report of the harvesting of asafoetida, in the form of a detailed narrative illustration in his *Amoenitatum exoticarum fasciculi V* 'Five studies of exotic wonders' (1712).

PLATE 15

An 18th-century camel caravan, from Engelbert Kaempfer's 'Five studies of exotic wonders' (1712).

Instrumentalists wearing unguent cones add both music and aroma to a scene of festivity in an ancient Egyptian wall painting, from a tomb at Thebes.

PLATE 16

Ancient Egyptian bottle for perfumed oil. Fancy shapes, ranging from lions to fish, were popular for these small luxury containers.

Early evidence for the use of aromatics in Western Europe: an Etruscan bronze incense-burner, *thymiaterion*, used to contribute aroma during ritual and festivity.

now lies. But there is a shorter route between Thailand and Cambodia and the West. This means crossing the isthmus of Kra, the narrow neck of the Malay peninsula. The Greeks and Romans were apparently unaware of this narrow isthmus, but Arab geographers, at a slightly later period, have plenty to tell us of Kra (*Kilah*) and its trade.

> Kilah is about half way to China. Nowadays this town is the general destination of the Muslim ships from Sîrâf and 'Omân, where they meet the vessels from China, but it was not always so. The Chinese vessels used to go all the way to the countries of 'Omân, Sîrâf, to the Persian coast and Bahrayn, to al-Ubullah and Basra, and the vessels from these places went all the way to China. It is only now that China has become so turbulent that this middle point has become the meeting place.[2]

That, rather briefly, was the height of Kilah's importance, around the tenth century. Another writer of almost the same period, Abû Zayd, adds a list of the local produce that one would look for at Kilah. 'This port is the centre of the trade in aloeswood, camphor, sandalwood, ivory, tin, ebony, brazilwood, spices of all kinds, and of many other things that there is no room to list.'[3]

Then as now the Malay peninsula, south of Kilah, was a byword for tin. 'This is the end of India, and as far as boats can go. If they continue beyond this point, they will be wrecked,' says the poet of Bukhara, Abû Dulaf Mis'ar, with his usual fairly close approximation to the truth. 'I found Kilah a great city, with strong walls, many gardens, copious springs. There are no bathhouses, but people bathe in the freshwater streams.' We noticed that Chinese traders in Cambodia liked to watch people bathing; perhaps Arab traders at Kilah did so too. 'There is a mine of tin, a metal found nowhere else in the world. The king is tributary to the king of China. I went on from here to the land of pepper,'[4] says Abû Dulaf, meaning the city of Aceh in northern Sumatra, a major source of pepper. Another feature of south-east Asian city life was noted by both Arab and Chinese visitors and is described for us by Zhou Daguan. Much local produce was grown in city gardens and sold in city markets, and 'women are the typical traders. Even a Chinese who arrives here and takes a temporary wife will profit greatly from her trading abilities. They do not have permanent shops, but simply spread a piece of mat on the ground. Each one has her own pitch. I am told that they make a payment to an official to reserve it.'[5]

Ambergris

Sailors from the West who came this way were crossing an ocean more productive in ambergris than any other in the world. Traditionally this was a speciality of the isolated Nicobar Islands, almost equidistant between India and south-east Asia. The Persian sailor Sulaimân reported in the ninth century:

The inhabitants of *Laṅgabâlûs* do not understand Arabic or any of the languages that the merchants speak. The men come out to the ships in canoes made from a single tree trunk, bringing coconuts, sugar canes, bananas and coconut wine. Sometimes they get a little ambergris, and trade it for iron. These exchanges are made entirely by signs, hand to hand, since those trading do not understand one another's languages. They are very agile swimmers – sometimes they snatch the merchants' iron and leave nothing in exchange.[6]

Once again we have a story of trading that takes place without any common language.

The origin of ambergris is unique. It is a secretion that solidifies in the intestines of the sperm whale, especially when it has been feeding on cuttlefish. Having been expelled from the whale's body, it is washed ashore as a solid, rather slimy mass, at first grey-white with a fishy smell; as it matures in the sea, and then dries and ages, it darkens to yellowish or reddish grey and eventually becomes almost black. Black ambergris, several years old, is highly aromatic. A piece may be anything from 250 g to 100 kg in weight.

The Nicobar Islands were not a convenient landfall for merchant ships. As can be deduced from the description just quoted, the hospitality they offered was limited. So the mainland kingdoms that bordered the Bay of Bengal came to be preferred as sources of ambergris, some of which had originally been bought in the Nicobar Islands by local traders.

In this area was the 'kingdom of *Qiranj*', as described once more by Sulaimân. They grew pepper, he said, but they ate it green 'because there was never enough of it', or possibly because they liked it that way. Sulaimân's description was borrowed by Mas'ûdî a century later. Mas'ûdî gets the name wrong – *f* and *q* are similar letters in Arabic. He is not interested in the pepper being eaten green, but he fills out the description with some nice antitheses: 'After Burma comes the kingdom of *Firanj*, both a land and a sea power. It is on a tongue of land that extends into the sea, and this sea produces a rich supply of ambergris. There is only a small harvest of pepper there, but many elephants. The king is brave and proud: indeed he has more pride than power, and more foolhardiness than bravery.'[7]

South again from Qiranj, which must have been in Tenasserim in southern Burma, was Phuket Bay, the district known in the sixteenth century by the odd name of Junkceylon, now the south-western extremity of Thailand. 'The kingdom of Junsalaom' was visited by English freebooters in 1591, and they 'sent commodities to the king to barter for Amber-griese'.

The Roman Empire already knew of the ambergris of the Indian Ocean. It continued to be used as medicine and perfume by the early Arabs and in medieval Europe. Its traditional name in Europe is simply 'amber' (Latin *ambar*, French *ambre*, early English *amber*). But in medieval times, perhaps first by the Arabs, ambergris was commonly likened to something rather different, the yellow substance most often found on the Baltic shores, chips of fossilized resin from prehistoric pines. This was *succinum* to

Romans, but *ambre jaune* ('yellow amber') in French, and nowadays simply *amber* in English. This is why English has now borrowed the long French form *ambre gris*, literally 'grey amber', for ambergris. Although they have different origins, and although the aroma of mature ambergris is powerful while that of amber is very light, the two substances do have several things in common. Both are found washed up on beaches; both can be ground and used as spices in food; both, as glassy solids, can be turned into mildly aromatic jewellery.

Westerners generally believed that ambergris was the dung or sperm of whales. Arabs and Persians were more varied in their opinions: it was solidified sea spray; it flowed from springs in the deeps of the sea; it was a kind of resin of the sea; it was a fungus that grew on the sea bed as mushrooms and truffles grow on the roots of trees. A sixteenth-century Indian author, Abûl Fazl 'Allâmî, lists some of these ideas along with a variety of others. 'Here is my own opinion,' he continues. 'We are told that on some mountains there is so much honey that it runs down into the sea. The wax separates from it [all honey, of course, came mixed with wax] and rises to the surface, where the action of the sun turns it into a solid substance. It is perfumed because of the aromatic flowers from which the bees gather the honey. Occasionally bees are found embedded in the ambergris,' concludes Abûl Fazl, and here, like the medieval writers, he is treating amber and ambergris as if they were all one.[8]

Early Chinese merchants had a very different view of ambergris, which – so the Arab and Persian merchants told them – was a product of the far West. They first heard of it, by its Arabic name *anbar*, in the ninth century, and linked it with Somalia, whose people 'have no dress or costume, using only some sheepskin below the waist to cover themselves. Their women are immaculately white, straight and tall,' and it is they, says Duan Chengshi, who sell amber and ivory to Persian traders. 'In the Western Sea of the Romans there are dragons in great number,' explains Zhao Rugua later. 'Now when a dragon is lying on a rock asleep, his spittle floats on the water, collects and turns hard, and the fishermen gather it as a most valuable substance.' The idea was so attractive that the story was soon embellished. Some said that sea birds, attracted by the perfume, gathered around the slumbering dragon, and it was by noting the movements of the birds that ambergris collectors were alerted to their opportunity. Others were sure that when a group of dragons fell asleep, a bank of clouds would form above, remaining stationary as they continued to sleep for weeks or months on end. The fishermen would approach only when they saw the cloud bank clearing, for this would mean that the dragons had gone away. Since it was so dangerous to collect, the Chinese paid a high price for their ambergris, both to early Persian merchants and to later Portuguese. It was a rare luxury, an occasional gift from distant and powerful monarchs, worth its weight in gold. Imperial courtiers would wear chips of ambergris as jewellery, and the very rich would sprinkle ground ambergris on boiling tea. It served also as an incense, to be burned in worship and festivity. 'When a quantity of genuine ambergris is mixed with frankincense, and is being burned, a straight column of clear blue smoke rises high up into the air. The smoke will not dissipate, and those present could cut the column of smoke with a pair of scissors. The cause of this is that the ambergris retains the power of the dragon's breath,' for dragon's breath, as every Chinese knew, was magically dense and solid: it appeared as clouds, but clouds upon which temples and pagodas stood.[9]

'I have seen a piece as large as a man,' states García de Orta, exaggerating slightly. 'Certain persons say that they have seen a whole island formed of ambergris. They noted the location, returned home, and set out again with sufficient food and water to make the return journey, but they could never find the island again. Possibly God preferred them not to find it, because of the castles of vanity that they would have built on it.' He says only a little of its medicinal uses. It is hot and dry in the second degree, he asserts; the Chinese, who value it so highly, consider it good for the heart, the brain, the stomach, and 'for intercourse with women'.[10]

Ambergris is one more of those spices that are not used in food nowadays, but it once was. In Arab cookery it was a flavouring, or rather an aromatic, in both food and drink: a small piece of ambergris, placed in the bottom of a cup, would aromatize successive cups of coffee for two or three weeks. In seventeenth century Europe sweets were scented with ambergris; Hannah Glasse's *The art of cookery made plain and easy*, published in 1747, called for ambergris in a recipe 'for icing a great cake', and the nineteenth-century French gastronome Brillat-Savarin's 'chocolate for invalids' was aromatized with ambergris.

Like musk, ambergris has the interesting and useful knack of serving as a vehicle for more fleeting scents, so it has traditionally been used a great deal in perfume-making. From the seventeenth century, when the fashion for perfumed gloves was at its height in Europe, we have this little catalogue in a play by Thomas Shadwell: 'I have choice of good Gloves, Amber, Orangery, Genoa Romane, Frangipand, Neroly, Tuberose, Jessimine, and Marshal.'[11] Amber – meaning ambergris – is near the top of the glover's list. In modern Europe it is less used: since whales are very rare – and are no longer killed for ambergris, as happened in the past – ambergris too is very rare and extremely expensive. 'Miss Dior' is one of the perfumes in which it is still used.

Aloeswood

'She breathes a perfume as pungent as musk rolled between the fingers,' writes a tenth-century Arabic poet, 'or as the aloeswood of Kilah.'[12] Aloeswood consists of the resinous, diseased wood of the tree *Aquilaria malaccensis*. It is not quite as ancient in human knowledge as sandalwood, but it is still among the oldest aromatics in the long-distance trade of Asia. It was well known both in early China and in the ancient Mediterranean.

In the Roman Empire in the first century AD the pharmacologist Dioscorides described *agalochon* as coming from 'Arabia and India'. As confirmation that the aloeswood of the early West came from India, its Greek and Hebrew names are borrowed, by way of other Near Eastern and Indian languages, from a south Indian form *akilu*. In the hills of eastern India are found the aromatic trees that provided the *akilu* and *agaru* of the classical Indian epics (written in the early centuries AD). From here, then, came the *agalochon* of Galen and Dioscorides, and – working backwards in time to the earliest known mention – the *ahaloth* of the *Song of Songs* and of the *Psalms*.[13] The aloeswood of India, thus familiar in the ancient West, is usually known in modern trade as Indian eagle-wood. It comes from as far east as Burma: the Arab geographer Ibn Khurdâdhbih writes that 'the king of Pegu has fifty thousand elephants. His country produces aloeswood of the kind called *hindî*', that is, the Indian kind.[14]

Chinese traders had early and detailed information on the origin of aloeswood and its varieties. It reached them from a little closer at hand than eastern India. The following curious classification comes from the fourth-century survey of the plant products of the south by Ji Han:

> The aloeswood tree has abundant white flowers, and leaves like those of the orange. To get the aromatic product, the tree has to be wounded several times. The following year its root, stem, branches and joints will all produce spices of different types. The heartwood and the joints are hard and black. If it sinks in water it is the 'sinking aromatic'; if it will float it is the 'chicken bone aromatic'. The roots are 'yellow ripe aromatic'; the trunks are 'timber aromatic'; the small branches, hard, solid and not decaying, are 'green cassia aromatic'; the root joints, big and light, are 'horse-hoof aromatic'.[15]

In medieval and later sources, both Chinese and Western, aloeswood is specially identified with the Muslim kingdom of Champa that once flourished in southern Vietnam. So it is, for example, in the bird's eye view of eastern Asia given by the Portuguese poet Luís de Camões.

> *Vês, corre a costa que Champá se chama*
> *Cuja mata é do pau cheiroso ornada;*

'Here runs the shore called Champa,' writes Camões, 'whose jungle is ennobled with the aromatic wood,'[16] and it is certainly aloeswood that he means. Even now the Chams, or rather the hill peoples who are their neighbours, specialize in the collection of aloeswood.

Seven hundred years before Camões, Ibn Khurdâdhbih had made the same association: 'Khmer produces the aloeswood called *Qmârî* and rice. From Khmer to Champa it is three days' sail along the coast. The aloeswood of Champa, or *Chanfî*, is superior to that of Khmer. Its quality is demonstrated by its weight, for it sinks in water.' We notice that while Chinese experts link quality with the type of wood, Arabs link it with geographical origin. The poet Abû Dulaf, never predictable, finds his place between the two: he believes that *Qmârî* aloeswood 'is dried in its country of origin, and continues to dry while it is adrift in the sea', while *Chanfî* aloeswood 'rots in its country of origin, and is washed up from the sea rotten'. Why the two kinds are named after Khmer and Champa, as they obviously are, he does not trouble to explain. All sources, Chinese and Arab, agree that aloeswood so dense as to sink in water is the best of all.

A less aromatic species, *Aquilaria sinensis*, comes from southern China itself. 'These spice trees grow both to right and to left of my house,' wrote a seventh-century local governor when the Chinese emperor asked him this very question. 'But the living ones lack the aroma: only when they are decaying do they begin to be aromatic.'[17]

It may once have been the case that Champa aloeswood was best, but later Arab authors prefer the *hindî* variety. The modern trade agrees: 'Indian eagle-wood' is better than 'Singapore agaru'. It is also said that the quality declined in the twentieth century, perhaps because too much is taken each year.

The use of aloeswood as a cosmetic, one that insulates against the cold, has already been mentioned; we shall hear later of an Arab king who had aloeswood burned in his palace during the winter months. Two thousand years ago in the Roman Empire, Dioscorides was already well informed on these uses of aloeswood, and of some others: 'Crumbled and boiled in water it makes a mouthwash for sweet breath and a paste to be applied to the whole body. It is also burnt like frankincense. One dram of the root, made up as a potion, is prescribed for fluidity and weakness of the stomach and for heartburn; drunk with water, it helps those with liver or kidney pain, or dysentery, or colic.'[18]

Medieval Arabic writers provide further details. Of all the varieties of aloeswood, nearly all sources agree, the best is the kind that is black, heavy, sinks in water, and is easy to grind because it is not fibrous. The aroma – especially that of the high-quality 'sinking' aloeswood – drives fleas away. When ground, good aloeswood takes on a grey colour. This grey powder is not only rubbed on the skin but also dusted on to clothes. It is often used as an ingredient in perfumes. It is also used as incense – that is, burnt in religious ceremonies: its odour when burning is reminiscent of roses, and is equally strong as it begins to burn and as it is entirely consumed. The better kinds burn very slowly. Older aloeswood is preferred for most of these uses, including perfumery, but fresh aloeswood is better as an ingredient in medicines. Champa aloeswood is slightly soft to the touch and has a taste so hot that it will burn and even ulcerate the tongue; yet, if you eat it, it makes you feel happy.[19]

In China, where the aloeswood of Champa had been an ancient and very popular exotic, it was important in medicine. If you boiled it down in wine, it cured internal pains, drove out evil spirits and purified the soul. As an incense or an ointment it healed wounds. Aloeswood water was used by courtesans to perfume their garments. Aloeswood was even used, in powder form, to aromatize buildings; and timbers of aromatic aloeswood – fearsomely expensive as they were – were used to make pavilions for Chinese and Mongol emperors. E. H. Schafer describes an antique Chinese box made for a manuscript of the teachings of the Buddha, still preserved in the treasure house of the Shōsōin in Japan. It is coated with aloeswood powder and decorated with cloves and the red 'love-seeds' of wild licorice.[20]

Aloewood oil, as it is known in the perfume trade, is distilled in India. As the aloeswood tree becomes rarer, the oil is nowadays a very costly ingredient in a few expensive perfumes.

Europeans in south-east Asia

We have seen that Malacca, modern Melaka, was founded by a Sumatran warlord around 1400; and that just a few years after their arrival on the west coast of India the Portuguese had pressed on eastwards, capturing Malacca in 1511. Although the trans-shipment route across the isthmus of Kra remained a theoretical alternative, the European spice hunters were never in doubt of the strategic position of the Straits of Malacca – not only because the trade between China and the Indian Ocean passed this way, but also because this was where all the spices from the archipelago joined the main trade routes.

And so for the next four and a half centuries the history of Malaya is, in part, the history of competition to control this focal point of the sea route to the 'spiceries'. The Dutch seized Malacca in 1641. They already ruled large areas of the archipelago and held the monopoly in cloves and nutmeg. The Portuguese, eventually driven out of the Moluccas and Java, managed to hang on in East Timor, the source of sandalwood. By 1685 the English had their own foothold on the west coast of Sumatra, the now for-gotten 'factory' of Bencoolen or Fort Marlborough, modern Bengkulu. In 1786 Georgetown (the island of Penang), north of Malacca, became the first British posses-sion in Malaya.

Fifty years later, not only Penang but also Malacca and the previously unimpor-tant harbour of Singapore were all three under British rule, as the 'Straits Settlements'. Malacca had been briefly seized from the Dutch in 1795 and was finally annexed in 1824. By the Treaty of London the Dutch in exchange acquired Bencoolen, the unpopular and malarial settlement of which Lord Cornwallis had written that it was an absurdity 'to have an establishment that costs nearly £40,000 at Bencoolen to facilitate the purchase of one cargo of pepper'.[21] Penang and Malacca retain their regional importance as two of the seaports of Malaysia.

Singapore was destined for a brighter future. It would eventually establish itself as an independent city state, as such almost unique in the modern world. As an Arab geographer described Kilah, so more recently the *Encyclopaedia Britannica* described Singapore: 'midway between India and China [it] forms the most important halting place on the trade route to the Far East.' Singapore's uniqueness is a fair testimony to the continuing importance of the seaway on which it stands – and spices are still among the cargoes that follow these routes – even if nowadays finance and the IT industry occupy more of Singapore's attention than nutmeg, cloves and sandalwood.

The above three paragraphs are no full narrative of the ups and downs of the ports that have dominated the sea route to the 'spiceries'. We have not mentioned that the Malay ruler of Malacca, when driven out by the Portuguese, founded the rival seaport of Johore, opposite Singapore. We have not mentioned the long independence of the kingdom of Aceh in northern Sumatra, or the French capture of Bencoolen in 1760, or the British seizure in 1824 of Tenasserim, the western coastal strip of the isthmus of Kra, destined eventually to become the southern extremity of Burma.

These harbours, 'factories' and 'colonies' had local products to deal in beside their long-distance trade. We have heard already of the ambergris of the Nicobar Islands, also to be acquired on the mainland coast opposite, from Tenasserim to Junkceylon (Phuket). The Englishmen who came here in 1591 'sent commodities to the king to barter for amber-griese, and for the hornes of abath, whereof the king onely hath the traffique in his hands. Now this abath is a beast which hath one horne onely in her forehead, and is thought to be the female unicorne, and is highly esteemed of all the Moores in those parts as a most soveraigne remedie against poyson.'[22]

The 'abath', whose horns no one but the king of Junkceylon was allowed to trade in, was no female unicorn. It was the rhinoceros, and its horn, ground to a powder, is strong medicine and powerful magic in traditional beliefs. 'Rhinoceros horn that is white and veined is the most valued: the black variety is inferior,' wrote Zhou Daguan;[23] but all kinds served the Chinese as antidotes to poison; even rhinoceros-horn cups were effective in protecting the drinker.

The cinnamon mountains

The cinnamon trees grow thick in the mountain's recesses,
twisting and snaking, their branches interlacing.

ZHAO YIN SHI.

Aromatics of Chu and Shu

The significance of spices and aromas in Chinese thought is profound. Nothing demonstrates this better than the oldest long poem in Chinese literature, the *Lament* (*Li sao*), the greatest work of the mysterious poet of Chu, Qu Yuan. When he wrote, in the fourth century BC, Chu was the southernmost of the Chinese kingdoms, occupying a wide region along the lower Yangtze valley.

To the prince who speaks the *Lament*, aromatic plants and spices denote sometimes a policy, sometimes an attitude or a state of mind. 'The three kings of old were very pure and perfect, and the fragrant flowers grew around them. They brought together Chinese pepper and cinnamon; melilot flowers were woven in their garlands.' This is, no doubt, allegorical; but the founders of the kingdom of Chu – if that is who these kings of old are – did indeed create the first Chinese realm whose territories grew both Chinese cinnamon (*jungui*, or *Cinnamomum cassia*) and one of the species of Chinese pepper (*jiao*, or *Zanthoxylum* spp.). The prince himself wove garlands of cinnamon and melilot, but his pursuit of traditional ways and policies got him nowhere; nor did his offering of peppered rice to the Shaman Ancestor Wu Xian. On whom can he rely? 'I thought that orchid was one to be trusted, but he proved a sham, bent only on pleasing his masters. He no more deserves to rank with fragrant flowers. Chinese pepper is all wagging tongue and lives only for slander, and even stinking dogwood seeks to fill a perfume bag. Since they seek only advancement and labour for position, what fragrance have they deserving our respect?'[1]

Within the unified Han kingdom of China, two centuries later, the old poetry of Chu was still cultivated. This style continued to depend on aromatic plants for emotional effects. 'The cinnamon trees grow thick in the mountain's recesses, twisting and snaking, their branches interlacing,' begins a short poem from this later period, evoking the inhospitality of a literal or a moral wilderness. 'One has climbed up by the cinnamon boughs and plans to stay there; a prince went wandering and did not return.'[2]

Soon, as China expanded southwards and westwards, interest in the exotic and entrancing aromas of the new borderlands grew greater. In due course the region of Shu, covering much of modern Sichuan, was incorporated in Chinese territory. Sichuan (Szechwan) is rightly identified in modern times with an especially hot and spicy style of Chinese cuisine. In ancient times the *Shu Capital Rhapsody* by Zuo Taichong gives a highly specific and accurate picture of the fruits and flowers, the spices and aromatics of this mountainous region: 'Qiong bamboo blankets the peaks; cinnamon trees look down from the cliffs.' As he glances towards the high mountains of the west, the botanist-poet finds further riches,

> every kind of medicinal plant in dense clusters, cold-resistant, fragrant in winter, unusual species in great numbers: what does this area not grow? Some places are thick with magnolia; others teem with Chinese pepper trees; selinum covers the central slopes; gold-thread ranges over the thoroughwort marshes. Red flowers are adorned with purple; branches and leaves grow lush and thick. The Divine Husbandman tasted them, Lu and Yiu made the prescriptions. Their aroma dispels foul humours, and their flavours heal pestilence and headaches.

Later he finds the hottest of the Chinese pepper species, known to us now as Sichuan pepper, growing in gardens in country towns, alongside 'melon patches and taro beds. Sugar cane and bitter ginger are alternately warmed by the sun and shrouded in shade; with each passing day they grow ever more luxuriant.'

Zuo Taichong returns to the Shu capital – Chengdu, still the capital of modern Sichuan – and explores the nexus of markets and shops, 'pool of a myriad merchants: its stalls stand a hundred rows deep, with thousands of booths nestled closely together,' offering delicate and beautiful craftwork, rare products brought from far countries, and the bustle of buyers and hagglers. 'Shu's knobbly bamboo was renowned in Bactria,' Zuo adds, with a very specific historical allusion to the exploration of the Silk Road, centuries earlier, by Zhang Qian: as we have seen, the adventurous general found Shu bamboo and cloth already on sale in the markets of Bactria.

Shu had another claim to fame, this one more closely linked to spices. 'The flavour of its sauce-betel was known in the villages of Panyu,' the poet continues,[3] this time alluding to the discoveries of Tang Meng, an explorer almost contemporary with Zhang Qian. On behalf of the Han emperor Tang Meng had made his way through the wild country that we now call south-western China, looking for trade routes. He had found something that he called sauce-betel on sale in the markets of the deep south, in Panyu (modern Guangzhou), and on enquiry he was told that it had come from the markets of Shu. What was it? Where had it originated?

The traditional interpretation, still the usual one among historians, is that Tang Meng and the other early Chinese writers who talk of *jujiang* or 'sauce-betel' actually mean a sauce made from betel leaves. But betel leaves grow ever more readily as one goes further south, so why a sauce like that should have been fetched to the far southern provinces from Shu would be hard to say.

There was another opinion. The botanical writer Ji Han asserted in the fourth century that 'sauce-betel' was a much more exotic product of Indian origin. 'The *jujiang* is the same as the long pepper. As the plant can be used in cookery, it was sometimes called "sauce-betel",' he writes. Long pepper, *Piper longum*, was a likely candidate and about as near as Ji Han could be expected to get. It is an explanation that makes very good sense of the strange name 'sauce-betel', because long pepper is a foreign member of the same botanical genus as the betel leaf that was already familiar in China – and betel leaf is not much used in cookery, while long pepper certainly is.

However, we can now get even closer to the truth than Ji Han. It seems in fact that Tang Meng's report marks the first appearance in far western China of a third member of the same genus, the true black pepper, *Piper nigrum*. It was evidently a product of great rarity, for it must have been carried along the difficult and mountainous trade route from Assam and Burma by way of Yunnan to Shu – and, from there, dispatched south-eastwards on the little-known roads that Tang Meng had set himself to discover.[4]

Chinese pepper

'In the rear palaces there are the lateral courtyards, the pepper rooms, the chambers of the empress and the concubines,' we are reliably informed in the *Two Capitals Rhapsody*, written by Ban Gu, the great historian of the Former Han dynasty, in the first century AD. The palace complex is that of Chang'an, the 'western capital' of the Han; the 'rear palaces' are the women's quarters; but what are the *jiao fang* or 'pepper rooms'? According to Yan Shigu, who wrote a commentary on Ban Gu's *Han History* in the seventh century, in this particular building the mud or plaster of the walls was mixed with Chinese pepper, to keep them warm and to give them an attractive aroma.[5]

Nothing can better demonstrate the power of this Chinese spice, or its importance in its native country. Several species of the genus *Zanthoxylum*, growing widely across China and in Japan, are used as spices and aromatics. They bear 'fruits that look like brown peppercorns twinned on a short stem. The whole looks like a tiny set of human male genitalia, providing the Chinese language with a simile that dates back to the *Book of Songs* [*Shi jing*, of the sixth century BC or earlier] and has been amply and lasciviously used from then to the present.'[6]

They are little known abroad. The most powerful of them all, regarded even in China in later times as the best, is the one that is native to Sichuan (*Zanthoxylum simulans*), sometimes known in English as Sichuan pepper. E. H. Schafer demonstrates how well it took the place reserved for pepper in Western cuisine, when he quotes the eighth-century monk Hanshan's supercilious reference to luxury dishes –

Steamed sucking-pigs dipped in garlic sauce,
Roast duck tinctured with fagara and salt[7]

– and he suggests that the combination of pepper and salt, which is so familiar to us that it is difficult for us to see its strangeness, must in Hanshan's time have been typical of southern Chinese cooking in particular.

Sichuan pepper is not so much biting, like black pepper, as numbing in its effect on the mouth. It has had many uses in China, both culinary and medicinal. One eighth-century emperor used to take his tea with clotted cream and Sichuan pepper.

Ancient and medieval northern China

So far we have looked at the use of aromatics in early southern China, and specifically at the old kingdom of Chu and the slightly later province of Shu. To Qu Yuan, a local author of Chu, aromatics had somehow defined one's approach to life. To the learned Zuo Taichong the neighbourhood of the Shu capital was a constant source of wonder for its exotic products, including its aromatic plants and spices.

We now turn north; and here archaeological evidence can be added to literary sidelights. The recent excavation of the Han tombs at Mawangdui, dated to the mid second century BC, tells us a great deal about Chinese food of that period, for the tomb contents – as in many other cultures – were intended to supply the deceased with most of the necessities of daily life. 'Han tomb no. 1' was the burial place of the wife of the first Marquis of Dai; she died about 165 BC. The contents of her tomb include ginger, a Chinese cinnamon species (identified as *Cinnamomum chekiangense*), two species of Chinese pepper (*Zanthoxylum armatum, Z. planispinum*) and lesser or Chinese galanga.[8] As if to supplement the basic diet, bamboo slips are found in the tomb lettered in Chinese characters to show that they represent other desirable ingredients and dishes: from these we know that wild ginger, sugar, soy sauce and fermented beans added their flavour to Han cuisine.

It is clear from finds such as this that besides Chinese cinnamon and Chinese pepper, both of which might have come from close at hand, a couple of flavourings from the southern country – sugar, ginger and galanga – were already reaching the Han kingdom. Just as important, there is a strong indication that spices from further afield were not yet known. The list of flavourings from 'Han tomb no. 1' is really quite short, and what is lacking is anything that might have arrived by way of the Silk Road – which we know was not yet opened to trade – and anything that might have come in trade from overseas: cloves, nutmeg, black pepper, long pepper, cardamom.

Not many years after the burials at Mawangdui came the movement to open up the borders of China and to make contact with what lay beyond. This is known from Zhang Qian's epic journey westward, Tang Meng's experience of 'sauce-betel' in far southern banquets, and other explorations contemporary with those. By 100 BC the Silk Road was open. In the centuries that followed, China's possessions extended rapidly westwards and southwards: to Shu, as we have seen; and to Lingnan, the great southern realm that extended even beyond the modern frontier of China far into Vietnam.

By the fourth century, when Ji Han compiled his 'Plants of the South', he can list a wide variety of spices and aromatics. His happens to be the oldest description in Chinese literature of cane sugar, a product of Tongking and of the independent kingdom of Fu-nan, which had sent sugar syrup as a gift to the Chinese emperor in the year AD 285. Ji Han lists products from beyond China's southern border such as Cambodian cardamom (*Amomum krervanh*) and aloeswood. Although he does not know their true origins, he can also list products that came from great distances like nutmeg, cloves (first recorded in China in the second century), frankincense and long pepper.

Ji Han provides the first mention in Chinese texts of the two finest aromatic species of jasmine (*Jasminum officinale, J. sambac*), originating in south-western Asia, and both of them important in later China as aromas and flavourings. Sambac now supplies the jasmine aroma so popular in Chinese tea. 'Jasmine and sambac were both brought in from the western countries by the foreigners and planted in the South Seas area,' he writes. 'The people of the south are now fond of their aroma and grow them enthusiastically. Women of the region string the flowers with coloured silk for use as hair ornaments. Sambac resembles white roses: its aroma is more powerful than jasmine.' In these few unexpected words Ji Han tells us that already in the fourth century some Westerners – Indians and Sassanian Persians, presumably, along with the odd Arab or Roman – had established themselves as traders and, and at least temporarily, as householders in a southern Chinese port.[9]

By the twelfth century the list of spices known in China is much longer. Two Western spices, mustard (*Sinapis alba*) and coriander, are by now being grown in China: coriander is first recorded in the sixth century, mustard about a century later. There is ginger; there is the still-popular *jiao* or Chinese pepper, derived from various native species; but black pepper has supplanted Chinese pepper in the dishes of the rich and powerful, and long pepper and cubebs are also much admired. Black pepper, incidentally, is no longer called by the early name of 'sauce-betel': it is now likened to Chinese pepper and is called *hujiao* or 'foreign pepper', a name first recorded in the third century. Beside sugar syrup there is now the newly popular 'sand sugar' or granulated sugar.

Nutmeg, cloves (still used for sweetening the breath) and cardamom are well known. Among newer exotics are aloes (*Aloe perryi*) and rosewater, first brought to court in the tenth century and said to be 'the dew of flowers in the lands of Rome. A substitute is made in China nowadays, but the flowers from which true rosewater is made are different from the Chinese rose.'[10] Ginseng – the best came from Korea – is used medicinally; licorice is popular as an antidote to possible poisons.

Aromatics are often used in incenses, for temple worship and for perfuming rooms. The incense candle, now a common gift in the West, is certainly a Chinese invention, but incense braziers were more usual, and some of these, presented to temples by rich worshippers, were highly elaborate, jewel-studded conversation pieces. Common ingredients in incenses are aloeswood (also used in medicines), sandalwood (said to surpass all other incenses in burning), frankincense, gum benzoin, rose-mallows, cloves, patchouli, elemi, lakawood, camphor, myrrh (also a medicine), storax and liquid storax. Most of these were also used in perfumes and in medicines. In China, myrrh was more a medicine than an incense, rather the opposite of its use in the West.

In incenses the mixture was everything, and some blends were, with a little exaggeration, called 'hundred-blend aromatics'. Here is a Tang period recipe for an incense blend actually used in a Buddhist temple in the north-west quarter of Chang'an: 'Grind finely together 1½ oz. aloeswood, 5 oz. sandalwood, 1 oz. storax, 1 oz. onycha, ½ oz. Borneo camphor, ½ oz. musk. Strain through gauze; mix with honey to make a paste.'[11]

And in Chinese cuisine, both medieval and modern, mixture is everything: spices, herbs and many other strong flavourings are called on not to impose themselves but to blend. This is the role both of Chinese 'flavour water' or cooking stock, and of the ubiquitous 'five-spice powder'. These are the reported ingredients of a five-spice powder manufactured for the Chinese community in Penang, Malaysia: 'Chinese cinnamon, cardamom, cumin, orange zest, star anise, cloves, coriander, nutmeg, rice, chilli.'[12] Five-spice powder contains more than five spices, it is true. In China itself the typical mixture is likely to include Sichuan pepper and perhaps fennel or licorice or dried ginger or galanga among the ingredients.

Galanga

From southern China comes a spice that was much more familiar in medieval England than it is in modern Britain – even though, in centuries past, spices took so much longer to travel across the world and were so much more expensive at journey's end. It is a root, comparable to and related to ginger. Greek and Roman doctors occasionally prescribed *galanga*: Aetius, for example, in his fifth-century textbook, mentions *galanga* three times as an ingredient in complex prescriptions. We are talking of luxuries here: if a single medicine for the kidneys contains '*zador*, *galanga*, lovage, hartwort, white pepper, long pepper, cinnamon, ginger, alexanders seed, cloves, tejpat leaf, spikenard, zachum, wild nard, putchuk, garlic, silphium, rhubarb, peony seed, hackberry seed, and cassia' and was administered 'in spiced wine or old wine or in an aromatic bath or as a lotion instead of bathing',[13] our physician is certainly dealing with a wealthy patient. Only such a one can afford a medicine containing no fewer than fourteen ingredients from beyond the borders of the Roman Empire.

There are in fact two species of galanga. The Indonesian (*Alpinia galanga*) is larger than the Chinese, which is named by the botanists *Alpinia officinarum* or 'the alpinia of the pharmacies'. Medieval European writers knew vaguely that some difference was to be looked for: '*Garingal* that is a very reddish violet when freshly cut is the best. Some is old, spoiled and as light as rotten wood: it is no good; the good kind is heavy and resistant to the knife.'[14] The red root is that of the Chinese species, whose white flowers, too, are spotted with red. Marco Polo remarked on the fine galanga that grew in profusion in Burma and several southern provinces of China, notably Fujian. In the same district, perhaps less reliably, he claims also to have found 'chickens without feathers, but with fur like cats, very good to eat'.[15]

As in so many other cases, it is García de Orta, writing in sixteenth-century Goa, who first makes a clear distinction between the two species of galanga:

> The small kind, from China, is very fragrant. It is a shrub or bushy plant two palms high, with leaves like myrtle, and the Chinese say it grows wild. The kind that comes from Java is called *lancuaz* [*lengkuas*]: it is larger, about five palms high, and not so fragrant or aromatic as the other. Its leaves are like a lance blade, and it bears a white flower. It does produce a seed, but the seed is not used; it is propagated from the root, like ginger, and not in any other way. Do not believe the authors who tell you otherwise, because Avicenna, Serapion and the other Arabic medical writers had only a very confused idea of galanga.[16]

Galanga, once much prized as a medicine and still used in India in treating rheumatism and catarrh, has now reverted elsewhere to use as a food spice. It provides heat and flavour that resemble those of ginger, though they are certainly not identical, and is a common ingredient in the cuisine of south-east Asia and Indonesia.

Rhubarb and licorice

The search for a north-east passage to the Indies, along the northern shore of Siberia, was destined to fail. There was a way, but even in summer it was almost impassable. The search, however, led English merchants to the Russian port of Archangel'sk. From there they found that by road and river routes they could reach the Caspian Sea, the Silk Road and the Persian Gulf. In spite of political uncertainties in Russia and Persia, this northern route seemed to offer a practical way in to the spice trade. Pepper, cinnamon, ginger, long pepper, nutmeg, mace and cloves could be bought in Persia far more cheaply than in Europe. In addition, new spices, almost legendary in their origins, became directly accessible for the first time.

Anthony Jenkinson, in 1557, reported on the trade of Bokhara, which he was perhaps the first Englishman to visit: 'their commodities are spices, muske, ambergreese, rubarbe, with other drugs.'[17] Rhubarb is one more of the unexpected names in early lists of spices, but this is the root of Tibetan rhubarb, *Rheum officinale*, a highly regarded medicinal spice in medieval times, of equal interest to the Chinese, the Persians and the physicians of Europe from about the tenth century. This or another species had been prescribed on occasion by physicians of the Roman Empire.

The first European to encounter it on its native territory had been the Franciscan emissary William of Rubruck in 1254. An Armenian monk whom he met at the Mongol court 'had a certain root, known as *reubarbe*, and he cut it up into granules which he put in water along with a little cross he had. He claimed that this enabled him to recognize when a sick man was due to recover or die. He used to give some of the water to drink to everyone who was sick. Naturally their innards were churned up by the unsavoury beverage, and this physical reaction on their part was regarded as a miracle.'[18]

Overshadowed in everyday knowledge by the garden rhubarb of modern Europe – itself originating from Manchuria – the dried root of Canton rhubarb still has its medicinal uses.

Licorice root, another central Asian spice, was also well known in early times. 'Of tonics for eyes, semen, hair, voice, skin and blood, and cures for sores and worms, licorice is best,' states the ancient Indian medical text *Caraksaṃhitā* among its neatly tabulated superlatives. The English adventurers of the sixteenth century found licorice grown in the lower Volga valley, then just brought under Russian rule. Half-way from Kazan to Astrakhan, reported Christopher Burrough in 1580, 'there groweth great store of licoris: the soile is very fruitfull: they found there apple trees, and cherrie trees.'[19] As a flavouring for sweets, licorice remains popular in northern Europe: as a culinary spice it is best known nowadays in China.

Ginseng and star anise

Meanwhile some newer Chinese aromatics have come to European attention. A pamphlet on China written in 1590 mentions several 'Chinese medicinal plants which are exported to Japan and elsewhere. Among these is the wood called simply China wood, which is especially good at expelling from the body the humours that cause contagious diseases.'[20] China wood, or China root, or Chinese sarsaparilla (*Smilax china*) was indeed highly regarded in the treatment of syphilis and of gout. But the most popular of the medicinal aromatics of China is ginseng (*Panax ginseng*).

Chinese ginseng first became known in Europe in the mid seventeenth century, and is carefully described by Engelbert Kaempfer in *Amoenitates Exoticae* (1712), but at that time it had already been essential in Chinese traditional medicine for a millennium or more. 'The ginseng that comes as tribute from the country of Silla [northern Korea] has hands and feet, and is shaped like a human being. It is over a foot long. One fixes it between pieces of *Cunninghamia* wood, and decorates it with bindings of red silk thread,' a tenth-century Chinese pharmacopoeia had explained.

Ginseng has been so much in demand in China that the native species are now very rare and expensive. So a related species discovered in North America (*Panax quinque-*

folius, colloquially 'sang') began to be exported to China in bulk in the early nineteenth century. The trade in American ginseng still thrives, while Korean and Manchurian ginseng remain luxury items both in China and elsewhere. Ginseng as extract, ginseng wine (with root still steeping in the bottle) and ginseng in many other forms are always on display in Chinese herbal stores and pharmacies.

The magical attractions of the anthropomorphic root are not, of course, the only reason why ginseng has a reputation as a medicine. An earlier writer had grandly claimed that 'ginseng overcomes the Five Labours and the Seven Lesions; it enhances the Five Organs and the Six Viscera.'[21] Many have attributed aphrodisiac properties to it. Although the *Encyclopaedia Britannica* in the 1950s asserted that 'there is no evidence that it possesses any pharmacological or therapeutic properties', modern medicine has since that time begun to take *P. ginseng* more seriously, especially for its apparent contribution to controlling blood sugar and blood pressure. For all that, James A. Duke, noting in the *Handbook of medicinal herbs* that sanchi ginseng (*P. notoginseng*) is 'suggested as an additive to chicken soup', hazards that 'the chicken soup is as valuable medicinally as the sanchi but not nearly so expensive'.[22]

The newest Chinese spice is star anise, which is ubiquitous in all modern Chinese 'five-spice powder' mixtures and in 'flavour water' as well. Star anise is the dried fruit of a small evergreen tree, *Illicium verum*, native to southern China and northern south-east Asia. The fruit is shaped like an eight-pointed star. The very similar fruit of *Illicium anisatum*, called shikimi or Japanese star anise, is used in Buddhist ceremonies. It is slightly poisonous: its Chinese name, significantly, means 'the mad herb'. People occasionally say that star anise is poisonous in large doses, but shikimi, not true star anise, is what they mean.

Star anise is often the only spice used in the 'soy-sauced' cooking method. It is the dominant flavour in the 'red-cooked' and 'red-steamed' methods, as in the famous red-steamed duck with taro of Canton. In fact, if there is any single spice flavour that asserts itself in modern Chinese cuisine, this appears to be it. Yet star anise makes no appearances as an aroma in earlier Chinese literature, and, like China root and ginseng, it was quite unknown in the West until, according to *Larousse gastronomique*, 'it was brought into Europe by an English sailor at the end of the sixteenth century'.[23] The following description comes from Schouten's voyage of Eastern discovery in the 1660s.

> *Badiane* is a seed gathered in the Indies, not unlike a melon seed but larger and thicker. Its colour is like that of cassia seed, but more lustrous and more uniform. It tastes like anise, whence some call it 'anise of the Indies', though its appearance and structure are quite different. It is enclosed in a thick, hard case shaped just like a star of seven rays, with a seed in each ray. It is mixed in sorbet and in tea, so that it is much sought after in countries where these things are liked. It is taken not only for the flavour but also because it relieves flatulence and strengthens the heart and stomach[24].

As Schouten suggests, star anise was briefly popular in seventeenth-century England, not only in tea but in recipes for fruit conserves. It is one of the aromatics used in some French anisette liqueurs.

The land of pepper

*Bales of pepper are brought to market from each house,
and gold received in exchange from the Roman ships is
brought to shore in sackfuls, at Muciri, where the music
of the singing sea never ceases and where King Kudduvar
loads his guests with the ambergris of the sea and the
cardamom of the mountains.*

PARANAR.

*We only want it for its bite – and we will go to India to
get it!*

PLINY, *Natural History*.

The Indian spice ports

Several great cities of the Indian subcontinent are centres of the world spice trade. India and Sri Lanka are well placed on the Indian Ocean route that links the eastern 'Spiceries' with their Western markets, and the Arabian spice producers with their customers in the East. Their pivotal position has long been recognized. In the sixth century the Greek merchant Cosmas had this to say of Sri Lanka:

> Serving as a centre of trade, this island receives many vessels from India, Persia
> and Ethiopia and sends out many too. From the lands on the far side, I mean
> *Tzinista* [China] and other markets, it receives silk, aloes[wood], cloves, cloves-
> wood, sandalwood, and all their other products. It transmits them to the places
> on this side, I mean *Male* where pepper grows, *Kalliana* where there is copper,
> sissoo wood and cotton (this is another important market), and *Sindu* too,
> where there is musk, putchuk and spikenard; also to Persia, southern Arabia
> and Eritrea. In exchange it takes in products from all these places and transmits
> them to the lands on the far side.[1]

This paragraph by Cosmas is a highly observant piece, typical of this deeply religious writer whenever he cares to lower his eyes to the world around him. It is supported by the Chinese pilgrim Yi Jing, who observed in the seventh century that 'areca nuts, nutmeg, mace, cloves and camphor of Baros' were to be found on sale in Sri Lanka.[2] In the thirteenth century an Arab geographer emphasized exactly the same points regarding Sri Lanka; from this later text it is also clear that Sri Lanka's traffic was increased by the great number of Buddhist monks and pilgrims from south-east Asia who visited the island.

> The island of *Sîlân* [Ceylon] is large, 800 parasangs in circuit. Here is mount *Sirandîb* upon which Adam was thrown down from Paradise. The wonders of China and the rarities of India are brought to Sîlân. Many aromatics not to be found elsewhere are met with here, such as cinnamon, brazilwood, sandalwood, nard and cloves.[3]

Cosmas had named three ports on the western coast of India, each of which had its own special products and was in contact with Sri Lanka: they were *Male* (see page 88), *Kalliana* and *Sindu*. All were important in the spice trade.

Kalliana, in Cosmas' list, still has the same name. It is Kalyân, a very ancient port at the head of an estuary north of Bombay. In the first century, at the date of the Greek sailing guide known as the *Periplus Maris Erythraei*, Kalyân was temporarily off-limits: foreign ships that landed there were sent under guard northwards to the equally famous port of Barygaza (Broach). Barygaza offered huge rewards to merchants, for it served the needs of the inland capital of Ujjain, named *Ozene* by the author of the *Periplus*. 'There are to be found on the market in Barygaza,' he observes, 'old silver drachms bearing the inscriptions, in Greek letters, of Apollodotus and Menander, rulers who came after Alexander.' This Menander was the greatest of the Indo-Greek kings of the second century BC; the Buddhist '*Questions of King Milinda*', in which he is the interlocutor, is quoted later in this book. The *Periplus* continues:

> Eastwards lies a city called Ozene, until recently the seat of a royal court. Through Ozene spikenard, putchuk and gum guggul are brought down from up country. In Barygaza there is a market for wine (they prefer Italian) and storax; Roman money, gold and silver, for which they pay a premium as against the local currency; also perfumery, but nothing too expensive and not in large quantity. For the court, in its day, one used to bring in silverware, slave musicians and dancers, pretty girls as concubines, fine wines, fine unadorned clothing, high quality perfumes. Exports are spikenard, putchuk, gum guggul, ivory, long pepper.[4]

Cosmas' third Indian port, *Sindu*, stands for the country of the lower Indus, still called Sind, and any one of the succession of ports near the Indus mouth – the current incarnation is Karachi. At the time of the *Periplus* the port known to Westerners was called by them Barbarice. 'Ships moor at Barbarice, but all the cargoes are taken upriver to the king at the capital. In this trading port there is a market for storax and frankincense. As return cargo it offers putchuk, gum guggul, *lykion*, spikenard.'[5] A thousand years later Arab and Persian mariners knew a port at the Indus mouth called Samandâr, and they looked to it for an additional aromatic product.

> Samandâr is a large, busy, rich city where there is plenty of profit to be made. It is a seaport dependent on the king of Kanauj, on the banks of a river that flows down from Kashmir. You can buy rice and other cereals, but particularly wheat of excellent quality. Here is brought aloeswood from the land of Kârmût fifteen days' journey away along a river of sweet water. This aloeswood is of high quality, with a fine aroma.[6]

Putchuk or costus

The ports at the mouth of the Indus were the embarkation point for one of the most famous spices of the ancient world, known in Sanskrit as *kuṣṭha*, in Latin as *costus*, in the modern world as putchuk or costus. It is not often called for in recipes – 'it has a burning taste and an exquisite scent,' says Pliny, 'but is otherwise useless.' Here is a recipe, however, from the book of dietary advice written in the early sixth century for King Theuderic of the Franks by the exiled Byzantine physician Anthimus: 'Hares, if they are quite young, can be eaten with a sweet sauce including pepper, a little cloves and ginger, seasoned with putchuk and spikenard or tejpat leaf. Hare is an excellent food, good in cases of dysentery.'[7]

As to Among these exotic spices that Anthimus casually expected to be available in sixth-century France, putchuk is now perhaps the least known in Europe. Roman poets used to call it *eoa costos*, 'putchuk from the lands of the dawn', or *Achaemenius costus*, 'putchuk from the Persian Empire'. 'In the island of Patale, just at the mouth of the Indus,' says Pliny, 'there are two sorts of putchuk plant, the black and the white, the latter being better. It sells at Rome at 5½ *d*. the pound.'[8] The price that Pliny gives makes putchuk one of the least expensive aromatics in the Roman Empire; it was used in the cheaper medical prescriptions and magical formulae.

As to its origin, Pliny was wrong. Putchuk came not from the mouth of the Indus – though that was where Roman merchants bought it – but from high in the Indus valley, from 'the highlands' as the *Periplus* puts it, that is, from Kashmir, which is still the only place where the kushth plant (*Saussurea lappa*) grows, a tall, stout herb demanding an elevation of at least 8,000 ft (2,500 m). An Arabic source of the tenth century describes the trade:

Hassan son of Omar told me that he had seen at Mansura people from Lower Kashmir, whose country is seventy days' journey away by land. They come down the river Mihran floating on packs of putchuk. This river when it is in spate flows out of Kashmir with a force equal to that of the Tigris and Euphrates. The packs are wrapped in skins dipped in pitch, which makes them waterproof. By tying them together they form a kind of raft and climb aboard, and so reach the port of Mansura in forty days, and the putchuk remains dry.[9]

Locally known aromatics have shared a name with putchuk. In the Far East the Chinese knew of a perfumed plant from the mountainous valleys of Yunnan which they called *mu hiang*. When they came to learn of the putchuk of Kashmir, they found its aroma so similar to *mu hiang* that they gave this new imported spice the same name. In the far West, in the fourteenth century, a new garden herb, *Tanacetum balsamina*, was introduced to England from some Mediterranean country. The aroma that it gave to ale was much appreciated, and someone must have thought it comparable to the expensive *coste* of Eastern trade: hence it was called in England *alecost* or *costmary*, though in France and elsewhere it seemed more like a kind of balm and was named after that.

There was no real confusion, though. 'Roots of costus both sorts, coming from beyond sea: hot and dry, break wind; being boiled in oil, it is held to help the gout by anointing the aggrieved place with it,' wrote Nicholas Culpeper, 'celebrated and useful physician', in the seventeenth century, about putchuk. His characterization of costmary is quite different, a herb 'so frequently known to be an inhabitant in almost every garden that I judge it needless to give a description thereof'.[10] In Europe putchuk is now very little used, but in India it is 'still used for scenting shawls', according to recent sources.

Spikenard

Several of the greatest of the spices of India have been not flavourings so much as perfumes and medicines. Another with a long history was spikenard, gathered high in the Hindu Kush and the Himalaya. It is an oil derived from the leaves and root of a herb, *Nardostachys jatamansi*, that grows in the mountains of northern India at heights up to 17,000 ft (5,200 m). The 'spike' is the spike or ear that grows from the rhizome. Spikenard was traditionally exported from the neighbourhood of the mouth of the Ganges.

Dacca and Calcutta are the current incarnations of this trading port. The writer of the *Periplus* – he had perhaps never been this far east himself – makes it clear that we are at the mouth of 'the greatest of all the rivers of India. It has a rise and fall like the Nile. On it is a trading port with the same name as the river, Ganges, through which are exported tejpat leaf, Gangetic nard [spikenard], pearls, and cotton garments of the very finest "Gangetic" quality.'¹¹ In modern times the floods of the Ganges are less predictable than those of the Nile, and far more devastating.

In the West there were alternatives to the costly spikenard of India. Medical writers tell us of 'Syrian nard', which was perhaps *Valeriana sisymbrifolia*, and of 'Celtic nard' which was the Alpine plant *Valeriana celtica*, and others too. But the really high prices, 40 to 75 *d.* the pound for the leaves, 100 *d.* the pound for the spike, were fetched by the 'tender spikes of downy nard' that travelled to the Near East, to Greece and to Rome by way of Barygaza or directly from the port at the mouth of the Ganges.

If the *nerd* mentioned in the *Song of Songs* (1.12), about the fifth century BC, is truly spikenard, it is the oldest evidence of this plant in Mediterranean lands. Theophrastus, in fourth-century Greece, was quite familiar with it. But why did the peoples of the early Mediterranean want spikenard? It contributed to the aroma of dining and festivity, as is shown by two very different sources less than a century apart. In both there is mention of a perfumed oil to anoint the brow, and of a carved onyx marble jar in which it is kept. The Roman poet Horace, in the first century BC, begins the explanation with a verse invitation that reads as a gentle jibe at his contemporary Vergil.

> It's a dry summer, Vergil, you pursuer of well-born boys! If you fancy tasting a good Italian vintage, you must earn your wine with nard: one little onyx pot of nard will get you a wine-jar now lying in a Roman warehouse, generous enough to give new hope and effective at washing away the bitterness of troubles. Come quickly, but bring your fee: I don't see you soaking up my wine if you come empty-handed.'¹²

St Mark's Gospel, written about a century later at the eastern end of the Mediterranean, helps us to clarify this picture. 'While Jesus was staying at Bethania in the house of Simon the Leper, reclining at dinner, a woman came with a carved pot of costly spikenard perfume. She broke open the pot and poured it over his head.' Afterwards there was complaint about the waste of money, and Jesus said, 'Let her alone; she has prepared my body for burial.'¹³ This was a clever response. It reminds us of two of the resonances of spikenard as a perfume: the woman's intention might have been to enliven the festivity and to honour an admired teacher or prophet by anointing his head, but it was equally true that costly perfumed oils were used to anoint the dead.

Classical Greeks and Romans loved the aroma of spikenard so much that they used it, just occasionally, in cookery.¹⁴ We have already seen the recipe for hare that was suggested in the sixth century by Anthimus – a recipe specially adapted to a sufferer from dysentery, hence its inclusion of five spices trusted for their medicinal powers. Perhaps two centuries earlier the Roman recipe book *Apicius* gives spikenard as a possible ingredient in two heady and expensive sauces:

Sauce for sliced cold meat. Pepper, lovage, caraway, mint, spikenard, tejpat leaf, egg yolk, honey, spiced wine, vinegar, fish sauce and oil. Stir with savory and leek; thicken with starch.

Glaze for roast venison. Pepper, spikenard, tejpat leaf, celery seed, dried onion, fresh rue, honey, vinegar, fish sauce; add Syrian dates, raisins and oil.[15]

The land of pepper

Male stands for the region of Malabar or Kerala. It may possibly be the first mention in literature of the port of Quilon (modern Kollam), so famous in medieval times, whose hinterland is often described as the 'pepper country'. The major ports in this region at the time of the early Roman Empire were Nelkynda (modern Niranom) and Muziris (Cranganore). The *Periplus Maris Erythraei* describes these cities and their trade for the benefit of Roman merchants. 'Ships at these trading ports carry full loads because of the volume and quantity of pepper and tejpat. They export pepper, grown for the most part in only one place connected with these ports, called Cottanarice. They also export Ganges spikenard and tejpat, brought from up country. For those sailing here from Egypt,' the anonymous merchant advises, 'the right time to set out is around the month of July.' He had never visited Sri Lanka, but he had seen in the ports of Kerala 'the very big *kolandiophonta* that sail across to *Chryse* [south-east Asia] and the Ganges mouth'. Though knowing very little of Chryse and nothing of the South China Sea beyond, he had been able to quote one Chinese phrase as a result of observing these exotic ships, his *kolandiophonta*: quite clearly in Chinese they would have been *kunlun bo*, 'South Sea ships'.[16] To match his description there is one by the Chinese trade official Zhao Rugua, writing twelve hundred years later.

> The land of the Nâyars is in the south-western extremity of India. From Sumatra you can reach it with the monsoon in a little over a month. The people are very dainty in their diet; they have a hundred ways of cooking their food, varying it every day. Its products are exported to Malaya and Sumatra, and the following goods are taken there to exchange for them: silk, porcelain, camphor, rhubarb, cloves, sandalwood, cardamom and aloeswood.

The Nâyar king of Malabar was attended by a troop of some five hundred foreign women selected for their shapeliness, Zhao Rugua adds. There were dancers at the front of the procession, bareback riders at the rear; all were dressed in loincloths, with filmy drapery, pearl necklaces and gold anklets. Their bodies were perfumed with camphor and musk and other aromas, and umbrellas of peacock feathers shielded them from the sun. The population were devout Buddhists.[17]

Long pepper

Of the two Indian species of pepper, the older in human history – and the stronger and hotter in flavour, everyone seems to agree – is the one that Europe has now almost forgotten. 'Long pepper' (*Piper longum*) is native to north-eastern India, from the southern edge of Nepal to Bengal and Assam; it was long ago transplanted to Kerala, in the south-west of the peninsula, and now grows wild there too. The root of this shrubby plant is used medicinally in India, but its main product, the spice, consists of the fruit pods: these are accurately compared to hazel catkins by 'Sir John Mandeville', quoted below.

In Sanskrit it is called *pippalī*, the origin of Chinese *pibo*, which continued to mean 'long pepper', and of all the European names for black pepper (see page 91). Long pepper is mentioned very early in Sanskrit literature, in the *Yajurveda* and *Atharvaveda*, collections of ritual and magical poetry that are possibly to be dated somewhere between 1000 and 500 BC. This is natural enough, because it grows very close to the region of north-western India where Sanskrit was spoken in those early times.

Dried long pepper is classed in Indian dietetics as a 'pungent' flavour, though with special properties: 'Long pepper, when fresh, provokes phlegm, is sweet in taste, heavy and oily. When dry, it is considered destructive of phlegm and wind; being pungent and hot, it is capable of increasing the semen. Foods of pungent flavour do not generally increase the semen, but long pepper and dry ginger are exceptions to the rule.'[18]

For nearly 2,000 years long pepper was one of the most valuable of Indian exports. It had reached Greece – as we know because it was mentioned in Athenian drama – early in the fourth century BC. Soon after 310 the botanist Theophrastus is able to add in the supplement to his *Study of Plants*: 'Pepper is a fruit, and is of two kinds: one round like bitter vetch, with a shell and flesh like bay berries, reddish; the long kind with poppy-like seeds, and this is much stronger than the other. Both are heating; thus, like frankincense, both are antidotes to hemlock,' and elsewhere he writes that vinegar, mixed either with pepper or with ground nettle seeds, had the potential to revive a suffocated patient.[19]

The Roman encyclopaedist Pliny, in the first century AD, gives Roman pepper prices, with a dash of his typical moralizing.

> Long pepper sells at 15 d. the pound, white 7 d., black 4 d. Why do we like it so much? Some foods attract by sweetness, some by their appearance, but neither the pod nor the berry of pepper has anything to be said for it. We only want it for its bite – and we will go to India to get it! Who was the first to try it with food? Who was so anxious to develop an appetite that hunger would not do the trick? Pepper and ginger both grow wild in their native countries, and yet we value them in terms of gold and silver.[20]

It was not only to food that Romans added pepper. They made peppered wine, adding also honey and sometimes other flavourings. They used pepper in medicines, such as the stimulating tonic described by Pliny that was based on elecampane 'flavoured with quinces, sorbs or plums, and sometimes enlivened – especially for jaded stomachs – with thyme or pepper;' it had become famous, he adds, since it was known that Augustus' daughter Julia took it every day.[21] This is a poignant aside: Julia, everybody knew, had been exiled by Augustus when he learnt of her extremely active sexual life. It is to be hoped that her daily dose of elecampane tonic with long pepper was not to blame.

In Europe long pepper is talked of as an important spice and drug throughout medieval times and down to the nineteenth century. Meanwhile, it also travelled east. In China it was mentioned, as if already fairly well known, by Ji Han in the fourth century. 'The Westerners bring it to us,' said Su Gong in the seventh century; 'we use it, for its flavour, to put in food,'[22] and they also used it as a drug, believing, like the Romans, that because it was more pungent it must also be more effective medicinally. Even the emperor Tai Zong was cured of some digestive ailment by taking long pepper boiled in milk.

The fact that long pepper continued to appear in all the European medical books, and in some of the cookery books, until the nineteenth century is deceptive. It suddenly dropped in price in the later sixteenth century. Soon after that it fell out of common use, although it was still in the reference books.

This must have been a source of frustration to the Dutch East India Company, which had meanwhile occupied the island of Java where another species of long pepper (*Piper retrofractum*) was native. The company developed the crop – indeed, some of the long pepper now used in India is imported from Indonesia – but it lost the European market. The reason, perhaps, was the discovery in central America of yet a third 'long pepper', the chilli. This is quite a different spice but it was occasionally called 'long pepper' in Europe because it had the same shape and served the same purpose of adding a powerful hot taste to food. And the chilli was cheap: unlike long and black pepper it propagated easily; it was readily transplanted – as it was to Spain and Hungary, for example – and it will grow indoors or in a greenhouse even in northern Europe. Philip and Mary Hyman, in 'Long pepper: a short history', suggest that on the sixteenth-century European market the competition offered by chilli was too much for long pepper. Its price eventually fell to only one-twelfth of that of black pepper, a price at which it no longer repaid the cost of gathering and transport. The trade to Holland continued longest, but it is now very hard to find long pepper in Europe, either the Indian or the Indonesian kind.[23]

Black pepper

'Black pepper is not especially hot. It does not increase the semen, but it is light and adds relish to food. It dislodges or dries up phlegm and the like; it is an appetizer.'[24] This milder form of pepper – the form that everybody knows nowadays – comes from the climbing tree *Piper nigrum*, native to southern India. Black pepper is the fruit, picked slightly unripe and dried; white pepper, less powerful to the taste, is the same fruit, picked a little riper, at which stage the pericarp is easily removed and the white seed remains.

It is called *marica* in Sanskrit. Marica is also the name of a demon, a pivotal character in the epic *Râmâyana* of the early centuries AD. Disguised as a deer, Marica was to distract Râma so that the villain Ravana was free to abduct the heroine Sîtâ. The demon's appearance when undisguised was certainly pepper-like, 'coloured like a black cloud', 'dressed in a black antelope skin', and as he contemplated the fatal endeavour that lay ahead of him 'shrivelled up in terror, passing his tongue over his dry lips' before bowing to the inevitable.[25]

Black pepper was known to the Greeks by the fourth century BC, as we have seen. They regarded it as a variety of long pepper, and called it by the same name (Greek *peperi*, Latin *piper*); the name *marica* was unknown in the West. At that early time black pepper, since it came from further away along land-based or coastal trade routes, must have been almost as costly as long pepper; being weaker in its power, it was less attractive. Five hundred years later the situation had changed. At the time of the early Roman Empire the Indian Ocean traders, having begun to take full advantage of the predictable monsoon winds, were able for the first time to reach the ports of south-west India easily. In their immediate hinterland was the 'pepper country', where black pepper grew easily and was cultivated on a large scale.

At Nelkynda 'they export pepper, grown for the most part in only one place connected with these ports of trade, called Cottanarice. For those sailing here from Egypt, the right time to set out is around the month of July, that is, Epeiph,' states the early Roman sailing guide. In the fourteenth century the fruit was 'picked in autumn and spread out on mats in the sun, as people do with raisins. They are turned repeatedly until they are quite dry and black; then they are sold to the merchants.' The ships from Roman Egypt would have been able to load in October or November and set out for home at the ideal time of year for sailing west.[26]

From that time on, black pepper, more than any other spice, was what the Romans wanted from India. The Caesars treated pepper as a currency, storing vast quantities of it, unused, in the Roman treasury. 'They arrive with gold and depart with pepper,' wrote the classical Tamil poet Tâyan-Kannanâr regarding the Roman traders who were to be seen at the port of Muziris in southern India. Pliny, not long before him, had lamented the vast quantities of Roman gold coin that were shipped eastwards to buy the aromatics of India. '100 million *sestertii* a year go from Rome to India, China and the Arabian Peninsula.'[27] And the *Periplus* reminds us that 'gold and silver coin' were a necessary cargo for ships on the southern India route because they were just about the only predictable bulk Roman export of adequate value to be exchanged for a shipload of aromatics.

Classical sources all agreed that long pepper was the most powerful medicine, the best to use in cases of poisoning. Thus gourmets and assiduous doctors might prescribe long pepper rather than black or white, but generally people talked about *piper* and listed it in recipes as if only one kind were in normal use.

How was pepper used in the ancient West? To take one text as an example: in Petronius' *Satyricon*, a Roman picaresque novel of the first century, pepper is wanted on one occasion in a cure for impotence. The peppered egg-yolk and peppered fish sauce that are mentioned elsewhere – in the episode called the 'Banquet of Trimalchio' – are typical Roman recipes, showing off the host's wealth, an excuse for one of his friends to say in a loud whisper, 'Don't think he ever needs to buy anything. It's all home-grown: wool, wax, pepper, if you ask for hen's milk you'll get it.'[28] We even have a recipe for the pepper sauce: 'Pound pepper, steeped overnight in wine, and add fish sauce to form a smooth, muddy fluid.'[29]

For a medieval use of pepper we may take John Russell's recipe from his *Boke of Nurture*:

> *Garlek or mustard, verjeus therto, pepur the powderynge –*
> *For thornebak, houndfysche and also fresche herynge,*
> *Hake, stokfyshe, haddok, cod, and whytynge –*
> *Ar moost metist for thes metes, as techithe us the wrytynge.*

In other words: garlic or mustard with verjuice (the juice of unripe grapes), and with pepper sprinkled over, are most suitable as flavouring, so our books tell us, for skate (*thornebak*), rock eel (*houndfysche*), fresh herring, hake, dried cod (*stokfyshe*), haddock, cod and whiting.[30]

Pepper was much the commonest and most typical oriental spice in medieval Europe. A perfunctory description of a rich meal will name pepper if no other spices. Here are the companions of Charlemagne on an imaginary visit to Constantinople, in a twelfth-century epic poem: 'Nothing that they wanted was denied them: they had plenty of game, venison and boar, cranes and wild geese and peppered peacocks. Wine and *claret* was served liberally, and the jongleurs sang and played their viols and their violins, and the French had a fine time.'[31]

Black and white pepper, as the Greeks and Romans knew, are varieties of the same product. Wrongly the Roman pharmacologist Dioscorides thought that long pepper, also, belonged in the same family – that black pepper was the fully ripened fruit from the pods of long pepper. Theophrastus had not made this slip, but once Dioscorides had started the story every later Western writer takes it up, Pliny in the first century, Galen in the second, Isidore of Seville in the seventh, Avicenna in the tenth; as late as the fourteenth century that curious book *The Travels of Sir John Mandeville* makes the same error.

> Pepper grows like a wild vine, planted near tall trees that support it just as they
> would a vine. The fruit grows like bunches of grapes, and the tree is so laden with
> them that it seems about to break. When the fruit is ripe, it is as green as a bean.

There are three kinds of pepper that all come from the one tree: first the long pepper, which ripens naturally; then white pepper, not burnt or toasted with fire or the sun's heat; then black pepper, dried by a fire or by the sun. The long pepper comes first, when the leaves are beginning to grow, rather as hazel catkins come before the leaves. Then follows white pepper, at the same time as the leaves, in great clusters like green grapes. Then comes the black pepper, very plentiful. They keep the white pepper for their own use, because it is more beneficial and more temperate in its operation, and retains its power longer.[32]

'These writers all concur in saying what is not true,' declares García de Orta, once more fated to correct a long-standing error. 'I don't blame Dioscorides, who relied on false information which came to him from a great distance, across a sea less often sailed than it is today.' García goes on to explain how the black pepper tree, a climber, is native to Malabar; its leaf is smaller than an orange leaf, bright green, sharp-pointed, slightly hot to the taste, very much like the betel leaf; however, the long pepper tree is different, and is native to Bengal. 'But pepper really is good as an antidote to poison: Dioscorides was right about that.' And García and his interlocutor nobly forbear to criticize Isidore, 'a saint, and a classic', who had been unwise enough to add to his encyclopaedia the information that each year when the pepper came ripe the natives of the 'Land of Pepper' set fire to the forest, for fear of the snakes, and so the snakes were burnt, and that was why the pepper turned black.[33]

The Land of Pepper, as mentioned above, lies inland from the ports of Kerala, ancient Nelkynda. The Latin encyclopaedist Pliny calls this pepper country Cottonara, the *Periplus* calls it Cottanarice: it is Tamil *Kuṭṭanâḍu*, the valley of the river Pâmbiyâr – noted locally for its fine pepper – which flows down to the site of ancient Nelkynda. Muziris (*Muciri*) is not far away. A Tamil poet of the second century sketches this trading port for us: 'Bales of pepper are brought to market from each house, and gold received in exchange from the Roman ships is brought to shore in sackfuls, at Muciri, where the music of the singing sea never ceases and where King Kudduvar loads his guests with the ambergris of the sea and the cardamom of the mountains.'[34]

To medieval visitors the Land of Pepper was equally well-defined and formed a distinctive landscape. 'The tree is like a vine,' writes Ibn Baṭûṭâ. 'They plant it at the foot of a coconut palm, and it grows up the tree just as a vine would.'[35] Even today there is little change. In the coastal districts of Kerala pepper vines are grown in gardens, but this pepper is mainly for domestic use. The commercial plantations are a short distance inland. But the Land of Pepper has gradually spread outwards as world demand has grown. The southern districts produce what is known in the trade as 'Alleppey' pepper, the northern 'Tellicherry'; from further north still, outside the traditional region of production, comes 'Mangalore' pepper.

Yet pepper will grow and has long been grown elsewhere. García de Orta knew of pepper in Java, in Sunda, in Sumatra, in Madagascar, in the Malay peninsula and elsewhere on the south-east Asian mainland – 'but all that is used up in China or in the districts that it comes from' – and, as usual, he was right. Arabic and Chinese observers had long known of pepper in south-east Asia: green pepper, they call it. Of Cambodia Zhou Daguan writes, 'Pepper is found occasionally. It climbs up bushes and entwines itself like a common weed. The green-blue variety is the bitterest.'[36]

Since the arrival of the Europeans, pepper has spread much further across the world. It is now an important crop in central Africa and in some of the Pacific islands. Green peppercorns – the unripe berries – are now a delicacy far outside the regions where pepper grows, even though conserved green pepper, a typically medieval delicacy, is almost forgotten.

Exotic spices in India

Because of India's position at the nexus of the trade routes, spices from both East and West reached India very early in recorded history. We have already seen, from the listings in the *Periplus*, that the ports on the west coast of India offered a market for storax, frankincense and some blended perfumes brought from the West. We know independently that frankincense was in demand in India: it is found in Indian literature, notably in Buddhist and Jain texts, of the early centuries AD. From the East cloves and nutmeg turn up in classical Indian poetry of about the same date. The classic Indian medical text, the 'Caraka collection', may be of this same date or rather later. It recommends cloves as breath-fresheners, along with several other eastern spices:

> One who wants clean, fresh, fragrant breath
> Must keep in the mouth nutmeg, cloves,
> Ambrette, areca nut, cubebs,
> Fresh betel leaves, camphor and green cardamom.[37]

Cloves were also prescribed for cough, hiccup, vomiting and inflammatory conditions of the mouth and throat; nutmeg for poisoning and also for rough skin and pruritus.

It is astonishing how many foreign aromatics were transplanted to India in the course of history. Chillies, which became a naturalized part of Indian cuisine in the sixteenth century, are only the latest and the best-known. Even in the third century BC the Buddhist emperor Aśoka, who reigned over all of northern India, was proud of his activity in transplanting aromatic and medicinal plants and encouraging his less meritorious neighbours to do the same.

> Everywhere in the dominions of the beneficent King, as well as in the border territories of the southerners, the Sri Lankans, the Greek King [of Syria] named Antiochus, and those kings who are neighbours of Antiochus – everywhere provision has been made for two kinds of medical treatment, treatment for men and for animals. Medicinal herbs, suitable for men and animals, have been

imported and planted wherever they were not previously available. Where roots and fruits were lacking, they too have been imported and planted.[38]

It is not possible to name for certain the spice plants that first reached India as a result of Aśoka's beneficence, but some can be listed that may well have arrived fairly close to this time. They include at least three foreign spices now extremely important in India: coriander, cumin and saffron. Poppy, ajowan and nigella also demand to be included in the list. All six of these are native to Europe or the Mediterranean shores. For their arrival in India we might make a bold guess that credit is due first to the Persian Empire, which stretched from Asia Minor to the borders of India and maintained a series of royal parks and botanical gardens; second to Alexander the Great, who seized the Persian Empire and was interested on his own account in transplanting European species to Asia; and third to Aśoka, who, as he claimed, transplanted useful plants to and within India.

Coriander first reached north-west India perhaps under Persian auspices, certainly before Alexander or Aśoka. It happens to be mentioned in Pânini's Sanskrit *Grammar*, generally dated to the fourth century BC. Its usual Sanskrit name, *kustumburu*, seems to be a loan from Aramaic, the lingua franca of the Persian Empire.

Saffron was certainly well established in Kashmir by the third century AD, when Chinese sources begin to describe it as a Kashmiri product. 'The habitat of saffron is in Kashmir,' stated the early Chinese medical writer Wan Zhen, 'where people grow it principally to offer it to the Buddha. The flower withers after a few days, and then the saffron is obtained. It is valued for its uniform yellow colour. It can be used to aromatize wine.'[39] How early had it reached Kashmir? According to Buddhist legend, saffron was planted there by Madhyântika, the first Buddhist 'apostle' to Kashmir. This, if related to historical fact, would put the first planting of saffron in Kashmir in the fifth century BC. Again, Persian gardeners might claim credit for transmitting saffron across western Asia.

Turmeric

Under the Sanskrit name *haridrâ* or *dâruharidrâ* turmeric occurs frequently in north Indian texts from about the first century BC onwards; it has been suggested – but cannot be proved – that Theophrastus, in fourth-century BC Greece, meant to refer to turmeric when he listed *khroma* ('colour') among exotic aromatics that he knew of. Independently of these texts, it seems certain that people in central India have been grinding the root of the native plant *Curcuma domestica*, to add to food and for magical and ritual uses, for much longer than two thousand years. This is one of those plants that survive only by human cultivation and are no longer known in the wild state, though a wild relative, yellow zedoary, still grows in eastern India.

The earliest history of turmeric is revealed by languages. While ginger was transplanted westwards from the Malay archipelago to India, turmeric travelled eastwards. We know this because it had reached eastern Indonesia or New Guinea early enough to be carried onwards, across the southern Pacific, by some of the early speakers of Oceanic languages, a subgroup of the Austronesian family. Their names for it are reconstructed as *yango* and *renga*; the word *lena*, which now means 'yellow' in Hawaiian, is one of the modern pieces of this linguistic jigsaw.

To the north-east, turmeric had reached southern China by the seventh century at the latest. It has its uses in traditional Chinese medicine, especially in controlling blood clotting and haemorrhage.

To the west, in the countries where saffron was traditionally available as an aromatic yellow colouring, turmeric, with its mild and undistinguished aroma, had few attractions in ancient and medieval times, because the cost of transport would have made it nearly as expensive as its rival. So early Western writers know little of turmeric. We may guess that it is the 'Arabian saffron' for which the Roman emperor Diocletian, about AD 300, laid down a maximum buying price for army supply: turmeric would have reached the Roman Empire by way of Arabian ports. We may guess also that turmeric is the 'kind of fruit that is like saffron, though it is not. Yet it is quite as effective in use as saffron is,' as noticed by Marco Polo in his visit to Fuzhou in south-eastern China.[40]

Elsewhere in the world, now that turmeric is a cheap spice and saffron remains expensive, turmeric is seen as a saffron substitute. It is given names like 'false saffron', *safran d'Inde* and perhaps 'Arabian saffron'. But in India, where saffron is the interloper, this is not really true: the two both have their independent uses.

Red sanders

While the subject of substitutes and crossed names is under discussion, red sanders demands consideration.

Sandalwood is powerfully aromatic – too powerfully, nearly everyone would agree, to be used in food. India, where so much sandalwood is used, has also another spice, sometimes described as 'a kind of sandalwood', and probably sometimes used by medieval doctors in place of the aromatic sandalwood that they intended. This is red sanders, the powdered wood of the tree *Pterocarpus santalina*. Since it has no sandalwood aroma and comes from an unrelated tree, there is no good reason for any confusion, except that in powdered form the two substances look rather alike.

Marco Polo's report of Madagascar (where he had never been) seems to give the first, apparently accurate, report of a new kind of sandal tree: 'They have many red sandal trees, as big as any of our trees, so many that there are whole forests of them.'[41] This is striking because sandalwood, *Santalum album*, is a parasitic tree which could not form a forest, so wherever he places his red sandal trees, Marco Polo is distinguishing them accurately from true sandalwood. In fact the main stands of this tree

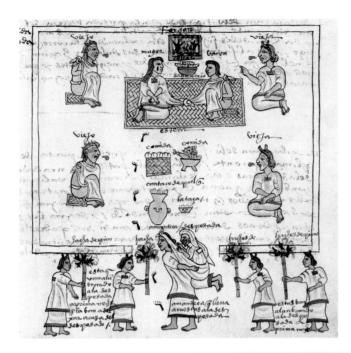

An Aztec wedding (*Codex Mendoza*, f.61r) shows aromatics in use in pre-Hispanic Mexico. The bride, her lips painted red with annatto, is carried in a procession lit by crackling, resinous pine torches (bottom). Then the newlyweds, their garments symbolically knotted together, kneel on a mat. Between them is a bowl of incense, which might be white copal (*Elaphrium jorullense*) and liquidambar, for tossing on to the hearth (top centre). Below them is a basket of tamales and a bowl of turkey stew; below again, a jar and bowl containing honeyed *pulque*, brewed from the agave plants that Columbus thought were aloes. The manuscript captions are in Spanish.

A page, captioned in French ('Balce'), from the 16th-century picture book *Histoire Naturelle des Indes*, compiled on one of Sir Francis Drake's expeditions, showing the collection of balsam of Peru, one of the most important discoveries among New World aromatics. 'Balsam is a resin very good for healing arrow wounds and others if applied with tobacco; also, taken with an egg, it relieves dysentery.'

Pepper, ripening on the vine. This species, originally from southern India, is the source of green peppercorns (unripe), black pepper (picked slightly unripe and then dried) and white pepper (picked ripe, dried and shelled). East India Company School, early 19th century.

The waterfront and foreign warehouses at Canton. Evidence for overseas communities at southern Chinese ports goes back to the 4th century AD, when Persians already grew jasmine there. This illustration is from an 18th-century Chinese porcelain punch bowl.

Market women and their customers in a north Indian bazaar. Indian painting from Benares, *c.* 1840.

A 17th-century French village épicerie, the scales and well-stocked shelves reminding us that they really did sell spices. The painter himself, Gérard Dou (1613–75), can be seen in the background at the left.

A sugar plantation at Pernambuco, Brazil. The freshly harvested cane is brought in from the fields on carts drawn by horses and oxen. It is then crushed in the water-driven roller mill before being boiled and allowed to crystallize. Vignette from the margin of a map in Carel Allard's *Atlas Maior*, 1710.

Le Déjeuner, 1739, by François Boucher (1703–70). But this is more than an everyday breakfast. Under watchful eyes the little girl is having her first, doubtful experience of chocolate, one of the legendary flavours of the spice trade: truly a dangerous taste.

are on the 'coast of Coromandel', as García de Orta puts it. From the point of view of the product rather than the tree, the Arabic trade author Abûl Fazl Ja'far, about a century before Marco Polo, states the facts clearly enough: 'there are two kinds of sandal, white and red. The red is used in medicines, the white both in medicines and in perfumery.'[42]

In India *P. santalina*, because of its red colour, serves as a decorative timber, 'for pagodas and idols', according to García. It has also been exported from India, for many centuries, as a powerful red dye. Because it is innocuous and without any strong taste, red sanders has been used sometimes in food as a colouring. It was popular in medieval Europe, and is still used in Switzerland for biscuits and in marzipan. Here is a recipe for 'Eels in red sauce', coloured with *sawndrys*, from a fifteenth-century English cookery manuscript:

> Skin eels. Chop them in pieces. Put them in a pot with onions and chopped herbs together with whole cloves, mace, cubebs, ground pepper, plenty of ground cassia, and fresh water. Make a sauce of breadcrumbs and wine, and add it. Put the pot on the fire, and stir. When it has boiled enough, colour it up with sanders; season it with ground ginger, vinegar and salt, and do not let it boil.[43]

Spices in Indian life

Alexander the Great is said not to have entered into diplomatic relations with any major Indian states; he came (in 327 BC), conquered a little, and went away. By contrast, his successor Seleucus, first ruler of the Greek kingdom of Syria (305–281), opened a more peaceful channel of communication. He sent Megasthenes as ambassador to the court of Chandragupta, emperor of northern India, and Megasthenes' reports on India were afterwards published. Now lost, they can be retrieved in part from references such as this: 'Megasthenes in *Indian Observations* book 2 says that at dinner the table that is placed before each person is like a pot-stand, and a golden bowl is set on it. In the bowl they first of all put rice – boiled just in the same way that we might boil cracked wheat – and then many different relishes prepared according to Indian recipes.'[44]

This is the very first surviving description of an Indian meal. With its 'golden bowl', it is evidently just the kind of meal that would be served to a diplomat. The variety of 'relishes' – that is, of meat and vegetable dishes to eat with rice – was to be recorded also by a later Chinese observer already quoted: 'The people are very dainty in their diet; they have a hundred ways of cooking their food, varying it every day.' And the Arabic diplomat Ibn Baṭûṭâ describes a royal meal in Kerala which fills out the picture, and gently hints that this one diplomat found the Indian diet not quite varied enough.

A beautiful slave girl, dressed in silk, places before the king the bowls containing the individual dishes. With a large bronze ladle she places a ladleful of rice on the platter, pours ghee over it, and adds preserved peppercorns, green ginger, preserved lemons and mangos. The diner takes a mouthful of rice and then a little of these conserves. When the helping of rice is all eaten, she ladles out some more, and serves a dish of chicken, again eaten with rice. When that is done, she helps rice again, and offers some other poultry dish, again eaten with rice. When all kinds of poultry have been served, she brings various fish, again eaten with rice. After the fish there are vegetables cooked in butter, and milk dishes, also eaten with rice. Rice is their only food: I once spent eleven months at that court without any bread. I had three years in southern India, the Maldives, and Ceylon, eating nothing but rice. I had to help it down with water.[45]

Here in a fourteenth-century narrative are the chutneys and pickles still so typical of Indian meals; here are 'preserved peppercorns', a local delicacy now unfamiliar elsewhere.

The variety of Indian cuisine, then as now, was achieved largely by the imaginative use of spices and other flavourings. It is in Indian texts, earlier than in those from any other part of the world, that we find theories and classifications of taste such as the 'six flavours' set out in the *Questions of Milinda*, probably written in the first century AD. These flavours are sweet, sour, salty, pungent, bitter and astringent. Each has its properties, its special benefits in the diet, its special ill-effects if taken to excess; the 'pungent' flavour includes what we would call 'hot', 'producing, on touching the tongue, a sense of pain and pinching; causing a burning sensation; leading to a discharge of water from the mouth, nose and eyes'.[46] In the early Indian medical texts there are long lists of the nutritional properties of foods, with special attention to spices and aromatics. In India, too, spices were used to give colour – examples include the saffron, turmeric and red sanders already discussed. 'That country produces wonderful colours,' wrote Onesicritus, who accompanied the expedition of Alexander in the fourth century BC.[47]

Chinese literature employs the symbolism of aromas; their use in perfumes, in incenses, in the life of the emotions has already been mentioned. In Indian literature, aromas are equally ubiquitous, and spices are used to define markets and cities as prosperous and peaceful.

According to the *Questions of Milinda*, the city of Sâgala was Menander's capital. 'Well laid out are its streets, squares, crossroads and market places; well displayed are the innumerable sorts of costly merchandise with which its shops are filled. Sweet odours are exhaled from the bazaars, where all sorts of aromatics and spices are laid out. There is laid up much store of property and corn and valuables in warehouses: foods and drinks of every sort, syrups and sweetmeats of every kind.'[48]

Aromas help too to define the beauty of landscapes, the desirability of men and women. India's classical poet Kâlidâsa, who wrote in Sanskrit in the fourth century, plays continually with the names and resonances of aromas. The cloud, the imagined *Cloud-Messenger* of one of his greatest poems, as it crosses the sky far above India, is to observe 'the caves of Udayâgiri, breathing out the perfumes of the courtesans who play lascivious games with their young lovers in the darkness'; it is to look down upon Ujjain, where the palace windows will exhale the heady scent of the royal ladies' perfumed hair; it is to notice the first snowy crags of Himâlaya, scented with the musk of the mountain deer; and it is eventually to recline upon the great mountain range, covering it as closely as a soothing ointment. There the beautiful recipient of the message is to be awakened with a cool breeze, as fresh as a recent shower and as a bouquet of jasmine.[49]

In a more everyday style, the Arabic traveller Ibn Baṭûṭâ describes the use of aromatics among the people of the hot and sweaty Maldive Islands in the fourteenth century. They were very concerned with cleanliness, washing twice a day, and used large quantities of perfumes such as sandalwood and musk. 'One of their customs is that after the dawn prayer each woman seeks out her husband or her son, bringing a box of ointment, rosewater and an oil of musk and ambergris. The men anoint their eyelids and perfume themselves with rosewater and musk.'[50]

Spices are at the centre of divine worship and of ceremonials from birth to death. In the fourth century the Chinese pilgrim Fa Xian arrived in Sri Lanka in time to attend the funeral of a revered monk. He saw

> a great pyre of firewood, perhaps thirty cubits square or more, and the same in height. Near the top were laid sandalwood, aloeswood, and other kinds of fragrant wood. They made a large carriage-frame like a Chinese funeral car, but without the dragons and fishes. At the time of the cremation the king and the people in multitudes from all quarters collected together and presented offerings of flowers and incense. While they were following the car the king himself presented flowers and incense. When this was finished the car was lifted on to the pyre, drenched in oil of sweet basil, and set on fire.[51]

The fact that Fa Xian remarked on them suggests that the burning of sandalwood and aloeswood, and the use of incense, must have been on a larger scale than in contemporary China, where all these products would have been more expensive. The use of aromatics in funeral rites is noticed again by the Jewish traveller Benjamin of Tudela, writing of southern India in the twelfth century: 'Pepper grows in this country. They plant the pepper vines out in the country, but each person knows his own plants. They are small, and the pepper is as white as snow. They dry it in the sun, and it turns black. Ginger, *calamus* and other kinds of spices are found there too. The inhabitants do not bury their dead but embalm them using certain aromatics.'[52]

Zedoary and zerumbet

In a prescription quoted on page 78 the fifth-century Greek physician Aetius calls for a new exotic ingredient, *zador*. This is the very first mention in the Western record of zedoary, an aromatic destined to become rather commoner in medieval texts. We have already encountered it in the French *Romance of the Rose*, and, under its alternative English name *setewale*, in Chaucer's translation of the *Romance*.

Medieval physicians were aware of two spices with similar names, zedoary and zerumbet. Both came from the East and both names percolated into European languages from Arabic (*zadwâr, zarunbâd*). The physicians disagreed on the differences between the two. '*Root of zedoary or setwall*,' writes Culpeper in the seventeenth century: 'this and *zerumbet*, according to Rhasis and Mesue, are all one; Avicenna thinks them different. I hold with Mesue: indeed they differ in form, for the one is long, the other round.' Culpeper seems to contradict himself: are they different or not? He means to say that although they look different, they have the same effects. 'They are both hot and dry in the second degree, expel wind, resist poison, stop fluxes and the menses, stay vomiting, help the colic, and kill worms. You may take half a dram at a time.'[53]

One Western author who is confident of being able to tell zedoary and zerumbet apart is García de Orta – and he, too, knows that zedoary will 'resist poison':

> I was working with the physicians of the Nizam of Hyderabad. They prescribed zedoary to someone who had been bitten by a scorpion, and he recovered his pulse and was restored to health. The root is as big as an acorn, and rather like one in shape, and its interior is translucent. The Nizam's children's private physician told me that it was of value for thirty-six different illnesses, but as an antidote to poisoning more than anything else.[54]

García goes on to explore the confusion between the two spices in medieval Arabic and European writers. He insists that zedoary was a costly rarity from far to the east – China, so he asserts, though Bengal would have been nearer the truth. Many earlier 'authorities', including Avicenna, had never seen it, though that did not stop them describing and prescribing it. But zerumbet was an easily propagated relative of ginger, widely grown in the neighbourhood of Goa.

It is surprising that so many of García's contemporaries disagreed with him. Duarte Barbosa, for example, lists the products of the 'kingdom of Calicut' in southern India as 'much pepper, plenty of good ginger valadine, cardamoms, myrobalans of all kinds, bamboo canes, zerumbet, zedoary, wild cinnamon'. All this is absolutely right except for the zedoary. Can he have meant the closely related turmeric, still unfamiliar in the West? However, García's assertion of the very high value of true zedoary root is quite in accord with the best-informed medieval physicians. Persian texts described *jadvâr* as a divine panacea, healing all ills, and a root of zedoary could fetch as much as four times its weight in gold.

García's confidence that the two roots were different is shared by modern botanists. They identify medieval zedoary as *Curcuma zedoaria*, a relative of turmeric growing wild in Bengal. Medieval zerumbet is identified with *Zingiber zerumbet*, a kind of 'wild ginger' found throughout India, now called kuchoora and best known in the perfume trade as the source of an essential oil with a hint of camphor.

But these are now neglected spices, except in the districts where they grow. So far from fetching four times their weight in gold, the roots of zedoary are used in India to extract *shoti* starch, which, like arrowroot, is used in thickening sauces. They are still allowed some minor medicinal uses.

Spices and European rule

'It is strange that we Portuguese have gone to so much trouble and expense to have all the world's pepper in our hands. We eat so little of it! Most of it is consumed in Germany and France,' remarks García de Orta's interlocutor. 'The Muslims take a large quantity of it to the Read Sea ports,' García replies, 'in breach of the King's monopoly. Nothing can ever be so well guarded as to prevent that.'[55] It was indeed a considerable trade, well worth the Portuguese king's attention. In the sixteenth century, it has been calculated, the Portuguese sold in Europe ten times more Indian pepper than grains of Paradise, and ten times more grains of Paradise than cloves or nutmeg.[56]

The search for spices had been from the beginning an impulse in the Portuguese voyages of discovery. Under this impulse, through the fifteenth century and with the untiring encouragement of Prince Henry 'the Navigator', they had pressed further and further down the west coast of Africa, and had long since found the regions where grains of Paradise grew.

Prince Henry died, and Vasco da Gama was born, in 1460. It was da Gama, in 1497, who led a newly built fleet of four ships that were fated to round the Cape of Good Hope (as Bartolomeu Díaz had done ten years earlier) and to press on, crossing the Indian Ocean, arriving in southern India at the port of Calicut on 20 May 1498. Calicut was the regular destination at this date of the merchant fleet that sailed annually from southern Arabia. 'Jedda is the name of the port where the whole trade of the Red Sea is at its most flourishing, a source of large and welcome profit to the Sultan of that kingdom,' explains the Portuguese epic poet Luís de Camões. 'From here, by treaty between the infidels, a fine fleet of great ships crossed the Indian Ocean to the Malabar coast each year in quest of spicery.'[57]

Whatever the combination of reasons that had brought the Portuguese to Calicut, it was jealousy over the spice trade that landed them in conflict there. Their opponents on the spot – Arab merchants in India and the Indian governments who took their side – hoped that this fleet, due to arrive any day, would engage with Vasco da Gama's four ships and destroy his expedition. Wisely, realizing what was in view, da Gama left in a hurry, carrying off with him a few captives and, more important, a cargo bought at local prices of 'burning pepper, and the nut and the black clove that have made the name of the new island of Molucca, and the cinnamon that makes Ceylon rich, renowned and beautiful'.[58] These four spices are specified by Camões – writing seventy years after da Gama's exploit – because they are specially appropriate to Portugal's future in the East. The Portuguese were soon to return in force to the Malabar coast, and pepper would be exported in Portuguese fleets from the port of Cochin. We already know of Portuguese involvement with the nutmeg and cloves trade of the Moluccas. And, for a century, a diamond in Portugal's crown of colonies would be Sri Lanka, producer of cinnamon: 'The noble island so well known under its ancient name of Taprobana, though today proud and independent on the profits of its hot and aromatic bark, is fated soon to pay tribute of the same to the Portuguese flag, rising tall and glorious on the tall tower of Colombo.'[59]

The fort was built in 1517, and from then the Portuguese dominated the ramshackle politics of the seven kingdoms of *Zeilaõ* for a hundred years, leaving a legacy of Portuguese surnames and of converts to Catholic Christianity. But, just as happened in the Spice Islands, so in Sri Lanka too the Portuguese dominion did not last long. From 1602 onwards the Dutch East India Company made inroads there, eventually ruling almost the whole island. It kept the price of cinnamon high, in accordance with its usual decisive approach to spice trading, by taking all supplies to Holland and burning any unsold surplus. The British, in turn, seized power in 1795 and held on to the island called by them Ceylon till it became independent in 1948, afterwards reverting to its old name Sri Lanka. Through all vicissitudes cinnamon is still a significant crop in Sri Lanka, and so is the island's other native spice, cardamom. But with the fall in the price of spices they have long ceased to be highly profitable, as they were when the Portuguese seized Colombo.

Amomum and cardamom

Of the many problems of identification posed by ancient Greek and Roman writings about spices, *amomum* is one of the most puzzling. It looked like a tiny bunch of grapes with leaves around, according to some descriptions. While the Romans' *cardamomum* was certainly what we call 'cardamom', it had very few mentions in ancient texts. It was something easily distinguishable from *amomum*, perhaps better than *amomum*, but the two had some similarities (and were sometimes confused). What, then, was *amomum*? According to Pliny, writing in the first century:

> The grapes of *amomum* are popular. They come from an Indian plant, a wild vine or, so some say, a contorted shrub one palm high. They are gathered stem and all, and packed gently by hand, being very fragile. The best kind is said to

have leaves like the pomegranate, not wrinkled, reddish in colour. The second best is pale, the third grass-coloured, the worst of all white: anyway *amomum* becomes white with age.[60]

Whatever it was, *amomum* was so sought after in the West, as early as the third century BC, that Seleucus, first Greek ruler of Syria, tried to transplant it to Arabia where it would be closer at hand.

The most likely guess is the one already made by the botanist Linnaeus, when in his modern scientific Latin he bestowed on a plant genus the name *Amomum*. By doing so he suggested that plants of this genus were the source of ancient *amomum*. They grow in south and south-east Asia, and they provide a spice that is rougher than cardamom but can be compared with it: some of them are now regarded as a poor substitute for cardamom, 'false cardamom', 'bastard cardamom'. One species is Nepaul cardamom, *Amomum subulatum*, which grows in Nepal and the southern Himalaya and is described evocatively by Janet Laurence as looking 'rather like a small cockroach'.

The problem with the identification is simply stated. *Amomum* was at its most popular in Rome in the first centuries BC and AD, and must therefore have been an important item of trade, yet it is never mentioned in the *Periplus*, the 'Sailing Guide to the Indian Ocean', which was written at just this time. The most likely answer is that *amomum* had always reached the Mediterranean by an inland trade route from northern India, and continued to do so even when other Indian spices were following the Indian Ocean route. Romans generally traced *amomum* to Pontus (north-eastern Turkey), to Armenia, to Commagene on the border between the Roman Empire and Parthia, to 'Assyria', and to Media in northern Iran: all these supposed sources make sense as stages on a land trade route to the Roman Empire from a real source of supply in northern India. Since *amomum* was never traded across the Indian Ocean, the author of the *Periplus* did not need to mention it, and he is a writer who always sticks to his brief.[61]

Amomum, to Romans, was the scent of men's hair: sometimes admired, sometimes overdone, as when it adorns the obsequious Syrian innkeeper of one satirical sketch, 'shiny with respectful *amomum*', running to welcome his free-spending customer.[62] It was a constituent of the Royal Perfume of the Parthian kings (page 108) – which included true cardamom too. *Amomum* was also one of the main aromatics in a flavoured wine recipe from the Roman Empire.

> *Making Aminaean wine.* Some put wine of Aminaean grapes in jars that have contained Italian wine, and bury them out in the open. Some also add a few bitter almonds and a little tejpat and concentrated must. Others, aloes 2 dr., *amomum* 3 dr., putchuk 4 dr., tejpat leaf 4 dr., melilot 9 dr., spikenard 2 dr., cinnamon 3 dr.: these quantities are for 7 amphoras of wine. Others again, 4 dr. each of myrrh, cassia, saffron; and some use *calamus* instead of myrrh.[63]

Amomum species were important in early China too. One kind, black or bitter cardamom, was known in China as 'seeds that increase wisdom' – a useful property – and these seeds were eaten in dumplings made of sticky rice or sticky millet. Bastard cardamom of Thailand had an aroma of camphor and was used to treat respiratory disorders. Round cardamom of Java had similar uses. The red flowers of *A. globosum*, which we call 'Chinese cardamom', were typical of the deep south to Chinese poets such as Li She, who imagined himself celebrating his meeting with an old friend somewhere south of Canton:

> *Above the river, by malarial hills, we see one another again;*
> *Immersed in drink, we look together at cardamom flowers.*[64]

Nowadays the larger (though still tiny) brown and black fruits of these 'false cardamoms' are sometimes used in cookery as cardamom is. For example, round cardamom or kepulaga (*A. compactum*), grown in Indonesia and Malaysia, is locally marketed as cardamom – to be added to curries and rice dishes, and to be finely ground and sprinkled on the top of Indian-style milk desserts.[65]

True cardamom is native to southern India and to Sri Lanka, where the wild form of the plant still grows. It is a large-leaved perennial grown high in the hills and reaching about 8 ft (2.5 m) in height; as a plant cardamom is very similar to those of the genus *Amomum*. In fact Linnaeus included it in that genus as *A. cardamomum*, but a later botanist revised this and it is now identified as *Elettaria cardamomum*.

Cardamom was sufficiently valued in India to reach the north-west of the subcontinent not later than the middle of the first millennium BC. Its Sanskrit name, *elâ*, came with it from the south, borrowed from a Dravidian language such as early Tamil. *Elâpattra*, 'cardamom leaf', is the name of a demon in the Sanskrit epic *Mahâbhârata*.

Theophrastus, far to the west in Greece, is able to report in 310 BC of *cardamomon* and *amomon* that 'some say they come from Iran, others from India, like spikenard and so many other aromatics'. He lists cardamom – and not *amomum* – among the plant aromatics that were used in perfumes, adding that it was especially suitable for combining with the aroma of cypress. 'It has a biting heat,' he observes, speaking now from the dietary point of view,[66] and other Greek and Roman writers agree; on the other hand traditional Indian medicine classes cardamom as cold.

In first-century Rome intelligence on the source of cardamom had not improved. Pliny says relatively little of *cardamomum*. It grew in Arabia, he thought. It did not, but from Sri Lanka it would certainly have passed through the Arabian ports on its way to Rome. There were four grades, Pliny continued, of which the best was very green and fleshy, with sharp corners, not easy to crumble; and this is fair enough. Romans used cardamom very little in cookery, so far as we know; but at the end of the Roman Empire, the short recipe book of the 'illustrious Vinidarius' advises the reader to keep cardamom in readiness in the kitchen, and includes 'asafoetida, ginger, cardamom' with fish sauce in a sauce for meatballs.[67] And here is cardamom in a powerful mixture from the *Apicius* recipe collection: 'Digestive oxygarum: ½ oz. pepper, 3 scruples Gallic parsley, 6 scruples cardamom, 6 scruples cumin, 1 scruple tejpat leaf, 6 scruples dried mint. Pound, grind, bind with honey. When required, add fish sauce and vinegar.'[68]

Like Jeeves' famous restorative, this Apician digestive seems likely to have given the patient the feeling that 'somebody had touched off a bomb inside the old bean and was strolling down my throat with a lighted torch'.

Far to the east, meanwhile, true cardamom is described in detail, relatively early, by the fourth-century Chinese botanical writer Ji Han:

> The young plant of the cardamom resembles a reed, and the leaves are like those of ginger. The flowers are slightly reddish; they form a spike, whose tip is darker-coloured. It is traditionally said that the eating of this flower will clear wind and dissolve phlegm, and allows wine to be taken in double the usual quantity. In AD 281 a bamboo chest full of cardamom came in tribute from Tongking. The Emperor tested it, found it effective, and shared it with his court.[69]

By this time, then, cardamom was being grown in Indochina; if we were uncertain of the fact, we would have gathered it anyway from Zhou Daguan's observation about Cambodia in the thirteenth century that 'cardamom is grown in the mountains by the wild people'.[70] It was, by that time, nearly a thousand years since the 'wild people' of the hills of southern Indochina had been in close contact with India. Cardamom is indeed grown at heights of about 3,300–5,000 ft (1,000–1,500 m) in forest clearings.

The camphor aroma more noticeable in some of the *Amomum* species is present in cardamom too, and some notice a hint of eucalyptus – two good reasons why cardamom has been used for breathing and lung problems in traditional medicine. 'The Indians use it a great deal against bad breath and as a masticatory; also to open the nasal passage and to clear the head,' writes García de Orta in the sixteenth century; and he concludes his dialogue on cardamom by serving his guest a fish flavoured with cardamom and the acid karanda fruit.

Cardamom is cultivated not only in Sri Lanka, southern India and Indochina, but nowadays also in Tanzania, Guatemala, El Salvador and New Guinea. In Sri Lanka grows the larger variety closer to the native wild tree. In India the best kind is var. *minuscula*, the pale green 'Alleppey cardamom'. This comes from a Mysore variety of the species, but it is grown in Malabar (Kerala).

Pliny's information was that green pods are best, and this is still said, but a better sign of good fresh flavour is if the seeds inside the pod are still sticky. The seeds soon lose their aroma when taken out of the pod, so it is not a good idea to buy cardamom seeds or ground cardamom.

Cardamom can be used in flavouring coffee. In fact half of all cardamom produced each year is required, in Arab-speaking countries, for precisely this. In northern Europe cardamom has been unusually popular – in Sweden and Finland, for example, it is used in baking, and around the Baltic in pickling herring. But it is most used in southern Asia: whole, in cooking various dishes, especially pulses and fish; also, ground, as an important ingredient in spice mixtures.[71]

The rarest of spices

Yours are the rarest of spices:
nard and saffron, calamus and cinnamon, and all the trees
that bear incense;
myrrh and aloes, and all the subtlest of aromas.

The Song of Songs.

The Sabaean harvest

The Arabian peninsula defines the region explored in this chapter. In its south-ern reaches lay the spice kingdoms already famous in Biblical and Classical times, Sheba or Sabaea the most notable among them, centred near modern San'a. At its north-western extremity, wide and beautiful, was 'the so-called Valley of Syria', between the Lebanon and Anti-Lebanon mountains, where many aromatics grew.' Across its northern edge flourished a succession of empires that drew part of their wealth from spices. They gathered in some of the spices of Arabia, and they transmitted, by river barge and camel caravan, spices and other costly products from the East to the Mediterranean and from the Mediterranean to the East.

Some of these realms have come into the story already. The Assyrians dominated the country that is now Iraq and Syria until the seventh century BC; theirs was one of a long succession of empires that took a tribute in 'all kinds of spices' from the Arab kingdoms to their south. The Assyrians are also the first people, anywhere in the world, who placed on record the transplanting of an aromatic plant species. The Assyrian monarch Ashurnasirpal II (883–859), having built himself a new palace at Calah, erected a commemorative inscription on which he proudly lists the trees that he had collected on his expeditions and planted in its garden. These trees included myrrh.

I collected and planted, from the countries through which I marched and the mountains which I crossed, trees and seeds wherever I found them: cedars, cypresses, myrrh trees, date palms, ebony, olive trees, tamarinds, oaks, pistachio trees, cornel trees, willows, pomegranates [and twenty-nine other species of trees, most of which cannot now be identified]. In the garden at Calah they competed with each other in fragrance. Pomegranates glow in that garden like stars in the sky.[2]

The ancient Persian Empire, which ruled all of south-western Asia from the sixth century BC to the fourth, claimed in its turn the tribute in Arabian spices – 'a thousand talents of frankincense per year', according to a Greek historian.[3]

The Persians inherited the Assyrian enthusiasm for gardens and also the Assyrian lavishness in royal pleasure-seeking. The Persian king was said by Greek moralists (who disapproved, on the whole) to have sent emissaries from end to end of his vast empire, searching for new dietary sensations: 'they travel the whole earth searching out what he will like to drink; tens of thousands work at what he will like to eat; and as to his sleeping soundly, no one can describe how busily they strive for it.' In response to his demand, many 'cooked dishes, sweets, incenses and perfumes' were newly invented for his use and enjoyment.[4] Alexander the Great, King of Macedon, seized the Persian Empire – and, in his short reign, had time to dispatch a fleet that explored the coasts of Arabia and investigated the sources of frankincense and myrrh.

On the death in 323 BC of Alexander, the Greek-speaking monarchs of the Seleucid dynasty emerged as rulers of the Middle East. We have seen already that Seleucus I, founder of the dynasty, tried unsuccessfully to transplant *amomum* to Arabia – a clear sign that, like his Assyrian and Persian predecessors, he took tribute from that region. His wealth in the spicery of Arabia, and of the Indian Ocean too, is symbolized by a rich donation in 288 BC to the Temple of Apollo at Didyma whose rebuilding he had financed. The donation included frankincense from Arabia, putchuk from Kashmir and cinnamon from wherever ancient cinnamon came from.

Seleucus' emissary to India, Megasthenes, had brought back a plethora of wonderful tales about that distant country, its festivities and its aromas. It is no coincidence that Seleucus' descendant Antiochus Epiphanes was said (by a severe observer) to have gone in for 'Indian revelry and orgies'.[5]

The Seleucid realm shrank in the first century BC to nothing, squeezed between the Roman Empire to the west and the Parthian kingdom to the east. Pliny, the Roman encyclopaedist, in the course of his survey of aromatics, gives a recipe for the Parthian 'Royal Unguent' – an excellent demonstration of the range of scents that were available to the King of the Parthians whenever he anointed his brow.

The *Regale Unguentum*, so called because formulated for the Parthian kings, comprises ben-nut oil, putchuk, *amomum*, cinnamon, *comacum* [unidentified], cardamom, spikenard, zatar, myrrh, cassia, storax, ladanum, balsam, *calamus*, ginger-grass, wild grape, tejpat, *serichatum* [unidentified], henna, thorny trefoil, galbanum, saffron, nut-grass, marjoram, cloves, honey, wine.[6]

We do not know Pliny's source for this recipe, so the careful historian must not ascribe to it a date earlier than Pliny's own, the mid first century AD.

Parthian rule gave way in 224 to a reborn Persian Empire. The Sassanian Persians in their turn profited from their proximity to the sources and the routes of the spice trade, using aromatics liberally in worship, festivity and medicine, as shown, for example, in a Roman description of the Persian ritual with which an agreement between Rome and Persia was concluded: 'The treaty is sworn at altars fragrant with heaps of incense and with the Sabaean harvest. Magi took blessed fire from the sanctuary and slaughtered calves by the Chaldaean rite. The King's own hand makes a libation from the jewelled cup, and invokes the mysteries of Bel and Mithras who guides the wandering stars.'[7]

The 'Sabaean harvest', in this poetic phrase, is the tribute of Arabian spices to which Persia still laid claim. And some Indian aromatics, including spikenard, *amomum* and putchuk, continued to reach the Mediterranean by a land route through Persia, or by way of Charax or Meson, the ancient port at the head of the Persian Gulf.

Gum guggul

By this route other spices, too, might have come to the West – if indeed it was true, as the Roman geographer Strabo had heard, that aromatic shrubs were so common in eastern Iran that the Macedonian troops had cut them down like brushwood. That inhospitable country, as he puts it, 'produces aromatic plants, in particular nard and myrrh: Alexander's army used them for tent-coverings and bedding, thus at the same time enjoying sweet odours and a more healthy air'. This is a version of one of the commonplaces about spices – that in certain far-off places they are so common that the local people place no value at all on them. In just the same way it was said, by those people who thought cassia came from Sabaea, that the Sabaeans used cassia as everyday firewood; in just the same way it was once said that the Sri Lankans allowed the Indians to take as much cinnamon as they liked from the logs lying untenanted on the shore.

The first ancient description of a native myrrh-like aromatic of Iran is given, as a direct result of Alexander's expedition, by Theophrastus. 'In the region called Aria there is a thorn tree which produces a tear of resin, resembling myrrh in appearance and odour. It liquefies when the sun shines on it.' Theophrastus assigns no name to his 'thorn tree', but he likens it to myrrh. Strabo simply calls one of his two Iranian spices 'myrrh'. Some Chinese texts, too, state that myrrh grew in Persia.

A little later than Strabo, the *Periplus* lists a spice called *bdella* as coming from Barbarice, the port at the mouth of the Indus. Ancient *bdella* or *bdellium* has been identified, ever since a medieval Arabic physician first made the link, with a myrrh-like resin called gum guggul (*Commiphora mukul*), which is native to eastern Iran and western India and might naturally have been traded at Barbarice: 'it is imported from the Beyla territory, west of Sind,' according to Henry Yule and Andrew Burnell. It is *gulgulu* in Sanskrit, hence the modern name; *muql* in Arabic, hence the botanical name. If *bdellium* is gum guggul, the unnamed myrrh-like tree of Theophrastus, Strabo and the Chinese sources is most likely gum guggul as well.[8]

Asafoetida or hing

One more spice that certainly did come to the early Mediterranean by land across Iran was in heavy demand in every self-respecting Classical kitchen. Europe has forgotten it now, and India is left to show the world the use and pleasure to be derived from asafoetida, better known in Indian English as hing. To define asafoetida to the uninitiated I can do no better than quote Yule and Burnell again: 'HING, *s.* Asafoetida. Skt. *hingu*, Hind. *hîng*, Dakh. *hîngu*. A repulsively-smelling gum-resin which forms a favourite Hindu condiment, and is used also by Europeans in Western and Southern India as an ingredient in certain cakes eaten with curry (*see* POPPER-CAKE).'[9] Asafoetida really does possess a remarkable aroma, combining something of leek and something of onion with much that is neither: it well earns the name of 'devil's dung' in some modern languages. It was never likely to be included in a Royal Unguent.

As we have seen, asafoetida emerges into history as a result of the conquering expedition of Alexander the Great, when, as they traversed the north-eastern provinces of the old Persian Empire (modern Afghanistan), his soldiers made the providential discovery of a plant they thought identical with silphium, the wonderful spice from Cyrene in north Africa. This Iranian 'silphium' turned out to be not quite so good. Dioscorides, in the first century, wrote that 'the Cyrenaic kind, even if one just tastes it, at once arouses a humour throughout the body and has a very healthy aroma, so that it is not noticed on the breath, or only a little; but the Median [Iranian] is weaker in power and has a nastier smell', while Galen considered it 'rather windy'.[10]

However, it could be substituted for silphium in cookery, and that was the providential fact, because not long after Dioscorides' time the true silphium of Cyrene became extinct. Asafoetida now came into its own; it was in heavy demand among physicians as well as cooks. The demand raised the price, and unscrupulous suppliers adulterated their asafoetida with sagapenum, the far less magical resin of *Ferula persica*.

Asafoetida is required in well over half of all the recipes in *Apicius*. Roman cuisine would have been a very different thing without it. Here it is in a nourishing barley broth:

Soak chickpeas, lentils, peas. Break barley and boil with the pulse. When it has boiled thoroughly, add sufficient oil and chop in green leek, coriander, dill, fennel, chard, mallow, young cabbage: put all these finely chopped greens into the saucepan. Boil cabbage leaves. Crush sufficient fennel seed, oregano, asafoetida, lovage. When crushed, blend with fish sauce, pour over the pulse, and stir. Finely chop the cabbage leaves over the top.[11]

Asafoetida was in demand both westwards and eastwards. By the seventh century the product had been heard of by the Chinese:

> *Awei* grows among the western barbarians and in Turkestan. Its sprouts, leaves, root, and stems strongly resemble *Angelica anomala*. The root is pounded: the sap thus extracted from it is dried in the sun and pressed into cakes. Its major characteristic is its foul odour, but it can also stop bad smells – a strange product indeed. The Indian Brahmins say that their *hungu* is the same as *awei*, and that the coagulated juice of the root is like glue; they confirm that it has a foul odour. In the western countries its use is forbidden to monks. Habitual use of it is said to cure bad breath. The barbarians think as highly of it as the Chinese do pepper.[12]

Meanwhile India, much closer to the region where asafoetida grows, naturally appreciated its properties to the full. Among the 'best and worst' aphorisms of the early dietary and medical manual *Caraksaṃhitâ* the following appears: 'Of catalysts, appetizers, digestives, and cures for wind and phlegm, asafoetida is best.' A later instruction in the same text advises the physician that asafoetida is pungent and hot, cures constipation, assists the appetite, helps in colic and 'adds relish to food'.[13]

From the end of the Roman Empire until the sixteenth century Europeans rarely encountered asafoetida, and then only as a medicine. 'If used in cookery it would ruin every dish because of its dreadful smell,' asserts García de Orta's European guest. Nonsense, García replies, 'nothing is more widely used in every part of India, both in medicine and in cookery. All the Hindus who can afford it buy it to add to their food. The rich Brahmins, and all the Hindus who are vegetarian, eat a lot of it. They add it to their vegetables and herbs, after first rubbing the cooking pot with it: it is seasoning, sauce and condiment in every dish they eat.'

Asafoetida had the most awful smell in the world, he adds, but in cooked dishes it was very good. Although Galen believed asafoetida provoked wind, García knew its value in treating it. A Portuguese merchant in Vijayanagar had a very valuable horse which was terribly flatulent, and for that reason the king would not buy it. The Portuguese cured it by giving it hing mixed with flour. The king paid a good price for it when it was healthy, and asked how it had been cured. 'With hing,' answered the Portuguese. 'I am not surprised,' said the king: 'what you gave it was the food of the gods; it is what poets call nectar.' The Portuguese said (but he said it in Portuguese and very quietly) that 'the food of devils' would have been nearer the truth.[14]

No Westerner, not even García de Orta, as yet knew the exact geographical origin of asafoetida, or what kind of plant it came from. The credit for determining this – and for drawing a detailed illustration of the process of harvesting the resin – goes to Engelbert Kaempfer, whose book *Amoenitatum exoticarum politico-physico-medicarum fasciculi V*, 'Five studies of exotic wonders, political, scientific and medical', was published in 1712.

The Romans had thought that they could distinguish Syrian, Median, Armenian and Persian kinds of asafoetida. Kaempfer's text begins by denying the reality of such distinctions. All had the same origin: they were the resin of a single species (whose modern scientific name, incidentally, is *Ferula assa-foetida*), a tall, stout umbellifer. 'I have been told by two Chinese druggists that it grows in China,' he adds, 'somewhere near the Great Wall, but I do not find it in the Chinese herbals.' The plant actually grew near Herat (in modern Afghanistan), which is not very near the Great Wall of China, and also in the mountains of Laristan in south-western Iran. The two plants were said locally to differ, but Kaempfer himself could not see any difference. The plant could be tapped only at a certain time of year. Cuts were made at regular intervals through the short collecting season, but if tapping was done in the proper way, growth would continue afterwards: the plant might flourish for many years.

One continuing source of confusion about asafoetida is whether the supplies usually found in the spice trade are 'adulterated'. The three classic scientific descriptions of this spice – Theophrastus on silphium, García de Orta and Kaempfer on asafoetida – all explain that the resin flows from the plant in liquid form and must be stabilized in order to turn it into the traditional asafoetida of trade. For this purpose various forms of meal, most often bean meal, are mixed with it. So 'adulteration' is the wrong word: the addition was not deceitful and there was no better way to handle the product. Since the seventeenth century, however, the essential oil of asafoetida has been available. Nowadays, from well-stocked herbalists, asafoetida essence can be bought as an alternative to the traditional lump or powder supplied by Indian food shops. Whether in Indian or in recreated Roman cuisine, it is to be used in tiny quantities!

One real adulterant of asafoetida in ancient times (possibly today as well) is sagapenum, a similar substance with a less interesting flavour: this resin of *Ferula persica* comes from Iran and counts as a spice in its own right. A third resin from the same genus of plants is galbanum, from *Ferula galbaniflua*. It is used as an incense and as an ingredient in perfumes, and is collected in the neighbourhood of Hamadan in Iran. In ancient times galbanum travelled widely, not only westwards to Rome but also eastwards to China. Early Chinese texts confirm what Greek, Roman and modern trade sources all assert: there is a second source of supply of galbanum, in Syria, but what species is tapped there no one seems to know.

Arabia the Blessed

Along the southern coast of Arabia lay the country that above all others in the ancient world was considered fortunate. This gave it its proper name, *Arabia Felix* in Latin, *Arabia Eudaimon* in Greek, or 'Arabia the Blessed', a name that is first heard in Greek poetry of the fifth century BC – long before any Greeks had been there – and was later given very precisely to the harbour city where Aden now stands. Why? The Arabian desert in general, and the hinterland of Aden in particular, is an inhospitable place. The unique blessing that southern Arabia was so fortunate in possessing was spices. 'Towards the midday sun,' wrote Herodotus in the fifth century BC, 'Arabia is the furthest inhabited land. This is the one country in the world where frankincense grows, and myrrh, and cassia, and cinnamon, and ladanum.' Ladanum is now the least-known of the spices of Arabia. 'Sweet-smelling substance though it is,' Herodotus continues, 'it is found in a most malodorous place: sticking, namely, like glue in the beards of he-goats which have been browsing among the bushes. It is used as an ingredient in many kinds of perfume, and is what the Arabians chiefly burn as incense.' This gum from the leaves of *Cistus ladaniferus* is still important in perfumery.[15]

For Greeks and Romans and their gods, these aromas accompanied worship, feasting and love-making. Arabia, whose whole harvests were spices, whose cooking fires were the wood of the incense and myrrh trees, must be permanently happy, so it seemed. 'There is a happy, far-off land in the extreme east, where the great gate of heaven stands open. This grove, these woodlands are the home of the matchless phoenix,' wrote the anonymous author of the Latin poem *The Phoenix*, five centuries after Herodotus. This mythical bird, rising from her fragrant ashes, each time rebuilt her nest with the aromas of Arabia and of all the world.[16]

The earliest full description of the Red Sea coasts, including the spice lands of southern Arabia, was given by the geographer Agatharchides, writing in Ptolemaic Egypt in the second century BC. He had apparently not been that way himself, and he used both good and bad sources.

In Arabia the Blessed, the region that we now call Yemen, Agatharchides reports the populous tribe of the Sabaeans, possessors of every sort of good fortune. But, as a counter-balance to her special blessings on the country, Fortune had also given it jumping snakes, particularly numerous in the aromatic forests. Agatharchides goes on to explain that the Sabaeans' senses were weakened and dulled, and their menfolk were rendered lethargic and effeminate, by continual exposure to these aromas (which were, by association, aphrodisiac to Greeks and Romans). They needed to revive themselves regularly by inhaling the smoke of pine resin and of burning goats' beards.[17] The story about the snakes was at least three centuries old in Agatharchides' time. It comes from Herodotus, who wrote: 'When gathering frankincense, they burn storax (the same substance that the Phoenicians import to Greece) and this storax raises a smoke that keeps away the small flying snakes. Great numbers of them keep guard over all the trees that bear the frankincense. Smoking them out with storax is the only way to get rid of them.'[18]

Nearly two centuries before Agatharchides, the botanist Theophrastus (who had little time for jumping snakes) had been able to draw on several sources in his description of the frankincense and myrrh trees, one of which was a first-hand report from the coastal exploration of Arabia ordered by Alexander the Great.

Neither tree is large, but the myrrh tree is smaller and nearer the ground. The frankincense tree has a leaf like bay and has smooth bark. The bark of myrrh is spiny and not smooth, and its leaf is like elm, but curled and spinous at the tip like kermes oak. Our people on the seaborne expedition from Heroonpolis said that they disembarked to look for water and saw the trees and how they were harvested. Both trees had cuts in the trunks, apparently made with an axe, and lighter cuts in the branches. The tears of resin were sometimes falling, sometimes adhering to the tree. In some places palm-leaf mats were put underneath; in others the ground was simply cleared of dust and dirt. The frankincense on the mats was clean and transparent, that on the ground worse. What adhered to the trees they scraped off with iron tools; some had bits of bark in it.

The whole mountain belongs to the Sabaeans. They behave honestly, so no one keeps guard; which is why our men, who had greedily taken some frankincense and myrrh to their ships, were able to load it and sail off. The place seemed deserted.

What follows is from hearsay. The myrrh and frankincense from all parts is brought in to the Temple of the Sun. Each makes a heap of his own frankincense and myrrh and leaves it with the guards, placing on each heap a tablet stating the number of measures and the price. When the merchants arrive, they look at the tablets, and whatever pile they like they take away, putting down the payment in the spot from which they took it. The priest reserves a third of the price for the god. He leaves the rest, and that remains safe for the owners whenever they come back to collect it.[19]

Here is one more version of the tale of 'silent barter' – it can still properly be called barter, although money is involved – the tale that recurs so often as we follow the spice trade through history.

Frankincense

This was Theophrastus' only eye-witness account of frankincense, but he had read other descriptions of the frankincense trees, here summarized by Pliny. 'The descriptions given by the Greeks vary: some have stated that it has the leaf of a pear tree, only smaller and of a grass-green colour; others that it resembles the mastic and has a reddish leaf; some that it is a kind of terebinth, and that this was the view of King Antigonus, to whom a plant was brought.' All this Pliny takes from Theophrastus, and then continues from a later source: 'King Juba in his volumes dedicated to Gaius Caesar, whose imagination was fired by the fame of Arabia, states that the tree has a twisted stem and branches closely resembling that of the Pontic maple and that it gives a juice like that of the almond.'[20]

The particular cargo of frankincense that was illicitly loaded by the men on

Alexander's Arabian expedition has a special place in legend. 'Alexander as a boy had been heaping frankincense generously on the divine altars when his tutor, Leonidas, interposed: "First you had better conquer the incense-growing tribes: then you may be generous with your incense." So Alexander, once he was master of Arabia, sent him a shipload of incense and told him to be sure to make a generous offering.'[21]

Juba's books on the exotic south were written in Augustus' time, when Rome was in expansionary mood. The emperor's Arabian ambitions were, naturally, aroused by the lucrative trade in frankincense and myrrh. But the expeditions of Gaius Caesar and Aelius Gallus were failures. Sabaea remained independent of Rome, and the trade continued under local auspices and for local profit.

Frankincense is a gum from the tree *Boswellia sacra*, which is unique to southern Arabia (modern Oman). *B. sacra* is an archetypal spice plant. It grows only in a limited, inaccessible, inhospitable location, far distant from the centres of civilization, and it must be transported over difficult roads and seas. It has never been grown outside its native habitat in commercial quantities, though a single frankincense tree was once established in a sacred precinct at Sardis, capital of the wealthy kingdom of Lydia, where Theophrastus knew of it 2,300 years ago. In modern times botanical gardens have occasionally emulated this *tour de force*.

In these fertile circumstances, history shades into romance. Herodotus has already told us of the jumping snakes. Pliny describes the soil of the frankincense country as milk-white in colour. Bordered by inaccessible cliffs and uncrossable mountains, only one narrow path gives access to it, and it is a capital offence for camels to turn off this path once they are laden with incense. Chinese texts, too, tell romantic tales of the production in the most distant West of frankincense, the 'milk aromatic' as they call it; of its origin in 'the depths of the remotest mountain valleys', its transport to the coast on elephants, and the thirteen qualities by which it was graded.[22]

From the earliest literary records onwards frankincense was needed in the worship of the Greek and Roman gods. Already, early in the fifth century BC, the Greek poet Pindar writes of 'the yellow tears of the green incense tree'; Sappho, a hundred years earlier, knew of the aroma of frankincense at wedding celebrations. Egyptians were well acquainted with it and are thought to have buried a supply of frankincense in royal tombs, but this was one aromatic that they did not use in mummification. 'Address Janus, Jove and Juno with incense and wine,' the elder Cato instructed his Roman readers in the second century BC.[23] Early Christians regarded incense as a typically pagan commodity: an 'incense-burner', in their eyes, was a renegade, one who had forsworn Christianity and gone back to the old ways.

Theophrastus described the power of frankincense as heating, whence it was used as an antidote to poisoning by hemlock; also astringent, biting and with a certain bitterness. Frankincense was hot and dry in the second degree, according to later pharmacologists both Roman and Persian: it healed wounds but might burn the blood; and the smoke was even hotter and drier than the resin itself, and was effective against eye disorders.

In the mid first century the *Periplus* describes two of the harbours from which frankincense was exported by sea – to Egypt and the Roman Empire, but also eastwards to India:

> All the frankincense grown in the land is brought into Cane, as if to a warehouse, by camel as well as by rafts of a local type made of leather bags, and by boats. The frankincense-bearing land is mountainous, has a difficult terrain and an atmosphere close and misty, and it has the trees that yield the frankincense. These are not large or tall; they exude frankincense in congealed form on the bark, just as some of the trees we have in Egypt exude gum. The frankincense is handled by royal slaves and convicts, for the districts are terribly unhealthy, harmful to those sailing by and absolutely fatal to those working there – who, moreover, die off easily because of the lack of nourishment.

At one nearby harbour, the *Periplus* continues, vessels trapped by the approach of winter are allowed to load frankincense, which stands there 'unguarded, thanks to some power of the gods who watch over this place. Frankincense cannot be loaded aboard a ship without royal permission, even secretly; if even a crumb is lifted aboard, the ship cannot sail, since it is against the god's will.'[24] The classic exploration of the inaccessible cliffs and almost uncrossable deserts, the incense roads and the traditional harbours of southern Arabia, from which myrrh and incense have been shipped for over 3,500 years, is Freya Stark's *The southern gates of Arabia*.

Both Theophrastus and the *Periplus* assert that the harvest is collected in a single place where it is under divine protection. By contrast, when it reached the factories of Egypt where it was incorporated in perfumed oils, 'no security is good enough. A seal is affixed to the workmen's loincloths; they have to wear a mask or hairnet with a close mesh; when they finish work they are strip-searched.'[25]

'Myrrh is common to Arabia and north-east Africa,' Pliny writes, 'but frankincense occurs nowhere except Arabia.' He is wrong. Two species similar to the frankincense of Arabia, *Boswellia carterii* and *B. frereana*, grow in Somalia; they produce what Roman merchants in Classical times used to call 'far-side incense', because they loaded it at African harbours beyond the straits of Bab el-Mandeb. The general agreement of all early sources that incense came from southern Arabia is slightly deceptive. The Sabaeans and their successors controlled the trade in Somali as well as Arabian frankincense, and it may at times have been the Somali species *B. carterii* that produced the most and the best. A fourth species, *B. serrata*, growing in the mountains of central India and on the Malabar coast, produces an incense of lower quality.

Myrrh

Frankincense and myrrh are well known to everyone familiar with the story of Jesus, as two of the three gifts brought to the newborn King by three wise men. Marco Polo was pleased to have discovered in Persia new information on this legend, which at the same time explained why the old Persians were fire-worshippers.

In Persia is the city of Saba, from which the Three Kings set out on their way to adore Jesus Christ. They are buried in this city in three very large and beautiful chambers, side by side, upon each of which stands a well kept masonry tomb. Their bodies are still preserved, with the hair and beards. They are called Jaspar, Balthasar and Melchior. Messer Marco Polo often asked the people of this city and its neighbourhood about the three magi, but he found no one who could answer his questions beyond saying that three kings had been buried there long ago. Three days later, at the Castle of the Fire Worshippers, he did find out what I shall now report. Why they worship fire I shall explain in their own words.

'In the distant past three kings of this country set out to adore a prophet newly born, taking three offerings, gold, incense and myrrh, in order to discover whether this prophet was a god, or a king upon earth, or a physician: they said that if he took the gold he would be a king, if he took the incense he would be a god, if he took the myrrh he would be a physician. When they came to the place where the child had been born, the youngest of the three went in and found the child of the same age as himself, and came out astonished. After him the next, who was quite young, went in and likewise thought that the child was of his own age; he too came out astonished. Then the next, who was very old, went in and had the same experience as the other two, and he came out deep in thought. When they were together each said what he had seen and found, and they were all astonished, and agreed to go in again, all together. So they did, and found the child to be thirteen days old, as in fact he was. They adored him, and offered him gold, incense and myrrh; and the child received all three offerings and gave them in return a closed box.

'The three kings set off for their own country. When they had ridden several days, they wondered what the child had given them. They opened the box and found a stone in it. Seeing this they wondered what this was that the child had given them, and what it meant. Since he had taken all three offerings, they had concluded that he was a god and a king and a physician. He had known their thoughts, and had given them the stone as a sign that the faith that they had begun to show should be as firm in them as a stone.

'But they did not know what the stone meant, so they threw it into a well. At once a burning fire came down from heaven and descended into the well. They were amazed, and much regretted throwing away the stone, for they saw now that it had a great and good meaning. At once they took some of the fire, returned to their own country with it, and placed it in the finest and richest of their churches. They caused it to burn every day, and adored it like a god.'[26]

Marco Polo's Saba is the city of Saveh in Iran – but the coincidence with the name of the Biblical spice kingdom in southern Arabia, Saba or Sheba, source of frankincense and myrrh, no doubt struck him forcibly.

Myrrh is the resin of the tree *Commiphora myrrha*, which grows in south-western Arabia and in Somalia. Myrrh was certainly known in ancient Egypt, well before the fifteenth century BC when it was a goal of Queen Hatshepsut's expedition to Punt, at the mouth of the Red Sea. The Egyptians worshipped their sun god Ra with an incense named *kyphi* that included (according to a later source) juniper and several aromatic herbs, mixed into honey and wine; but the only exotic spice in it was myrrh,[27] which would have come from the 'land of Punt'.

Myrrh was known too in Israel and in Assyria (where its name was *murru*): there, as we have seen, Ashurnasirpal II (883–859) had transplanted a myrrh tree to his botanical garden at Calah. It was known to the ancient Greeks by the sixth century BC (as *myrrha* or *smyrna*), and in due course Theophrastus was able to say something of its origin, thanks to Alexander's Arabian expedition. Pliny, in his encyclopaedic *Natural History*, gives fuller details:

> The myrrh-producing tree is likewise tapped twice a year, at the same seasons as the frankincense tree, but in its case the incisions are made all the way up from the root to those of the branches that are strong enough. Before it is tapped the tree exudes a juice called *stacte*, which is the most highly valued of all myrrh. Next after this comes the cultivated kind, and also the better variety of the wild kind, the one tapped in summer.
>
> Throughout the region it is brought in by ordinary people and packed into leather bags. Our perfumiers have no difficulty in distinguishing the different sorts by the evidence of the scent and consistency. There are a great many varieties [and at this point Pliny lists several, from both shores of the Red Sea]. Broadly speaking, however, myrrh is of good quality if it comes in small pieces of irregular shape, forming as the juice solidifies and whitening as it dries; also if it shows white marks like fingernails when broken, and has a slightly bitter taste. Prices vary with demand; that of *stacte* ranges from 3 d. to 50 d. the pound. Myrrh is adulterated with lumps of lentisk resin and with gum: the latter can be detected by its sticking to the teeth.[28]

The Greek observer Herodotus, in the fifth century, noted how important was the use of myrrh in embalming in Egypt – and he had a story to tell that helped to explain the choice. Once every five hundred years the newly born phoenix (a bird so often linked with spices in legends) was said, according to Herodotus, to form an egg-shaped container made of pure myrrh resin, to enclose the body of its just-dead father inside this egg, and to carry it from Arabia to be cremated at the Temple of Ra at Heliopolis in Egypt. 'This is what they say the bird does,' Herodotus warns his audience, 'but I myself do not believe it.'[29]

In ancient Jewish, Greek and Roman practice, myrrh was wanted in divine worship but also in very human festivity: it was a scent typical of love-making. 'Myrrh, cassia and frankincense rose in smoke,' writes Sappho in the sixth century BC of the ceremonial surrounding a wedding. 'I have sprinkled my bed with myrrh, with aloeswood and with cinnamon,' says an adulteress in the Hebrew book of *Proverbs*; 'come, let us drink deep of love.'

Myrrh was the first example that occurred to Theophrastus in discussing the spicing of wine. 'It appears that it is not only the perfume of certain aromatics that contributes to their taste effect, but also their pungency and their heat. This is why such aromatics are mixed with some wines, as if to give them a sting. Myrrh, for example, is hot and biting, with astringency and some bitterness.' Cinnamon, putchuk and cassia are his next examples. Myrrh remained a favoured ingredient in Roman spiced wine: in a recipe that has been quoted fully above, '4 *dr.* each of myrrh, cassia, saffron' were required for seven amphorae of wine.[30]

Equally important is the use of myrrh in medicine. This use was strongly implied by the story of the Three Wise Men as retold by Marco Polo. In fact in earlier times it was at least as important as its use in perfumes and incenses. '*Smyrna* is the tear of a tree that grows in Arabia, like the Egyptian thorn,' Dioscorides begins, and follows up with a careful description of its varieties and their qualities. Theophrastus had considered that myrrh would keep for ten years, and the older the better. Dioscorides disagrees: 'Choose myrrh that is fresh, crumbly, light, even in colour, in small lumps; showing small white cracks inside, like *onycha*, when bruised; sharp-tasting, fragrant, pungent, heating. Any that is heavy and pitchy in colour is of no use.' Then he gets down to its medical qualities, in one of the very longest of his monographs.

> Its power is heating, soporific, sealing, drying, astringent; it relaxes and opens the closed womb, and rapidly causes menstruation or abortion if applied with wormwood or the water from cooking lupin seeds or the juice of rue. It is applied to the face, mixed with cassia and honey, for acne; used with vinegar, it clears sycosis; rubbed in, with ladanum, wine and myrtle wine, it strengthens falling hair. It heals sores in the eyes, cures white patches and blind spots in the pupils, and smooths away trachomas.[31]

Myrrh first arrived in China as long ago as the fifth century. In the twelfth, Zhao Rugua knows of myrrh both from southern Arabia and from the opposite shore of north-east Africa (modern Somalia). To Chinese users, as to early European ones, myrrh was as much a medicine as an incense. Its medicinal uses in the modern West are few: 'occasionally used in mouthwashes and gargles for ulcers in the mouth', says the pharmaceutical handbook *Martindale*.

Several trees related to myrrh, classed by botanists in the genus *Commiphora*, produce resins that are not unlike myrrh but are generally allowed their own names. Balsam of Mecca, resin of *C. opobalsamum*, native to Arabia, has already been described, as has gum guggul, *C. mukul*, native to eastern Iran. In southern Arabia and north-eastern Africa a further species is found. The resin of *C. erythraea* is now known as opopanax or bissabol, and may be the *cancamum* that was once of interest to Roman merchants.[32]

The Arabs and the Indian Ocean trade

The lands where frankincense, myrrh and balsam of Mecca were found lay close to the trade routes that carried many other spices from the East to the Mediterranean. Thus the people of Sabaea were ideally placed to become mediators in the spice trade, as were their southern neighbours and successors the Himyarites, with their capital city at modern Yarim. To the north was the Arabian desert, crossed by caravan routes; to the west was an alternative route northwards, the Red Sea. Both routes carried cargoes of spices destined for the Mediterranean. Immediately to the south was the Indian Ocean coast, with the various harbours at which not only frankincense, myrrh and balm, but all the spices of the Indian Ocean shores, were on the market. Beyond, across the water, was east Africa, on whose coast southern Arabian merchants had set up trading posts and colonies, thus controlling the important trade in local spices which otherwise might have competed with their own.

Several observers, including the author of the *Periplus* at the beginning of the Roman Empire, and the merchant Cosmas at the end of it, regard east Africa rather than southern Arabia as the real centre of production, at least of frankincense and myrrh; Arabia was simply where the traders came from and the trade was controlled. To Cosmas, the 'land of incense' (or Barbary) corresponds with modern Somalia.

> The land of incense is at the extremity of Ethiopia, and extends far inland; its further side is bordered by the Ocean. The people of Barbary, who live near, go inland to trade, returning with many of the aromatics of commerce including incense, cassia, *kalamos*. They send them on by sea to Adulis [in Eritrea], to the Himyarite country, to India proper and to Persia.
> We read in the book of *Kings* that the Queen of Sheba (known to us as the Himyarite country) brought Solomon 'the spices of Barbary'. Naturally: Barbary was her neighbour to the south, only two days' voyage away. She also brought ebony, apes and gold from Ethiopia, because all of Ethiopia borders on the Red Sea.[33]

Offshore, equally accessible from Arabia and Somalia, lay Socotra, 'the Fortunate Islands', where all the cattle were white and none of the females grew horns (so an early geographer assures us). Here, in ancient times, merchant vessels from all over the Indian Ocean could be seen riding at anchor – the greatest number from the ports at the mouth of the Indus, with others from Persia, Carmania and elsewhere. Socotra, generally controlled by the Arabian kingdoms to the north, was the particular source of aloes, a medicine proverbial for its bitterness; the best aloes came from the juice of *Aloe perryi*, which grew only on Socotra. 'Dragon's blood' or 'Indian cinnabar' was another speciality of the markets there. This red pigment (actually the product of a plant of the genus *Dracaena*) was long believed to have unequalled power in medicine because of its unique and magical origin as a mixture of dragon's blood and elephant's blood. The sixteenth-century navigator Richard Eden tells the story well.

> [Elephants] have continual warre against Dragons, which desire their blood, because it is very cold: and therfore the Dragon lying awaite as the Elephant passeth by, windeth his taile, being of exceeding length, about the hinder legs of the Elephant, and when the Elephant waxeth faint, he falleth down on the serpent, being now full of blood, and with the poise of his body breaketh him: so that his owne blood with the blood of the Elephant runneth out of him min-gled together, which being colde, is congealed into that substance which the Apothecaries call *Sanguis Draconis*, that is Dragons blood, otherwise called Cinnabaris.[34]

In Greek and Roman times the immediate destinations for the various spice routes were Egypt, long an independent realm, eventually a private estate of the Roman emperor, and always a major entrepôt in the spice trade; and Nabataea in north-western Arabia, a kingdom with a settled capital in the remarkable city of Petra but with a largely nomadic and trading population. Probably the majority share of the Red Sea trade rested with Greeks and Romans of Egypt. Nabataeans were masters of the caravans; but they also had a hand in the Red Sea trade, and had once fought the Ptolemaic kings of Egypt for control of it. The eventual incorporation of Nabataea as a province of the Roman Empire (called by the Romans 'Arabia') left the actual trade routes still outside Roman control; a later Arab monarchy, that of Ghassân, took full advantage of the spice trade in its turn. At the Ghassânid court – according to the early seventh-century poet Ḥassân ibn Thâbit – 'when king Jabala would drink wine he sat on a couch of myrtle and jasmine and all sorts of sweet-smelling flowers, surrounded by gold and silver vessels full of ambergris and musk. During winter aloeswood was burned in his apartments, while in summer he cooled himself with snow.'[35]

There were no true monopolies in the spice trade, in ancient times or later. An Arabic geographer of the ninth century offers a reminder that, in the Indian Ocean as in the Mediterranean (the 'Western Sea'), Jewish merchants were a significant force. Kolzum has now replaced the earlier Heroonpolis as the harbour at the north-western extremity of the Red Sea.

These Jewish merchants speak Persian, Roman [Greek], Arabic, Frank, Spanish and Slavonic. They travel from West to East and from East to West, partly by land, partly by sea. They carry from the West eunuchs, slave girls, boys, silk, furs, swords. They set out on the Western Sea from the Frank country and make for Farama; there they load their merchandise on to pack-animals and go by land to Kolzum, five days' journey away. At Kolzum they set out across the Eastern Sea and make for Jedda, and onwards to Sind, India and China. On their return journey they carry musk, aloes, camphor, cinnamon and other Eastern products, and return to Kolzum and Farama where they set out once more on the Western Sea. Some make for Constantinople and sell their wares there; others go to the Frank country.[36]

Sind is the newly Muslim-conquered region of the Indus valley, already named Sindu in a sixth-century quotation from Cosmas (page 83). 'Frank' is the Latin or Romance language of Italy and France. Farama and Kolzum are replaced in modern times by the passage through the Suez Canal from Port Said to Suez.

In spite of all the competition the southern Arabians, ideally sited, well buffered from Persia, Egypt and Rome, had sufficient influence in this great nexus of trade to become and to remain wealthy. Greek and Roman texts – well-informed or not? – mention royal prerogatives over the Sabaean harvests of frankincense and myrrh. Later, we know, power lay in the hands of merchant families; and we know of the growing influence of Mecca, a great trading city on the caravan route from south to north. This was where the prophet Muḥammad grew up, a member of a merchant family, who made several journeys with trading caravans to Syria in company with his uncle and guardian Abû Ṭâlib, at the precise time when the poet Ḥassân ibn Thâbit had described the wealth of the Ghassânid court, its spices and its singing girls. Later, established at Medina, Muḥammad took advantage of his knowledge of the Meccan spice trade by raiding and plundering the caravans.

With their control of the caravan routes and their participation in the Indian Ocean sailings, Arabs have continued to be at the centre of the spice trade. The story of Sindbad the sailor and his seven voyages, incorporated in the standard recension of the *Thousand and One Nights*, is the tale of a dealer in spices and other exotic products – 'emeralds, pearls, rubies', but also 'pepper, cinnamon, Champa aloeswood and Assam aloeswood'. Sindbad's hair-raising adventures, shipwrecks, maroonings and providential meetings have very close parallels in narratives that are supposed to be factual, such as the *Marvels of India* by Buzurg ibn Shahriyar and the anonymous *Book of Marvels*. The six-times-repeated formula, 'For many years after my return I lived riotously in Baghdad, feasting with my boon companions and revelling away my riches. But I once again longed to sail new seas and explore new lands...,' surely resembles the life histories of some of the real traders who, like the fictional Sindbad, took passage and cargo space in a succession of merchant ships and hoped each time to show a massive profit on return.

Cargoes of complacence

The great Galees of Venice and Florence
Be well laden with things of complacence,
All spicery and of grossers ware.

Libel of English Policie.

The Mediterranean and the spice trade

We do not think of Europe and the Mediterranean as lands of spices. In fact some peoples' definition of spices requires them to be of tropical origin, and one traditional story of the origin of aromatic plants relies on the fierce heat of the sun in arid lands as an explanation.

Several spices that have become important across the world for their flavour and aroma are native to the Mediterranean shores: poppy, caraway, coriander, cumin, anise, sumach, ajowan, saffron, not to mention the ancient and long-lost silphium. Only the last two of these have been highly valued in their region of origin. Silphium, as long as it lasted, made the fortune of the Greek colony of Cyrene; saffron is a costly product and always will be.

To Mediterranean peoples, rare aromatics from distant lands have always over-shadowed the native spices. It is on the former that we have spent most of our money – cinnamon, pepper, ginger, cardamom and nutmeg among the oldest; vanilla and *baies roses* among the newest.

Our spending goes back at least 3,500 years. In the fifteenth century BC Queen Hatshepsut of Egypt sent an expedition to the far south-east, to the region known to Egyptians as Punt (modern Eritrea or Somalia). One of her successors, Amenhotep III, who ruled around 1400 BC, boasts of Egypt's continued dominance of the Horn of Africa, modestly putting the boast into the mouth of the god Amon-Re: 'When I turn my face to the east,' says Amon-Re to King Amenhotep, 'I work a wonder for you: I make the countries of Punt come to you, bearing all the sweet plants of their countries, to sue for peace and to breathe the breath of your generosity.'¹ Those sweet plants of the countries at the mouth of the Red Sea were myrrh, frankincense and balsam of Mecca.

Across the eastern Mediterranean, in Greece, the seventeenth-century BC wall paintings from the Minoan town of Akrotiri, buried by the eruption of Santorini, depict the picking of saffron. Aromatics catalogued in the fourteenth-century BC Linear B tablets of the Mycenaean palaces include cumin, fennel and sesame. Classical Greeks, of the sixth to fourth centuries BC, prized the aroma of silphium in food and as a medicine, whether or not they founded Cyrene especially to assure the supply of it. They knew and valued frankincense and sumach. They had begun to appreciate certain costly products from further afield, including pepper and cassia. Theophrastus, at the end of the fourth century, puts together a list of *aromata*:

> Cassia, cinnamon, cardamom, nard, *nairon*, balsam of Mecca, *aspalathos*, storax, orris, *narte*, putchuk, galbanum, saffron, myrrh, *kypeiron*, ginger-grass, *kalamos*, marjoram, *lotos*, anise; the aromatic consists of their roots, bark, branches, wood, seeds, tears, flowers, as the case may be. Some of them are found widely, but the best and most fragrant come from Asia and the sunny countries. Not one of them comes from Europe, except orris.²

The availability of spices and aromatics in the Mediterranean lands grew with Alexander's conquests. Demand grew also. By Roman times great quantities of Eastern spices made their way to the Mediterranean each year. The papyrus from unwanted secondhand books was torn up to be reused as wrappers for incense, pepper and other costly spices. In Rome it was a sign of wealth to use aromatics lavishly – in food, wine, perfumes, in human festivity, divine worship and funerals. At the dictator Sulla's funeral in 78 BC the procession had included a model of the great man himself – preceded, as in life, by an attendant bearing the *fasces*, the bundle of rods that were the insignia of a consul – and the whole model was made up in cassia and frankincense. By the first century AD, according to Pliny, human – and especially feminine – uses of aromatics took up much of the supply. 'By the lowest reckoning,' he calculates, 'India, China and the Arabian Peninsula take from our empire 100 million *sestertii* every year. That is the sum which our luxuries and our women cost us; for what fraction of these imports, I ask you, now goes to the gods or to the powers of the lower world?'

Roman emperors were the trend-setters in this form of conspicuous consumption. Not at all worried by the contradiction, Pliny provides another comparison from the very recent past: at the funeral rites for an imperial lady, in AD 65, 'experts say that Arabia does not produce as much spice in a year as the emperor Nero burnt in one day along with the body of his beloved Poppaea.'³

As Rome decayed, the Byzantine Empire inherited the eastern Mediterranean and appeared to outsiders equally rich and spendthrift in aromatics. Here is a fictionalized Byzantine emperor, in a French epic of the twelfth century:

In the quarter of St Sophia, near the cathedral, he lodged each French prince in a noble house. There you would have seen new silk strewn underfoot; you would have scented many a spice, for he had balsam burning everywhere. No other king matched his wealth. When he had shown them the relics of the Apostles, he took them to his vaulted chamber, its floor strewn with many-coloured gems. He gave them rings, brooches and cups, new silk and purple and samite, and vases full of theriac and balsam.[4]

By that time the spice market of Constantinople, modern Istanbul, was already in existence. We know of regulations for this and other trades laid down in the tenth century. Observers noted the regular shipping of 'musk, spices and sugar' from Egypt to Constantinople. When the Venetians diverted the Fourth Crusade, in 1204, and the rich and populous city of Constantinople was sacked and pillaged, the Venetians themselves emerged as possessors of Pera, overlooking the Golden Horn, the city's harbour. They controlled the trade of Constantinople from that time on.

By that time, too, Venice and other Italian city states dominated the sea trade that brought these Eastern spices to France and eventually to Britain. An English pamphlet of the fifteenth century, with its lines

> *The great Galees of Venice and Florence*
> *Be well laden with things of complacence,*
> *All spicery and of grossers ware,*[5]

is concerned to emphasize the economic and political problems caused by this trade. Pliny was making a similar point, more than a millennium earlier. And these were the precisely the thoughts in the minds of Portuguese, Spanish, French and English monarchs and governments, as they began to look seriously, from the fifteenth century onwards, for other choices. Could they avoid buying spices that had come by the traditional route, generally by way of Arab merchants into the hands of Venetians and Genoese, at whatever price these merchants cared to charge?

They found that they could avoid it. The Portuguese led the way to the East, by the new route around the Cape of Good Hope, and thus they learnt to buy traditional spices at the laughably low prices charged by local producers. Fortunes were made by those lucky enough to return unscathed from the dangers of the long journey. The Spanish led the way across the Atlantic, where a whole range of new spices was waiting to be 'discovered'. Both did their very best to set up new monopolies and to keep prices high, as did Dutch, French and English in their turn, but all such efforts were doomed. The seventeenth and eighteenth centuries were remarkable for the astonishingly low price of spices in Europe and for the range of uses that they found. This was the epoch of the scented glove, of the perfumed and sugary sweetmeat, of aromatic 'water' or liqueur; this was the heyday of chocolate and of anise-flavoured tea.

In western Europe sugar and chocolate, which remain highly popular, are not now considered to be spices. The same might be said of paprika in Hungary. Apart from these, although the romance of spices has never faded, the day-to-day use of exotic spices seems to have declined. Perhaps they became too cheap, too commonplace? Yet in the markets of the southern and eastern Mediterranean the aromas are as powerful as ever, and trade remains brisk. The native spices of the Mediterranean have their full share of it.

Coriander or cilantro

The excavators of Frankhthi cave, near Portokheli in southern Greece, a site that was inhabited for many thousands of years in prehistoric times, found a tiny coriander fruit in a layer dated to the seventh millennium BC. If this was really something that the ancient cave-dwellers might have used – and not a red herring, dropped by one of the excavators – it makes coriander one of the very oldest spices in human use, quite as old as the ginger and sugar cane whose prehistory is traced above.

Coriandrum sativum is certainly native to Greece and the eastern Mediterranean. It was familiar in Egypt in 1352 BC, for it is one of the foodstuffs found in Tutankhamen's tomb. As *korianna* its small dry fruits were listed in the Linear B tablets, in Greece of around 1300 BC. Coriander played a major role in ancient Greek and in Roman cuisine, and has never ceased to be popular around the Mediterranean.

Its popularity has spread far eastwards and westwards. We have already seen that it was introduced to India, probably at the time when the old Persian Empire stretched to the Indus valley. It advanced from there to south-east Asia, to the extent that coriander now seems a typical Indian spice and a typical south-east Asian herb. By way of Persia, coriander was also introduced to China. Later Chinese tradition suggested that this happened at the moment when Zhang Qian opened up the Silk Road, in fact that he personally brought coriander back with him in 125 BC. This is unlikely, not only historically – he had other things on his mind than coriander during his year-long imprisonment among the Huns and his lucky escape – but also because the earliest certain mention of coriander in Chinese texts is dated to the sixth century AD. In due course the Spaniards planted coriander in their American colonies: cilantro, as it is better known in America, is now one of the typical flavours of Mexican cuisine.

It is an extremely versatile aromatic. Its leaves, garnishing meat dishes and stews, give an unmistakeable pungent aroma – 'soapy', perhaps, to those who cannot get the taste for it. Its spicy roots are specially useful in Thai cooking. Its tiny black fruits (often called 'seeds') are the most powerful part, described as 'cooling' by traditional pharmacologists in spite of their spicy heat.

Cumin, caraway, anise, ajowan and nigella

'Cumin has the most fruits of any plant,' writes Theophrastus in the fourth century BC. 'There is an odd thing that is said of this plant: when people are sowing it they must curse and slander it if they want it to be healthy and prolific.' I omitted to do this, I now realize, when planting cumin this year in my garden in France. It did badly.

Cumin, like coriander, was listed in the Linear B tablets, so it was a significant commodity in the stores of the Mycenaean palaces in the fourteenth century BC; it is recognized, as *kamunu*, in Akkadian cuneiform tablets from Mesopotamia, and it was an important spice in ancient Egypt in the second millennium BC. It was well known to the later Greeks as *kyminon*, and to the Romans as *cuminum*. Cumin is called for in a great many of the recipes in the late Roman cookery book *Apicius*, including a sauce for shellfish already quoted.

Cumin is the seed of *Cuminum cyminum*, native to the eastern Mediterranean and the Near East. Like coriander, the plant has gradually spread eastwards. Still a typical flavour of the southern and eastern Mediterranean, cumin must have arrived in India in the last centuries BC, possibly as a long-term result of the conquests of the Persians or of Alexander in the Indus valley. Its Sankrit name *jiraka* recurs as a loanword in many other Eastern languages.

Caraway, the seed of *Carum carvi*, is the central European equivalent of cumin. They are closely related plants, but the seeds give a very different flavour. Caraway was not known in classical Greece, though the peoples of the Roman Empire became familiar with it as *karo* or *careum*. It is popular in Europe in baking and in the flavouring of liqueurs, such as the German *Kümmel*. This is, incidentally, the German name for both caraway and cumin: in several European languages the two spices share one name. In French caraway is *cumin des prés*, 'meadow cumin'.

In seed cake, one of the glories of English cuisine, the seeds are (of course) caraway:

4 oz (115 g/½ cup) butter	1 oz (25 g/¼ cup) ground rice
4 oz (115 g/½ cup) caster sugar	3 teaspoons caraway seeds
2 eggs, beaten	3 tablespoons milk
5 oz (150 g/1¼ cups) self-raising flour	2 tablespoons demerara sugar

Cream the butter and caster sugar and gradually beat in the eggs. Fold in the flour, ground rice and caraway seeds. Add the milk. Spoon into a greased 7-in (18-cm) cake tin (having lined the base with greaseproof paper). Smooth off and sprinkle the demerara sugar on top. Bake for about an hour at 180°C (350°F/gas mark 4). Turn out on to a wire rack as it begins to cool.

Unlike coriander and cumin, caraway has never found an enthusiastic audience outside its native Europe.

Western Anatolia is the native habitat of another related spice, anise, the seed of

Pimpinella anisum. We can be fairly sure that its range did not originally extend to Europe because in the fourth century BC Theophrastus, who was a native of the eastern Greek island of Lesbos, made a list of Asiatic aromatics (quoted on page 124), specifically adding that they did not grow in Europe, and he included anise in the list. If in his time it grew in his native island, as it does now, he would surely have known of it. Modern visitors to Lesbos – and particularly to the ouzo distilleries there, which consume a large quantity of anise each year – will be assured that the finest, sweetest anise now grows on this particular island; having tasted fresh Lesbian anise at the Barbayiannis distillery at Plomari, I will admit that it may be true.

Anise is used all over the Mediterranean as a flavouring for popular spirits and liqueurs, the best-known of the family being the pastis and anisette of France. Anethol, the essential oil of anise (also present in dill and fennel), dissolves in the alcohol, but it is precipitated when the proportion of water increases, hence their unusual white colour when diluted. Anise is popular in sweets, too: aniseed balls spring to mind. In making sweets and spirits true anise is nowadays sometimes mixed with or enhanced by or even replaced by star anise, quite different botanically but almost identical in flavour.

At the south-eastern extremity of the native range of cumin, from Egypt eastwards, is found ajowan, another related spice plant. Botanists now classify it as *Trachyspermum ammi*, though it has had many other botanical names, including *Carum copticum*, *Ptychotis ajowan* and *Ammi majus*. Little known in Europe, this spice came to the attention of Roman pharmacologists as a variety of cumin: they called it *ammi*. It may be the same, or nearly the same, as the 'Ethiopian cumin' known to some ancient Greek writers and once supplied to the Persian king's table.

Nowadays ajowan is used as a culinary spice from north Africa all the way to India. It must have reached the sub-continent from the West at about the same period as cumin; its Sanskrit name *yavânî*, meaning 'the Greek spice', suggests that it came by way of one of the Greek kingdoms of the Middle East. From this word *yavânî*, by tortuous etymological routes, derive not only the Indian English word 'ajowan', modern name of this spice, but also the 'omum' of Indian English 'omum water', a digestive medicine made from ajowan in southern India. Gripe water, an English digestive medicine for children, has a similar formulation.

The small triangular black seeds of nigella (*Nigella sativa*) are one more spice native to the Mediterranean but now a part of Indian cuisine and medicine. The plant is a close relative of love-in-a-mist, often grown in European gardens. Ancient pharmacologists, while observing differences between them, used both in their prescriptions. Nigella has many names: gith in India; black cumin, onion seed, nutmeg flower and small fennel elsewhere, though it is quite different from cumin, onion, nutmeg and fennel!

PLATE 17

(*Above*) Roman silver casket, the 'Projecta Casket', for perfumes and cosmetics, a 4th-century wedding present to Secundus and Projecta. This panel shows the bride on her way to the baths: attendants carry caskets and other utensils.

(*Left*) Flask for medicines and digestives, the 'Highdown Goblet'. Made in Byzantium, with a motto in Greek, this costly objet d'art would have contained the aromas of many exotic spices. It was found in an Anglo-Saxon burial.

(*Below*) Roman 4th-century domed silver casket for perfumes and cosmetics, belonging to Projecta.

Plate 18

The Atlantic and the spice lands of the New World: detail from the manuscript world map of Pierre Desceliers (1550). The Amazon is represented only by a rough sketch of the lower river: Desceliers, usually well informed, had not heard of Francisco de Orellana's epic voyage (see p. 153). The map was designed to be placed on a table and read from all sides.

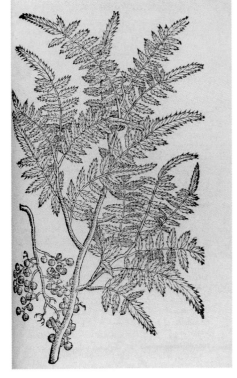

The true Peruvian pepper. Known in Quechua as *mulli* and in modern botany as *Schinus molle*, this aromatic plant now thrives in California. From Carolus Clusius' Latin reworking of Nicolás Monardes' researches (1579).

PLATE 19

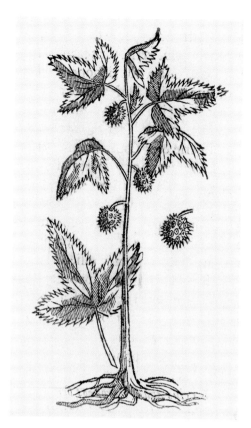

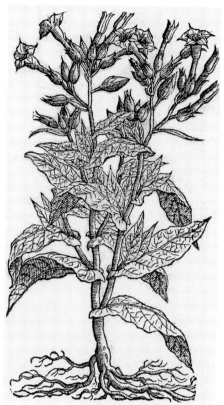

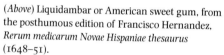

(*Above*) Liquidambar or American sweet gum, from the posthumous edition of Francisco Hernandez, *Rerum medicarum Novae Hispaniae thesaurus* (1648–51).

(*Above right*) Tobacco, from Carolus Clusius, *Exoticorum libri decem* (1605).

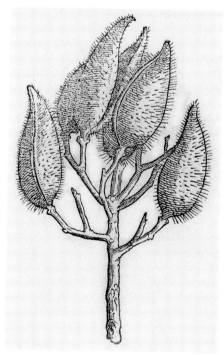

(*Right*) Annatto, source of a red pigment important in Aztec food and ritual, from Carolus Clusius, *Exoticorum libri decem* (1605).

PLATE 20

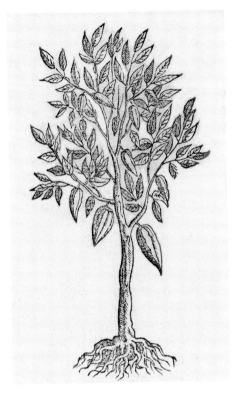

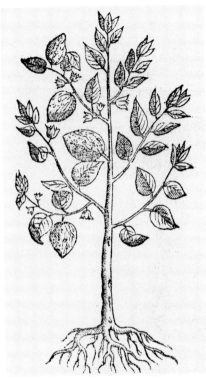

(*Above left and right*) The two cacao species, from the posthumous edition of Francisco Hernandez, *Rerum medicarum Novae Hispaniae thesaurus* (1648–51).

(*Below*) Cacao beans, from Carolus Clusius, *Exoticorum libri decem* (1605).

68   PII

Axi.
Capsicum.

Forma.

Capsici hi-
storia.

Axi seu Capsicu
nigro, cùm sapori

ALTÆ cuiuf
crassitie quidem fi
tudine, constans v
diculum oblongur
dispositis, seminis
ptis, pediculus nu
est, sole maturefca
tio gradu.

NEC præter
nostris missum, qu
dicum vsum recep
lentissima, & tot
lus est hortus, in
chritudinem.Vidi
ad arboris altitud

FOLIO est v
albo, ex quo pull
longus, rotundus, Melopepo

PLATE 21

CAPSICVM.   CAPSICVM BRASILIANVM.

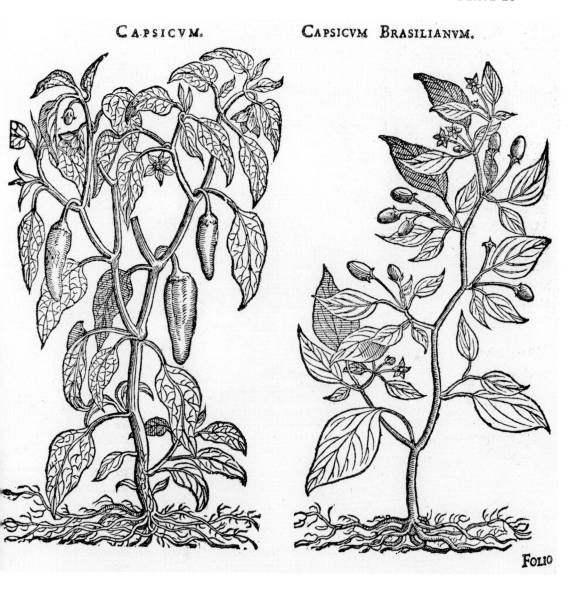

FOLIO

(*Opposite below right*) 'This capsicum or Indian pepper (American, actually) is now grown assiduously throughout Spain, by gardeners and by women in their windows ...': so wrote Carolus Clusius in his reworking of Monardes' researches (1579). He also re-used Monardes' woodcut, which looks more like long pepper than chilli. Monardes had surely never seen a fresh chilli.

(*This page*) In his 1579 edition, Clusius also used a new, much more accurate woodcut of a whole chilli plant (*left*, labelled *Capsicum*). By the time he compiled his definitive 1605 volume, *Exoticorum libri decem*, Clusius had also seen and drawn another species of capsicum, something close to the modern Brazilian piri-piri (*right*, labelled *Capsicum brasilianum*).

PLATE 22

HAGIS·ROGES·   HAGIS·IANNE

HAGIS·VERT·

Hagis haulz autant adire en langue dinde
Comme poiure Et en y a de troix sortez
Mais le plus petit qui est le vert est le
plus fort et la foeulle est fort bonne a
mettre au potaige et en sallades Les yndariens
la poiure auec du sel Et le mettent
dans la robbe de mil Et quand Ilz sont sur le
pais loingtain ou Ilz ne peuuent trouuer deaue
douce pour boire Mengent le plus de ce poiure
quilz peuuent en cheminant et ne sont aucunemen
Alterez estans fort soutz fraiz Combien que la challeur
soit fort violente Et se sont tous ...

PLATE 23

(*Right*) Mechoacan was 'commonly called ruibarbe of the Indies' according to Nicolás Monardes – perhaps the 'rhubarb' that Columbus said he had found. Illustration from the posthumous edition of Francisco Hernandez, *Rerum medicarum Novae Hispaniae thesaurus* (1648–51).

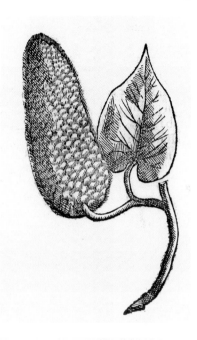

(*Opposite*) Red, yellow and green chillies, as depicted by the anonymous artist of the 16th-century picture book *Histoire Naturelle des Indes*, compiled on one of Sir Francis Drake's expeditions: 'Hagis, in the language of the Indies, means pepper. There are three sorts, but the smallest, which is green, is the hottest. Its leaf is very good to put in stews and salads. The Indians mash this pepper with salt and wrap it in a corn shuck; then, when they are far from home and cannot find fresh water to drink, they eat as much of this pepper as they can along the road, and they are never thirsty and always cool, although the heat is so violent and they are completely naked.'

(*Below*) The sassafras tree, from the *Histoire Naturelle des Indes*, captioned in French (see p. 151).

PLATE 24

Sir Thomas Stamford Raffles' house as governor of Fort Marlborough (Bengkulu, Sumatra), with newly planted clove trees beginning to flourish (*c.* 1820).

Aromas in wine and food

It is safe to say that Mediterranean Europe is the world centre for spiced wines and spirits. Wine itself was probably invented somewhere in the triangle whose points are Greece, Palestine and the Caucasus. It is definitely in ancient Greece that the practice of adding exotic aromas to wine was first recorded. Early information comes, once again, from Theophrastus, whose statement on this topic now reads somewhat strangely: 'One might wonder why exotic and other fragrances improve the taste of wines when, so far from having that effect on foods – whether cooked or uncooked – they invariably ruin them.'[6] A surviving, quite simple, recipe for peppered wine seems to originate from Greece in the Hellenistic period, after the conquests of Alexander: 'Washed, dried, finely ground peppercorns, 8 scruples. Attic honey, 1 pint. Old white wine, 4 or 5 pints.'[7]

Romans spiced their wine much more enthusiastically than this. Myrrh, little used in food or drink now, became a popular aroma for wine. *Mulsum*, or spiced honeyed wine, was a typical aperitif at Roman feasts, and we have a recipe for it.

> Put Attic honey in an earthenware vessel and set it in hot ashes to drive off the scum; and after it has heated add 4 pints wine to 1 pint honey; then put the honey wine in well-resinated jars and hang in them linen bags containing 12 scruples chopped dried putchuk. Cover and store in the loft. – Some add 12 scruples tejpat leaf to the honey wine, and after 15 days find it surprisingly good; when kept longer, incomparable. – Others make honey wine thus: they mix myrrh 6 scruples, cassia 12 scruples, putchuk 2 scruples, spikenard 4 scruples, pepper 4 scruples, Attic honey 6 pints, wine 24 pints and stand in the sun from the rise of the Dog Star for 40 days. Some people call this 'nectar'.[8]

Mulsum, in the later centuries of the Roman Empire, was outshone by a more fashionable spiced wine, *conditum*. As we know from Byzantine medical texts, *conditum* should not be the same all the year round. The spices, being powerful medicaments, must be adjusted in accordance with the seasons to keep the human constitution in balance: nothing too heating in summer; nothing too cooling in winter; nothing too drying in spring. But here is a relatively simple recipe, perhaps from the fourth century.

> To make novelty spiced wine: 15 lbs honey are put in a bronze jar already containing 2 pints wine, so that you boil down the wine as you cook the honey. This to be heated over a slow fire of dry wood, stirring with a stick as it cooks: if it begins to boil over it is stopped with a splash of wine; in any case it will simmer down when the heat is taken away, and, when cooled, re-ignited. This must be repeated a second and a third time; then the mixture is finally removed from the brazier and, on the following day, skimmed. Next 4 oz. ready-ground pepper, 3 scruples mastic, 1 dram each tejpat leaf and saffron, 5 roasted date stones,

and also the flesh of the dates, previously softened in wine of the same kind and of sufficient quantity to give a smooth purée. When all this is ready, pour on 18 pints smooth wine. If the finished product is bitter, coal will correct it.[9]

In medieval Europe spiced and mulled wines were as popular as ever. A Muslim observer – temporarily held hostage at the court of Christian Constantinople – describes the spiced wine that was stored in a hidden tank, from which water was usually piped to a fountain. On Christmas Day this tank was filled with ten thousand jars of wine and a thousand jars of white honey, and the whole was spiced with a camel's load of nard, cloves and cinnamon. When the Emperor left the Palace to go to church, he saw the spiced wine flowing from the mouths of the statues and gathering in the basin below. Each person in his procession, as they went towards the church, was given a brimming cup of this wine.[10]

Meanwhile the fashion for ready-made spiced wines was well under way. Flavours were already to be found that were ancestral to some of Europe's modern favourites. The bitters of Italy can be traced back two thousand years, when, according to Pliny, 'one wine merchant even falsifies the flavour and colour of his wine with aloes.'[11] Modern vermouth and the now-outlawed absinthe go back just as far. The French term *absinthe*, incidentally, derives from the Greek and Latin name for wormwood; the English *vermouth* derives from the German name for wormwood, *Wermut*. The following recipes for wormwood wine are from the first century AD.

Some add to 48 pints of must one pound of wormwood and boil down to two thirds: then adding 90 pints of must and half a pound of wormwood and mixing carefully they bottle and (after straining) store. – Others chop 3 (or 4) oz. wormwood and 2 oz. each Syrian nard, cinnamon, cassia, *calamus*, ginger-grass, crushed date stone into one amphora of must, seal and set aside for two months, then strain, bottle and store.[12]

Where Romans liked their *mulsum*, their *conditum* and their wormwood wine, medieval Europe had a new favourite in hippocras, popularly supposed to be a health-giving drink, not only because of its spice content but also because of its name, which is that of the father of medicine, Hippocrates. According to John Russell, in the fifteenth century, the expensive kind of hippocras demanded four different spices, all of which were costly. 'For common people' a slightly cheaper recipe was available, and colouring was unnecessary.

Good sonn, to make ypocras, hit were gret lernynge,
And for to take the spice therto aftur the proporcionynge,
Gynger, synamome, graynis, sugur, turnesole, that is good colourynge;
For commyn peple gynger, canelle, longe pepur, hony aftur claryfiynge.[13]

The comparison tells us something of the relative costs of spices in medieval Europe. For expensive sugar, naturally, cheap honey can be substituted; for cinnamon we can use the lower-quality cassia (*canelle*). Ginger, though costly, is unavoidable (is hippocras one of the ancestors of ginger wine?). Long pepper, once expensive, had evidently fallen from favour by John Russell's time and become cheap: it has been supplanted in fashion by the African 'grains of Paradise' or melegueta pepper. The fifth ingredient in the expensive hippocras recipe is turnsole – not sunflower, but a blue-purple colouring derived from a western Mediterranean plant, *Chrozophora tinctoria*. Expensive hippocras had not only to taste right but to look right too.

For those who would like to try making up one of these recipes, and need an idea of quantities, here is hippocras as described in the sixteenth century, a quotation borrowed from Charles Corn's *The scents of Eden*: 'a gallon of wine, an ounce of synamon, two ounces of ginger, one pound of sugar, twentie cloves bruised, and twentie cornes of pepper big beaten: let all these soake together one night, and then let it run through a bag.'[14]

Today Europeans still expect spices in their drinks: ginger in ginger wine and ginger beer: anise or star anise in pastis; caraway in Kümmel; cinnamon, as well as gold leaf, in Goldwasser; juniper berries in gin; not to mention the cocktail of herbs and spices in Bénédictine, Chartreuse and Drambuie.

The fashion for spicy food in Europe dates back almost as far as that for spiced wine. In a scrap of Greek comedy of the third century BC a pontificating cook lists the old-fashioned flavourings that he and his friends are putting out to grass. My teachers, he says, 'have wiped out the old hackneyed seasonings from the books, and made the pestle and mortar disappear from among us; I mean, for example, cumin, vinegar, silphium, cheese, coriander, the seasonings that Cronus used.'[15] Cronus himself, grandfather of the gods, was superseded by Zeus, just as the old spices were being superseded by new flavours from the East. Alexander's conquests opened the way, and Alexander's booty made some Greeks rich enough to buy all the spices they wanted. Yet these fashions came in slowly, so that as late as the second century AD a Greek author observed that many elderly people had never learnt to enjoy the taste of pepper.[16]

Classical Roman cuisine is, as everyone knows, laden with spices. In *Apicius* pepper is called for in practically every dish. On occasion, just like a modern gourmet for whom everything must be 'just so', a Roman will demand that it be white pepper: 'This is my sauce for lamprey: Venafran oil of the first pressing, Spanish fish sauce, five year old Italian wine to be added during the cooking (if adding after, Chian wine will serve at least as well as any other), white pepper, and vinegar from the vineyards of Methymna on Lesbos. My own little innovation is to add fresh rocket and bitter elecampane.'[17]

In this extract from the Roman poet Horace's satire on gastronomes the speaker is Nasidienus, boastful host at a disastrous dinner whose climax came when the wall hangings collapsed, covering his guests in very dusty curtainings. Satire though it is, we can feel fairly sure that someone, just around Horace's time, had used almost exactly these ingredients in a sauce for lampreys. Horace liked to get things right. And, yes, there are occasions when it must be white pepper: pepper ice cream, I assure those unlucky enough not to have tasted it, must be pure white to have its full effect.

Pepper is only one of the exotic spices of Roman cuisine. I have already quoted the recipe for hare suggested by the dietician Anthimus, in the early sixth century, to his patron Theuderic: 'Hares, if they are quite young, can be taken with a sweet sauce including pepper, a little cloves and ginger, seasoned with putchuk and spikenard or tejpat leaf.' I translate *folium* as 'tejpat leaf'; Theuderic's cooks might well have substituted bay leaf, just as they might have substituted Gallic nard for spikenard and juniper berry for pepper. Anthimus was more familiar with the southern cities of Byzantium and Ravenna on the Mediterranean trade routes, where the spices he calls for were always available; but it is not incredible that the six Eastern spices listed here would have reached Theuderic's court, somewhere in north-eastern Gaul, in the ruins of the Roman Empire, for travel and trade continued from end to end of the Mediterranean.[18]

Although so many spices entered into Roman cuisine, an emphasis on pepper is nearly always there. We have seen the importance placed on pepper in the Roman *Periplus* or sailing guide to the Indian Ocean; from this, and again from contemporary Indian sources, we know that Roman merchants 'came with gold and departed with pepper'.

Just so, if a medieval writer or poet mentions valuable spices and flavourings, pepper is likely to be what comes first to mind. So it is with the earliest of the troubadours, William IX Duke of Aquitaine, sketching in this lyric an intimate *dîner à trois*.

> *A manjar mi deron capos,*
> *E sapchatz ac i mais de dos,*
> *E no.i ac cog ni cogastros,*
> *Mas sol nos tres,*
> *E.l pans fo blancs e.l vins fo bos*
> *E.l pebr' espes.*

'For dinner they gave me capons, more than a brace of them, and there was no cook and no waiter but just the three of us, and the bread was white, and the wine was good, and the pepper was thick!'[19]

And yet in medieval times, too, many other exotic spices besides pepper were in demand in wealthy kitchens. A recipe from *Le Mesnagier de Paris* gives us a fine medieval sauce:

> *Spiced green sauce.* Grind finely ginger, cloves, grains of Paradise. Remove from the mortar; then grind parsley or herb bennet, sorrel, marjoram, or any one or two of these, and white breadcrumbs soaked in verjuice, strain, grind again finely. Strain again, mix all together and season with vinegar. Some people use none of the spices, simply substituting rosemary leaves.[20]

In southern Europe, where the myrtle is native, dried myrtle berries (fruit of *Myrtus communis*) have occasionally been used as a local substitute for pepper.

Dried juniper berries (the fruit of *Juniperus phoenicea*, *Juniperus communis* and other species) were used from very early times in embalming, medicine and cookery in Egypt – baskets of two non-Egyptian species of juniper were found in Tutankhamen's tomb. Their use in Roman cookery is really one more indication of the popularity of pepper, because juniper berries also served as a cheap pepper substitute. Yet juniper berries have their own special flavour, and in several European countries are regularly used, crushed, to flavour meat dishes. Gin (the name derives from French *genièvre* or 'juniper') owes its distinctive aroma, at least in part, to juniper berries. Oil of juniper is important in aromatherapy and perfumery.

A favourite aroma of the eastern end of the Mediterranean is sumach. It is the ground fruit of a tree whose relatives are now familiar in northern gardens; but *Rhus coriaria* grows best in Syria, and that is where this dark red spice is produced. 'The fruit reddens like the grape, but it looks like lentils crowded close together,' writes Theophrastus. The sweet-sour scent of sumach, at its best and most colourful when sprinkled on rice, has a longer history than rice in the West, its first mention in literature coming in a list of aromatics in a poem by the law-giver of Athens, Solon, written about 600 BC. Its medicinal uses were familiar to ancient Greeks and medieval Persians.[21]

Mustard

The mustard best known in Europe is the seed of white mustard, *Brassica hirta* (sometimes classified *Sinapis alba*), a plant familiar in Greece at least four thousand years ago –a bag of mustard seeds turned up in the excavation of the Bronze Age site of Marmariani. An Egyptian find, of large numbers of mustard seeds in a twelfth-dynasty tomb, is almost as old as this. Until the beginning of the pepper trade, around 400 BC, mustard (*napy* in Greek, *sinapi* in Latin) was certainly the hottest flavour of the Mediterranean. It was so hot, and so cheap, that fine Indian long pepper, hotter than black pepper and a very expensive item in Roman times, was sometimes 'fraudulently mixed with Egyptian mustard' on its way to Rome.[22]

European white mustard was attractive enough to others that white mustard had been transplanted to India and China by early medieval times. They had their own native mustards; these were so familiar that the ancient Indian law code *Manusmṛti* names the smallest weight in the scale *sarṣapa* 'one mustard seed'.

For at least two thousand years the popular way to enjoy mustard has been as a smooth sauce. The oldest recipe is given by the first-century Roman writer on farming, Columella.

Carefully cleanse and sieve mustard seed, then wash it well in cold water. Leave it in the water for two hours. Take it out, squeeze it in the hands, place it in a new or well-cleaned mortar, and grind it with pestles. Then collect the whole mass in the middle of the mortar and squeeze with the flat of the hand. Then scarify, place a few hot coals on it and pour on water mixed with nitre, to leach away all its bitterness and pallor. Lift up the mortar at once for all the liquid to drain away. Add pine kernels as fresh as possible and almonds; grind finely, adding sharp white wine vinegar, then strain. You will find this an excellent sauce for your dinner parties, and also attractive in appearance: if well-made, it will be very brightly coloured.[23]

The old French *moustarde*, origin of the English word, is first recorded in the thirteenth century. It originally denoted a prepared mustard sauce of just this type, but fruity as well as hot because it was made with 'must' or grape juice. Soon, in both French and English, 'mustard' came to be the new name of the plant as well. The sauce that people prefer varies from country to country, the hottest and the yellowest being the English kind – but some of the yellow comes from adding turmeric, and that is true of American mustard too. The making of *moutarde de Dijon*, the most popular French type, can be traced in Dijon to the fourteenth century. Many in Europe would echo the French proverb, recorded in 1680, that begins –

De trois choses Dieu nous garde:
Du boeuf salé sans moutarde...

God save us from three things:
From salt beef with no mustard...

Poppy

The power of spices to restore humans to health has been an article of faith in traditional medicine for millennia. Mediterranean spices are among those to which very powerful effects have been attributed. In the early first century BC King Mithridates of Pontus (north-eastern Turkey), having at least as many enemies as most kings, took a daily dose of an antidote against all poisons that had been formulated especially for him by the royal physician Crateuas. A recipe for the *Mithridaticum* follows, as recorded a century later by the Roman medical writer Celsus.

Putchuk, $\frac{5}{12}$ dram; sweet flag, 5 drams; St John's wort, gum, sagapenum, gum arabic, orris, cardamom, 2 drams each; anise, 3 drams; Celtic nard, gentian root, dried rose petals, 4 drams each; poppy latex, parsley, 4½ drams each; cassia, hartwort, darnel, long pepper, 4¼ drams each; storax, 5¼ drams; castoreum, frankincense, hypocistis, myrrh, *opopanax*, 6 drams each; tejpat leaf, 6 drams; nut-grass flower, terebinth resin, galbanum, Candy carrot, 6⅙ drams each; spikenard, balsam of Mecca, 6¼ drams each; shepherd's purse, 6¼ drams; rhubarb root, 7 drams; saffron, ginger, cinnamon, 7¼ drams each. These to be ground and mixed into honey; a quantity equal to a walnut to be taken daily, in wine, against poison.[24]

Mithridates had a long and adventurous life, so his antidote served him well – until his final defeat, when he decided to commit suicide by taking poison, and the poison would not work.

Among the more active ingredients in the *Mithridaticum* – though with alterative rather than curative properties – is opium. Poppies produce both a mild aromatic, their dried seeds, and a powerful drug, poppy latex or opium, which can be extracted by cutting into the unripe seed pod. The best species for both seeds and opium is the opium poppy, *Papaver somniferum*, native to Mediterranean Europe. A third product, poppy-seed oil, can be made from the seeds of this same species, but is usually made from those of the corn poppy, *P. rhoeas*. The distinction between the two species is already set out by Pliny in the first century AD: 'There are two kinds of poppy, white and black, the latter cultivated for edible oil. The seed of white poppy used to be served roasted with honey at dessert, and even nowadays peasants sprinkle it on loaves, using egg to bind it.'[25]

The seeds of the opium poppy have been used as a spice for at least 2,600 years: 'poppy-seed bread' was first mentioned, so far as we know, by the archaic Greek poet Alcman, and poppy seeds are still sprinkled on bread in just the same way. At the grandiose 'banquet of Trimalchio', centrepiece of Petronius' great Roman novel *Satyricon*, 'a row of dormice, glazed in honey and rolled in poppy seeds' is among the tastier of the hors d'oeuvres.[26] Opium, too, was used by Classical Greeks and Romans, who found it an effective pain-killer and soporific.

Like coriander and cumin, poppy is one of the spices that have gradually spread eastwards from Europe. Poppy differs from those two, however, in that European states have in the last two centuries taken a very close interest in the growing of the opium poppy in certain other countries, not, of course, because of the market in poppy seeds but because of the demand for opium and its derivatives, morphine and heroin.

The addictive nature of these products was not recognized by early physicians, and the widespread condemnation of opium as a harmful drug is a relatively recent development. Opium addiction was a grave problem in China by the early nineteenth century, and the earliest serious steps against it were taken by the Chinese government, whose ban on the import of opium led to the first Opium War, against Britain, in 1839–42, and the second, against Britain and France, in 1856–60. Both countries were profiting massively by selling opium to China. These wars were lost, but China persisted in opposing the trade and in 1906 succeeded in persuading the British government of India to collaborate in a plan to wipe out the opium trade and opium addiction in the two countries in ten years. Interrupted by the First World War, the plan was never completed. The League of Nations and then the United Nations took up the continuing fight.

Mastic

A second European spice of medicinal importance is mastic, the resin of a local variety of *Pistacia lentiscus* that grows only in twelve villages in the southern half of the island of Chios. In the mastic-harvesting season, in late summer, the trees are wounded; mastic flows to heal the wound and is collected from carefully cleaned ground at the foot of the tree. This early description of the harvest was written in the eighteenth century:

> They begin the tapping of the lentisks on the first of August, making several diagonal cuts into the bark with a long knife but not touching the young branches. On the day after cutting, one observes the nourishing sap flowing out in drops, which gradually coagulate into tears of mastic. They harden on the ground: this is why the bases of the trees have to be kept so clean. The bulkiest harvest is in mid August, if the weather is dry and fine. The ladies of the Harem consume most of the mastic that goes to the Palace. They chew it, all through the morning, on an empty stomach, both to pass the time and to sweeten their breath. Tears of mastic are also put in stews, and in bread before it is baked.[27]

Mastic has certainly been known for 2,400 years, and probably for much longer. Its simplest and most obvious use is as a natural chewing gum for cleaning the teeth and freshening the breath: 'chewing mastic' is the phrase in which mastic is first heard of, in a scrap of ancient Greek comedy, and it is no coincidence that in English 'masticate' means 'chew'. Mastic is still used in just this way in Greece and Turkey, and its unique flavour is popular partly because of its subliminal connection with fresh breath. In these countries you can buy synthetic chewing gum to which mastic flavouring has been added, as well as liqueurs and sweets flavoured with it.

Spices in religion

> Take the choicest spices: of liquid myrrh five hundred shekels, half this weight of fragrant cinnamon, and of scented cane two hundred and fifty shekels; of cassia five hundred shekels, and one hin of olive oil. These you are to compound into a holy chrism, such a blend as a perfumer might make.
>
> Take sweet spices: storax, onycha, galbanum; sweet spices and pure frankincense in equal parts, and compound an incense, such a blend as the perfumer might make, salted, pure, and holy.[28]

These instructions, from the book of *Exodus*, are accompanied by strict regulations: the recipes are to be used only in worship, never as perfumes for people. Death is threatened to anyone misusing them. The recipes surely do not date from when the story of *Exodus* was first written down, still less from when the exodus from Egypt took place, for few of these spices would have been available to the Israelites in their wanderings, during which they had other priorities than the precise formulation of incense.

These recipes are part of the instructions for the Jewish 'tabernacle' or tent and its contents, and they show us just how crucial spices and aromatics had become, in the ritual surrounding divine worship in Mediterranean lands, by the last few centuries BC. Without these scents – frankincense, myrrh, storax, cinnamon and the rest – the God of Israel, like the gods worshipped by other peoples, could not properly be addressed.

In these two recipes 'scented cane' is a product familiar in ancient times, not identified for certain, referred to elsewhere in this book as *calamus*. Onycha (now known in perfumery as sweet hoof) is the operculum or membrane sealing the mouth of various shellfish; ground, it formed an aromatic that was equally prized in the ancient Near East and in early China.

Storax

Storax, sometimes spelt 'styrax', was originally a sweet-smelling red gum from the tree *Styrax officinalis* of Syria. It was widely popular, known in ancient Egypt, exported to India in the first century AD and as far as China very soon after that, though it was said to 'pass through the hands of many middlemen before reaching China, and lose much of its fragrance in the process'. Storax was not only an incense but also a medicine: 'a small dose dispels melancholy, but a larger one causes it,' according to Pliny.[29] It was also widely regarded as an effective fumigant: we remember that the Arabs were imagined to burn storax to drive away the snakes that clustered around their frankincense trees. For some reason, storax is no longer obtained from this Syrian species. Nowadays liquid storax or Levant storax comes from an alternative source, already drawn on in ancient times, the worm-eaten rotted wood of the tree *Liquidambar orientalis*, which grows in southern Asia Minor. A medieval Russian pilgrim, Daniel, gives an engaging description of the production of storax.

[South-western Asia Minor] produces red incense or benzoin. This is how it comes: it runs from a tree like a sort of pith, and is collected with an iron blade. The tree is called *zyghia* and resembles alder. Another small tree, resembling the aspen and called *stiouriaka*, is gnawed under the bark by a fat worm, a sort of big caterpillar. What it has gnawed, resembling wheat bran, falls from the tree and collects on the ground like the resin of cherry trees. It is collected, mixed with the product of the first tree, and cooked together in a cauldron. That is how they prepare the benzoin incense, which is sold to merchants in skins.[30]

Daniel may not be right about the two trees, but he is certainly right about the skins. Pliny, a thousand years before, had already said that storax came in goatskin bags.

In the Far East a similar sweet gum, from the tree *Altingia excelsa*, is popular under the odd name of rose-mallows, borrowed from Sanskrit *rasamâlâ* or 'perfume garland'. Similar again is a North American species, *Liquidambar styraciflua*, whose resin has many names: sweet gum, American storax, red gum, bilsted, to mention a few. All three of these are used in perfumes and cosmetics. It may be that only the Byzantine Greeks, who would try almost anything, were bold enough to try the effect of adding storax (it was probably *S. officinalis*) to their spiced wine.

Saffron

Last but not least, saffron is the most expensive of Mediterranean spices; probably it always was. It consists of the dried stigmata of the purple saffron crocus (*Crocus sativus*), which have to be picked laboriously by hand. Is it possible, as suggested by a Cretan wall painting, that monkeys were once trained to do this work?

Saffron is perhaps native to Asia Minor. At any rate it was well known in the Aegean islands before the eruption of Santorini, which buried the Minoan town of Akrotiri with its wall paintings showing the picking of saffron. It was known to the poet of the *Iliad*, composed around 700 BC. And in Roman times the best saffron in the world grew in coastal Cilicia (southern Asia Minor) at the Corycian cavern, an awe-inspiring cauldron-like depression in the limestone, irrigated by a river that emerged from a natural spring in the rocks and, after crossing the basin, disappeared underground once more. Among the luxuriant vegetation, plots had been established to grow the saffron crocus.

In early Europe, saffron was a dye and an aromatic. It coloured cloth either yellow or deep red, depending on its age. It was burnt in sacrifice for its aroma, and it was used in a subtle and seductive aromatic oil, *crocinum*, to be applied to the hair; in the first century AD the best *crocinum* was made in Rhodes. Typical additives included wine, dragon's blood and alkanet, the last two to adjust the colour. The Romans combined its colouring and aromatic effects in another special use: saffron was mixed with sweet wine and the resulting sticky yellow mixture was sprayed liberally about at theatres, filling the air with costly fragrance.

Grown in Iran from very ancient times, saffron reached Kashmir, as we have already seen, no later than the third century AD and possibly as early as the fifth century BC. It became a staple of the local economy; and in due course, when Kashmir was part of the Mogul empire of northern India, the official memoirs of the emperor Jahângîr (reigned 1605–27) provide a fine description of the saffron harvest in Kashmir.

As the saffron was in blossom, His Majesty left the city to go to Pâmpûr, which is the only place in Kashmir where it flourishes. Every field, as far as the eye could reach, was covered with flowers. The stem inclines towards the ground. The flower has five violet petals, and three stigmas yielding saffron are found within it. That is the purest saffron. It is the established custom to weigh the flowers, and give them to the maufacturers, who take them home and extract the saffron from them, and upon giving the extract, which amounts to about one-fourth weight of the flower, to the public officers, they receive in return an equal weight of salt, in lieu of money wages.[31]

Westwards, saffron now grows in southern Spain, which is where the highest quality comes from today. Not long ago it was a speciality of Saffron Walden in England and of Pithiviers in France.

Safflower (*Carthamus tinctorius*), though not aromatic, finds plenty of use as a much cheaper substitute for saffron in its role as a colorant; in addition, safflower oil serves as a base for perfumes. Safflower has been used in these ways for so long, in so many parts of the Old World, that no one can now be sure where it first grew. It is so well adapted to cultivation that it will not propagate in the wild, and no wild form is known.

'I have found cinnamon!'

In Española there are many sources of spices, as well as large mines of gold and other metals. I believe I have found rhubarb and cinnamon.

CHRISTOPHER COLUMBUS.

Spices of the Inca Empire

The two great powers conquered by the Spaniards in the New World were very different in nature. The Aztecs dominated a relatively small region of central Mexico, though their trade links extended much further, and Mexico was a colourful patchwork linguistically and ethnically. The Incas, by contrast, ruled a vast empire along the chain of the Andes. Quechua, the language of their administration and their army, had spread rapidly: it was spoken from southern Colombia to northern Chile. Both these states had their traditional foods and cuisines; both had their typical spices and aromatics.

According to legend the three brothers of the first Inca, Manco Cápac, were Ayar Cachi, Ayar Uchu and Ayar Sauca. *Sauca* is 'happiness'; *cachi* is 'salt'; *uchu* is...*uchu*. Their legendary family history, through many generations, was evidently still present in the minds of the Inca nobility, from one of whom, Garcilaso de la Vega, '*el Inca*', we know the story. Garcilaso was the illegitimate son of an Inca princess and one of the Spanish *conquistadores*. His great work, the 'Royal Commentaries of the Inca', gives a unique picture of the already lost civilization of pre-Columbian Peru.

The Incas and their subject peoples knew many medicinal plants. For example, 'they made many uses of the herb or plant the Spaniards call tobacco and the Indians *sairi*. They inhaled it as a powder to clear the head. Many have experienced the virtues of this plant in Spain, where it is now called "holy weed".' This was the so-called 'wild tobacco' of South America, *Nicotiana rustica*. But the three ancestral names of the

Inca, given above, are meant to guide us to a list of three basic ingredients of human civilization, seen through Inca eyes. They prepare us for the information that when Pizarro and his band entered the borderlands of the Inca empire in 1531, *uchu* was among the symbolic gifts sent by the emperor Atahuallpa to the men who would soon destroy his realm.

Uchu, rocoto and ulupica

Uchu is the best-known Peruvian species of capsicum, *Capsicum pendulum*, or *C. baccatum* in an alternative classification. It is still nowadays a major crop in Peru, where it has been grown since about 2000 BC, having been familiar as a wild plant some centuries earlier still. Naturally it was among the major crops of the Inca dominion. At altitudes where it would grow, farming communities paid tribute to the Incas by farming those fields that were set aside for the Sun and the Inca, and by harvesting and storing such crops as *uchu* for supply to the government. When new lands were irrigated and taken into cultivation by this most paternalistic of governments, colonists were directed to grow *uchu* whenever the altitude and climate were suitable.

In the extract that follows, from his survey of Peruvian fruits and vegetables, Garcilaso sets out exactly why *uchu* was so important in Inca cuisine.

> With these fruits – and at the head of them all according to the taste of the Indians – we might include the condiment they invariably take with everything they eat, whether stewed, boiled or roasted. They call it *uchu*, and the Spaniards say 'pepper of the Indies', though in America generally it is called *ají*, a word from the language of the Windward Islands. The inhabitants of Peru are so attached to *uchu* that they will eat nothing without it. Because of the pleasure they obtain from it, they used to prohibit the eating of it when they were obeying a strict fast, which was thereby rendered the stricter.

The Spanish phrase *pimiento de las Indias* or 'pepper of the Indies' was used equally for all capsicum species. So is *ají*, which Garcilaso correctly identifies as a Carib word and which even now remains a general term for capsicums in Spanish America. He continues with a survey of all the capsicum species (as we would now define them) that were available in pre-Columbian Peru, taking *rocoto*, *uchu* and *ulupica*, each in turn. Now living in poverty in Seville, Garcilaso is trying to recall the lost flavours of his youth:

> The 'pepper of the Indies' is found in three or four varieties. The commonest is thick, rather long, and not pointed. It is called *rócot uchu*, 'thick pepper', to distinguish it from the next sort: it is eaten either ripe or green, that is before it

takes on its final red colour; others are yellow or purple, though I have seen only the red kind in Spain. There are other peppers about as thin as the bigger finger, which were regarded as nobler than the others and therefore used in the royal household and among all the royal kin: I cannot remember its separate name: it is also called *uchu*, but the adjective escapes me. Another small round pimento resembles exactly a cherry with its stalk. It is called *chinchi uchu*. It is incomparably tastier than the rest, and only small quantities of it are found, wherefore it is the more esteemed. Poisonous creatures avoid the capsicum and its fruit. I heard a Spaniard from Mexico say that it was very good for the sight, so he used to eat two roast chillies as a sort of dessert after every meal. All the Spaniards who come to Spain from the Indies are accustomed to it and prefer it to Oriental spices.

None of the South American species of capsicum is well known abroad – unlike the chilli of Mexico, which has taken over the world. Nowadays *rocoto* (*Capsicum pubescens*) is used in Peru rather as sweet peppers are used elsewhere: For example, the seeds can be removed and the fruit stuffed with minced meat or cheese and baked. But it is also strong enough in flavour to be used as a spice. *Ulupica* (*Capsicum cardenasii*) is carefully described here by Garcilaso as *chinchi uchu*, and it has never ceased to be sold in the markets of Bolivia, yet no botanist had noticed it until 1958. Very small, very hot and also pleasantly aromatic, it is often pickled in oil or vinegar. The *uchu* itself is often sold dried, *cusqueño*, and it remains Peru's traditional condiment.

Pink peppercorns

Uchu is sometimes called 'Peruvian pepper'. A second Peruvian pepper is a medicinal plant known to the Incas as *mulli*. 'They understood the virtues of the juice and resin of a tree named *mulli*, which the Spaniards call *molle*. This has a remarkable effect on fresh wounds: it seems almost supernatural.' In botanical Latin it is *Schinus molle*, now grown in Mexico and California as well as Peru. It has a close relative, *Schinus terebinthifolius*, native to Brazil, whose berries are currently enjoying a vogue as a culinary spice under such names as pink peppercorns, red peppercorns, *baies roses* or Brazilian pepper. They have been much used by chefs who aim at nouvelle cuisine, though some diners suffer adverse reactions to them.

Coca

Uchu, like other capsicum species, has never commanded the high price fetched by traditional Old World spices. Given a suitable climate, these fruits are simply too abundant, too easy to grow. For a time, after the Spanish conquest, Peru's economic success story was the export of coca, the leaf of the high-altitude shrub *Erythroxylum coca* and of its relative *E. novogranatense*. Traditionally the leaves are part-dried in the sun. They must not be completely dried or they lose their effect; but they must not stay damp, or they rot in the baskets. These coca baskets were made of split canes, covered on the outside with the leaves of the canes. Packed in this way, coca leaves used to travel long distances in America.

They are traditionally chewed together with lime and the ash of certain plants. Coca has been a stimulant much needed by hard-working Peruvians and Bolivians under Inca and Spanish rule – and even after independence. It enables the user to overcome tiredness and postpone appetite for food, at the cost of an addiction which leads inexorably to ever-increasing use. Garcilaso tells the story of a poor Spaniard, left alone to care for his disabled daughter, who thus explained his use of coca leaves: 'Sir, I used to hate it no less than others do, but necessity forced me to imitate the Indians and chew it. I can tell you that if I didn't I couldn't carry her weight. It is because of coca that I feel strong and vigorous enough to cope with the task.'[1]

The method for the extraction of cocaine from coca leaves was discovered in 1860. In 1892 the description of the new fictional detective hero, Sherlock Holmes, as 'alternating from week to week between cocaine and ambition' simply added a colourful detail to Holmes' Bohemianism – though, soon afterwards, his doctor was said to be advising him to give it up.[2] About this same date the name Coca-Cola was invented for a new fizzy drink. Whether or not the original recipe contained coca leaf or cocaine, the name was used because it suggested harmless stimulation (not drug addiction). Cocaine does have value as a stimulant and a local anaesthetic, and retains some medical uses, but it has gradually earned an evil reputation as an addictive drug; in addition, very small doses can kill those who have a special sensitivity to it.

Spices of pre-Columbian Mexico

The Aztecs, too, had a foundation myth. Their ancestors had been barbarians from far away in the north of Mexico, whose wanderings brought them to the Valley of Mexico and the city of Tenochtitlán in the early fourteenth century, two hundred years before the Spanish invasion. One of their legends told of an expedition to retrace their steps, at the end of which the powerful emissaries of the Aztecs were admonished by the aged goddess of their ancestral home: 'You have become old, you have become tired because of the chocolate you drink and because of the foods you eat. They have harmed and weakened you.' In spite of the puritanical impulses evidenced in this legend, the Aztecs did not cease to eat their universal condiment, chilli (though admittedly they ate no chilli on religious fast days); they did not stop smoking tobacco; and they certainly did not stop drinking chocolate.

Bernal Díaz, an eye-witness of Cortes' conquest of Mexico in 1519–21, wrote memoirs of the fateful event many years later. He recalled how, as a young soldier, he had had his first fascinated glimpse of the pleasures of the Aztec court.

> They brought to Montezuma, in cups (or the like) of pure gold, a drink made from this *cacao*. They said he took it before going to his women, and we took no more notice of it than that. I saw them bring into the hall more than fifty big bowls of good cacao, all frothed up, and I saw him drink some of it, the women presenting it to him with great respect. Montezuma enjoyed music, dance and poetry, and he would send the leftovers and the bowls of chocolate to the performers.
>
> After Montezuma the Great had dined, his guard and many others of his household dined next. I believe they got a thousand platefuls of the dishes I have listed, and more than two thousand bowls of chocolate all frothed up Mexican fashion, and more fruit than I can count. With all his women and maids and bakers and chocolate-makers, what it must have cost him! They also placed on the table three tubes, all painted and gilded, in which they put *liquidámbar* mixed with a herb called *tabaco*. When he had finished his dinner, and they had sung and danced, and cleared the table, he would take the smoke from one of these tubes, just a little of it, and then would fall asleep.[3]

Montezuma's cigars contained true tobacco, *Nicotiana tabacum*, blended with sweet gum, *Liquidambar styraciflua*. Of the three sensual pleasures bequeathed by the Aztec Empire to the world at large, it is hard to know whether chocolate, tobacco or chilli should have the first rank.

Chocolate

Chocolate comes from the seeds – roasted, fermented and ground – of the cacao tree, *Theobroma cacao* L. This 'L.' is the great botanist Carl Linnaeus himself, evidently a chocolate-lover, since the generic name he invented, *Theobroma*, means 'food of the gods'.

Having traced its progress through the language families of Mexico, most linguists believe that *cacao* is in origin a Mixe-Zoque word, *kakawa*. This connects the use of chocolate with the early Olmec culture of Vera Cruz and Tabasco provinces of Mexico, dated between 1500 and 400 BC. But Olmec hieroglyphs have not been deciphered, so we cannot read what they themselves might have said about it.

After the Olmecs, cacao was well known to the classic Maya of Yucatan. Alongside dead Maya were buried implements for use in the after-life, including jars and bowls for their chocolate. The identification of the word *ka-ka-w* in the inscriptions on these pots was a breakthrough in the decipherment of Maya phonetic writing – and traces of theobromine and caffeine, the active constituents of chocolate, have been found in some of them.

An eighth-century painted vase shows chocolate being poured from a cylindrical jar, held high, into a bowl, thus demonstrating how the Maya raised froth in their chocolate: to them the froth was the best part. The Maya liked to drink their chocolate hot, as they still did under Spanish rule. They added chilli and vanilla to flavour it. The Aztecs, who preferred it cold, sometimes sweetened their chocolate – by adding honey – and sweetened chocolate is what almost the whole world now prefers. Among many other aromatics, the Aztecs liked to add to chocolate the sassafras-scented leaves or the pepper-like fruits of *acuyo* (*Piper sanctum*). Modern Central American peoples some-times add its relative, black pepper, which was not available in pre-Columbian America. Allspice is also used nowadays. In the late eighteenth century the French still occasionally flavoured their chocolate with chilli, in the old Mexican and Spanish style, but they always added sugar as well.

Sometimes, in Central America, annatto is added to chocolate: this contributes flavour and also colours the drinker's mouth red, a reminder that drinking cacao was, in Aztec thought, parallel with drinking blood. Annatto is the fruit of the plant *Bixa orellana*, which provides a red dye still used for cloth, and in Central America and the Caribbean is much used in foods too. In the seventeenth century it served as a sun blocker, as does sandalwood in southern Asia: 'The Carib women dissolve some annatto in a little carap oil, take it up in a brush and paint their husbands' bodies all over with it. This cosmetic shields their skin, so that it will not crack or burn in the sun and wind, and it protects them from the bites of mosquitoes.'[4]

To the Maya and the Aztecs the ceremonial importance of chocolate was profound. It was provided generously at the banquets at which noblemen and merchants dis-played their wealth. It was offered to the gods, and was used to anoint newborn child-ren on the forehead, face, fingers and toes in a rite resembling baptism. To the Aztecs, chocolate was a drink for warriors and the elite. Aztec soldiers on campaign were sup-plied with tablets of ground cacao, to be stirred into water as 'instant chocolate'.

Cacao beans had become a trade commodity, an object of warfare, and also a cur-rency, long before the Spanish reached Mexico. In fact Columbus, on his third voyage to the New World, on 15 August 1502, captured a Maya trading canoe laden with cacao beans and other produce, described in his biography as 'the almonds which the Indians of New Spain use as currency'. He never found out that a drink was made from them.[5]

The use of cacao beans as currency continued under Spanish rule. 'These cacaos goe among them for meate and money,' reported a bemused English pirate after burn-ing the Mexican seaport of Aguatulco in 1587. 'They are very like unto an almond, but are nothing so pleasant in taste. They eate them, and make drink of them.'[6] According to one source, in sixteenth-century Nicaragua a rabbit was worth ten beans, a slave fetched as many as a hundred. One hundred and fifty to two hundred beans – the rate varied with time – equalled a silver dollar.

Meanwhile, when the Spaniards under Cortes invaded Yucatan and then the Valley of Mexico itself, between 1517 and 1526, they soon realized the full value of the black 'almonds'. At first disgusted by this frothy beverage seen at every Aztec banquet and festival, the *conquistadores* soon learned to like it. They thought it aphrodisiac, and argued whether it must be ruled out during Lent. In contrast to the Aztec view of it as a drink for warriors, chocolate has sometimes been seen by Europeans as a woman's drink. This may have something to do with the fact that the *conquistadores* were taught to like it by their Mexican wives, concubines and domestic servants. By 1590 'the Spanish men – and even more the Spanish women – are addicted to it,' wrote José de Acosta of his Mexican observations.

It was from an innovation of this period that the name 'chocolate' originally comes. Hot water with a mixture of ground cacao and ground sapote kernels, maize and other flavourings made a refreshing drink first described by the Spanish natural-ist Francisco Hernández in the late sixteenth century. Its new name, *chocolatl*, appears to be a Spanish-inspired blend of Maya *chocol* ('hot') and Nahuatl *atl* ('water') – an appropriate formation for the melting-pot of cultures that was colonial Mexico.

The Spaniards in Mexico also appear to have invented a new means of producing the much-loved froth of drinking chocolate. Where Maya and Aztecs had achieved the effect by pouring, colonial Mexico developed the *molinillo* or swizzle stick, which required a chocolate pot with a well-fitting, pierced lid. Meanwhile cane sugar, intro-duced to America in early colonial times, became an ever more popular flavouring in chocolate drinks. Other flavourings, including cinnamon and anise, were also tried.

Chocolate reached Europe in 1544, when a party of Maya paid a visit to the future Philip II of Spain. They brought him chocolate, maize, sweet gum, sarsaparilla and chillies. As a commodity of trade cacao beans began to reach Spain in 1585. In the seventeenth century the Spanish court was well known throughout Europe for its prowess in preparing chocolate drinks. By 1644 chocolate was known in Italy as a medicine; soon the court physician to Cosimo III de' Medici was experimenting with new flavour combinations, aromatizing the Grand Duke's chocolate with ambergris, musk, jasmine, citron peel and lemon peel. A century later Italian cooks were adding chocolate to savoury dishes and to ice creams. The French, meanwhile, tried flavour-ing biscuits and sweetmeats with chocolate; and the English thought of adding milk to their drinking chocolate. In the French Caribbean another idea was developed:

Cacaos confits: The beans must be picked white and tender, some days before they are fully ripe. Soak them in clear water for five or six days, changing the water daily. Insert in each bean five or six slivers of lemon peel and tiny chips of cinnamon. Make a thin sugar syrup, and while it is still hot add the beans to it. Leave them for twenty-four hours, then drain them. Make a fresh sugar syrup, thicker than the last; again add the beans to it while it is still hot and leave them in it for twenty-four hours. Repeat this process four more times, with a thicker syrup each time. To the last syrup, in which you will be conserving them, add a little essence of ambergris or musk or other aromatic.[7]

By 1671, according to the letters of Madame de Sévigné, chocolate was much in vogue at the Court of Versailles, alternately praised for its medicinal virtues and blamed for unexpected side-effects: 'The Marquise de Coetlogon took so much chocolate during her pregnancy last year that she produced a baby as black as the Devil. It died.'

Chocolate was first sold in London about 1657 by a Frenchman with a shop in Gracechurch Street. He advertised it as 'an excellent West India drink [which] cures and preserves the body of many diseases'. An enlightened entrepreneur, he not only sold chocolate ready to drink but also offered to teach his customers how to make it themselves, with the help of a recipe book which they were encouraged to buy. The diarist Samuel Pepys, in the 1660s, several times recorded a morning drink of 'Chocolatte'. England's supply of chocolate came from the plantations of Jamaica, captured from the Spanish in 1655. The chocolate houses which sprang up in London at this period became fashionable meeting places, precursors of men's clubs, and were briefly banned by Charles II in 1675 as hotbeds of radical politics. The Garrick Club began life as 'The Cocoa Tree', the early headquarters of the Jacobite party.

The rich chocolate produced from the beans of the criollo cacao tree was the only kind known to the pre-Columbian peoples of Central America, and it was the sole variety known in Europe down to the eighteenth century. The Caracas cacao of Venezuela came from trees of the same variety, found there as early as 1570. As disease and serfdom reduced the population in the Spanish colonies, criollo trees were planted elsewhere – especially in Jamaica and Trinidad – to maintain the supply of chocolate.

In Ecuador and in parts of the Amazon basin in the seventeenth century Spanish and Portuguese prospectors found, growing wild, a distinct variety of the cacao tree named 'forastero'. The chocolate it produced was bitterer, less delicate in flavour, but the tree was much hardier than the temperamental criollo, and the Jesuits of Brazil took to growing it. As the Caribbean plantations of criollo chocolate succumbed to blights, forastero replaced them. Soon it was growing in west Africa, and by the early twentieth century in many other tropical countries. Forastero and the hybrid trinitario varieties account for almost all of modern world production. This is no longer the sweet, rich, exotic chocolate that the Maya and Aztecs knew, or that was so popular in Europe in the seventeenth and eighteenth centuries. Criollo chocolate, still available in small quantities from Nicaragua, is now a rare luxury, and the only remaining trace of the original spice.[8]

Vanilla

The vanilla vine, *Vanilla fragrans*, grew on the edge of the Mexican forests. Its long, narrow pod, harvested unripe and fermented, produces a marvellous, sweet aroma and flavour which made it a favourite additive to chocolate for the Maya and after them the Aztecs. This was at first how the Spanish used it too. The first European to describe it – he wrote in classical Aztec – was Friar Bernardino de Sahagún; after him came the naturalist Francisco Hernández. It was Hugh Morgan, apothecary to Queen Elizabeth I, who is said to have suggested the use of vanilla as a flavouring for other foods.

The flowers do not pollinate easily, and a French attempt to naturalize vanilla in Mauritius, Madagascar and Réunion did not succeed fully until a method of artificial pollination was invented in 1840. Even now, when most of the world's production comes from Réunion, vanilla remains an expensive spice. It cannot be effectively synthesized: the only inexpensive vanilla is 'vanilla flavouring', containing a low proportion of real extract of vanilla. The cheap 'vanilla ice cream' of Britain, which contains very little vanilla and less cream, is surely destined for renaming.

Chilli

Although not mentioned in the description of Montezuma's banquet quoted above, the chilli of Mexico, the country's almost universal condiment, had already come to the attention of the Spanish invaders. The less observant took it to be the same bonnet or Tabasco pepper that they had encountered in the Caribbean islands, which they had learnt from the Caribs to call *ají*. This is why an exhausted Spanish soldier, on a long march to Tenochtitlán, complains of 'our misery of maize cakes, *agi*, prickly pears and green herbs'. Columbus himself had already observed of the Maya country that 'according to reports they are all acquainted with "pepper of the Indies"'.⁹ But in fact this mainland capsicum was not quite the same, and the so-called 'Anonymous Conqueror' is right, in his narrative of the Spanish conquest of Mexico, to give it a new name: 'The Aztecs cultivate a great diversity of plants and garden truck of which they are very fond, and these they eat raw as well as in various cooked dishes. They have one, like a pepper, as a condiment which they call *chili*, and they never eat anything without it.'¹⁰

Chilli is the Nahuatl (Aztec) name for the fruit of *Capsicum annuum*. People in this region were using wild chillies for food by about 7000 BC, and were purposefully growing chillies probably by 4000 BC. By the time the Aztecs, and then the Spaniards, arrived in central Mexico chillies had developed into numerous varieties, of all sizes, flavours and strengths, in the hands of Mexican gardeners. The great naturalist of sixteenth-century Mexico, Francisco Hernández, was to divide them into seven different categories: the *quauhchilli*, tree chilli, which is the smallest and hottest; the *chiltecpin*, flea chilli, which seems even hotter but loses its fire more quickly; the summer *tonalchilli*; the *chilcoztli*, which tints yellow any food prepared with it yellow; the *milchilli*, small and pointed; and the *texochilli*, large and sweet, which, if smoked and dried, was called *pocchilli*.¹¹ But the market trade in chillies in all its richness is set out for us incomparably by Bernardino de Sahagún, the Franciscan friar who – with the worthy aim of replacing the Aztec with the Christian way of life – set to work with his Nahuatl-speaking assistants to make an Aztec encyclopaedia, a full survey of Aztec life, all in classical Aztec rhythmical prose.

> The good chilli seller sells mild red chillies, broad chillies, hot green chillies, yellow chillies, *cuitlachilli, tenpilchilli, chichioachilli*. He sells water chillies, *conchilli*; he sells smoked chillies, small chillies, tree chillies, thin chillies, beetle-like chillies. He sells hot chillies, early-season chillies, hollow-based chillies. He sells green chillies, pointed red chillies, late-season chillies, chillies from Atzitziuacan, Tochmilco, Huaxtepec, Michoacan, Anauac, the Huaxteca, the Chichimeca. Separately he sells strings of chillies, stewed chillies, chillies with fish, chillies with white fish.
>
> The bad chilli seller [in Aztec rhetoric there must also be a bad chilli seller] sells stinking chillies, sour chillies, foul chillies, rotten chillies; waste from chillies, runty chillies, chaff from chillies. He sells chillies from the wet country, chillies without heat, chillies without taste; malformed chillies, flabby chillies, unripe chillies, embryonic chillies.[12]

As it has spread across the world – for this at last is the chilli that everybody knows and a great many people grow – *Capsicum annuum* has taken many new forms and almost as many new names. In British English it is usually 'chilli', in American English 'red pepper' or 'chile pepper' (or sometimes just 'pepper'). But each new variety or cultivar will have a name of its own, sometimes more than one; and then there are the chilli powders and sauces, which different peoples like in different strengths, from the very hot Cayenne pepper to the various mild-to-hot versions of paprika that have become the national condiment of Hungary.

New spices of tropical America

Columbus' aim, already stated in his earliest plans, to find a route to the 'Spiceries', had been fulfilled as soon as he began to explore the Indies. Or so he insisted in his first report to Ferdinand and Isabella.

> In Española there are many sources of spices,as well as large mines of gold and other metals. I shall give their Highnesses spices and cotton at once, as much as they shall order to be shipped, and as much as they shall order to be shipped of mastic, which till now has never been found except in Greece in the island of Xio,[13] and the Seigneurie of Genoa sells it for whatever price it pleases; and aloes as much as they shall order to be shipped; and slaves as many as they shall order to be shipped, and these shall be from idolatrous peoples. And I believe I have found rhubarb and cinnamon.[14]

The special mention of mastic is interesting because Columbus, himself Genoese, had visited Chios (which was at that time under Genoese rule) and seen the tapping of mastic. But the Genoese monopoly of mastic and the resulting high price had made an impression on other explorers besides Columbus himself. Dr Chanca, in his own report to the municipality of Seville, repeats the claim that mastic had been found in Hispaniola:

> There are a great number of terebinth trees which are very remarkable and very fine; also much tragacanth, which is very good too, and some trees which I think bear nutmegs but at present no fruit. I say 'I think' because the smell and taste of the bark is like that of nutmegs. I saw a root of ginger, which an Indian had tied round his neck. There is also aloes, and though not of a kind which has hitherto been seen in our country it is no doubt one of the species used by doctors. There is also very good mastic.[15]

None of the Old World spices named by Columbus or Chanca was truly duplicated in the West Indies, though they had found some useful new aromatics. In his private log-book Columbus is less assertive, and a good deal nearer the truth. At the island of *Isabela* as he obsequiously named it (now Crooked Island) he notes: 'I think that many trees and plants grow here which will be highly valued in Spain for dyes and medicinal spices. But I am sorry to say that I do not recognize them.' And two days later: 'The trees are of many kinds, each with its own fruit, and all have a marvellous aroma. It grieves me extremely that I cannot identify them, for I am quite certain that they are all valuable and I am bringing samples of them and of the plants also. I recognized aloes, and tomorrow I intend to have half a ton brought aboard, for they tell me it's very valuable.'[16]

One of the things that Columbus particularly wished to do was to find pepper – not quite the most expensive spice in medieval Europe, but the one in most demand. He and his followers came to call the capsicum species 'pepper of the Indies'. Meanwhile, however, they learned that there was in the Caribbean islands something that more closely resembled pepper, a kind of myrtle bush bearing tiny round fruits that gave a spicy taste to food. Columbus perhaps never saw it himself, but he was assured it was there and was ready to be brought into cultivation.[17] Now best known in English as allspice, it is mainly cultivated today in Jamaica. Jamaica pepper, *pimienta de la Jamaica*, has always been an alternative name for this spicy berry of the shrub *Pimenta dioica*. The Spanish explorers were the more ready to recognize its possibilities as a flavouring because they were already familiar not only with expensive black pepper but also with cheaper European substitutes, juniper and myrtle.

Many other new spices and herbs were waiting to be 'discovered'. The bay rum tree, or West Indian bay, *Pimenta racemosa*, produces an essential oil once used in medicine and still in demand as a skin lotion. Sarsaparilla, the root of *Smilax* spp., noticed in the early sixteenth century, was for a long time considered to have powerful medicinal properties. Now it is a bitter flavouring in commercial soft drinks. Sassafras comes from the bark of the root of *Sassafras albidum*, and this was described enthusiastically by one of Francis Drake's crew as 'a tree growing in Florida well up in the interior. The Indians make wine from the root, whose aroma is as good as cinnamon. It is as fine as muscadel.'[18] There is plenty of enthusiasm for sassafras in early texts; it is true that there is something of cinnamon in the aroma, and it is true that the southern United States once had a taste for sassafras tea. Sassafras is less used than formerly, even as a flavouring and perfume: sassafras oil is now outlawed as a food ingredient in the United States.

These and other 'new spices' of tropical America are not new in the sense that nobody at all had known of them. Local people knew them perfectly well. But they had not entered into trade until the very moment that we hear of them, and in this they differ from all the other spices dealt with in this book. Those that had been found by Columbus on his first voyage are very minor spices – with one exception – but others, discovered a little later, have a real world importance. Columbus' so-called mastic tree, which was plentiful enough in Cuba to be burnt for firewood, and was 'very similar in leaf and fruit to the mastic of Chios, but considerably larger',[19] was apparently the gumbo-limbo tree (*Bursera simaruba*); the aloes, of which Columbus enthusiastically loaded half a ton although Chanca was uncertain of the identification, are thought to have been one of the *Agave* species, from whose juice *pulque* is fermented. The rhubarb might have been some such plant as *Trimeza juncifolia*, known in the Portuguese of Brazil as *ruibarbo-do-brejo*, 'marsh rhubarb'. The cinnamon? More space is devoted to the cinnamon below.

Tabasco pepper and Scotch bonnet

The one new aromatic noted on Columbus' first voyage that is nowadays a significant food spice is one of the *Capsicum* species. The natives, according to Dr Chanca, 'use as seasoning a spice called *agi*, with which they also flavour their fish and birds when they can get them'. This was perhaps *C. chinense*, called in the West Indies 'country pepper' and also native to northern South America. Its best-known cultivated varieties today are Scotch bonnet in Jamaica, *habañero* in Spanish America, *piri-piri* in Brazil and Angola: from the latter comes the fiery sauce called *molho de piri-piri*.

A second capsicum species, *C. frutescens*, the one to which Tabasco pepper belongs, is also native to the Caribbean, along with Florida and the northern edge of South America. Tracing the historical meanderings of the cultivated capsicums is far from easy. Confusion was first introduced by the Spanish explorers, to whom these fruits were all new and very similar to one another. And so, having described the first they met as 'pepper of the Indies', and having learnt the Carib name of *ají* for it, they went on giving these same names to the different species that were in use in each cultural region. The English names, red pepper and chilli, add further confusion: chilli, though it is historically the Nahuatl word for *C. annuum*, is generally used for all the hot-tasting capsicums. And finally *C. annuum* is so easy to grow that it spread very rapidly to other regions with the initial help of the Spanish explorers. This is why *C. chinense*, on its Caribbean home ground, is now called, almost pejoratively, 'country pepper'. *C. annuum* is almost everywhere regarded as the best species, and has swept the field.

Canella

Columbus, we remember, wrote home: 'I believe I have discovered rhubarb and cinnamon.' And Dr Chanca went along with this. 'A kind of cinnamon has been found as well,' he writes, 'though it is true that it is not so fine as the cinnamon we know at home. This may be because we do not know the right season to gather it, or possibly there are better trees in the land.' Cinnamon was among the most costly of spices in ancient and medieval Europe, and although it was known to come from somewhere far to the east, no one knew exactly where. No wonder the explorers had been anxious to find the source of supply. What they had actually found was *Canella winterana*, the tree that is known in Jamaica now as 'wild cinnamon' or 'white cinnamon'. The aromatic part – just as with cinnamon – is the bark, which has been called 'whitewood bark' or 'Winter's bark'; it is used in perfume sachets and in potpourris. Canella is also native to Florida and is useful enough to be cultivated outside its homeland, but it was soon clear that it was not the valuable prize that Columbus and Chanca had been seeking.

The hunt for cinnamon was still on. The hope of finding a forest of this costly spice was what ensnared Gonzalo Pizarro, brother and lieutenant of the man who destroyed the Inca Empire. Gonzalo's ill-starred expedition set out east from Quito in 1540 to find a province called by the Incas *Sumaco* or *Zumaque*. The Spaniards themselves named the province, hopefully, *La Canela*, 'the Cinnamon'.

> In this province of *Sumaco*, which is on the equator or near it, grew the trees called cinnamon, of which the Spaniards were in search. They are very tall and have big leaves like laurels; the fruit consists of bunches of small fruit growing in husks like acorns. And though the tree and its leaves, roots, and bark all smell and taste of cinnamon, these husks are the true spice. A great many such trees grow wild and produce fruit, but it is not so good as that obtained from trees planted and tended by the Indians, who trade in it with their neighbours, though not with those of Peru. These latter have never wanted any other spices but their *uchu*.[20]

Garcilaso is a good and honest writer, but he went beyond his knowledge here. The Spanish demand for cinnamon, and local anxiety to please, created in everybody's mind in Peru the conviction that there were regular plantations of this wonderful spice waiting to be found in the trackless mountain jungle of eastern Ecuador. Even Garcilaso believed it. The search for the cinnamon of Ecuador is one of the most horrifying stories in the history of spices.

What Gonzalo and his fearless band were after (we now know) was the tree *Ocotea sassafras*, or a relative. Plants of this genus are sometimes called 'canela' in English after the Spanish and Portuguese word for cinnamon.

Two thousand strong, a hundred and fifty of them on horseback, they set out east from Quito driving a herd of pigs along with them for food. Their intelligence methods were limited, and similar to those used in the search for El Dorado: they consisted of torturing village headmen till they told them where the cinnamon country was. The result was also similar: they were always assured that it was about ten days' march further on. It never was. It rained continuously for months; there were no paths, and certainly no tracks suitable for horses or even for herds of pigs. Every one of the native porters died; more likely, perhaps, some quietly abandoned the party. The pigs and horses were soon gone. After nearly a year of wandering in the rain forest, the survivors came to a great river, the Napo. They built a ship, on which a group led by Francisco de Orellana was embarked with instructions to search for a rumoured city, three days downriver, and to return with supplies. They never returned. The remainder of the party struggled downriver on foot, in a death march lasting two months, and arrived at the confluence with an even greater river (which must have been the Amazon), where one mutinous member of Orellana's group had been left behind to greet them. From him they learnt that Orellana had abandoned them. There was now no option: Gonzalo Pizarro led them back upriver and over the Andes to Quito. Eighty of the two thousand arrived there, naked and starving, more than two years after they had set out. They brought back no cinnamon.

Orellana, unable to row upriver against the current, had gone on down, miraculously avoiding the numerous rapids, and he became the first man to trace the course of the greatest river of South America all the way to its mouth. He also claimed to have met and defeated the tribe of beautiful warrior women, long known from Greek mythology, after whom the Amazon is named. The little ship went on, crossing the Atlantic to Europe, and Orellana became, and still is, a hero of exploration. The town later founded at the fateful confluence is named after him Francisco de Orellana. Gonzalo Pizarro never forgave him.

The genus *Ocotea*, notably *Ocotea sassafras* of Brazil, is now important as the source of Brazilian sassafras oil, a useful perfume ingredient with a hint of cinnamon.

Balsam of Peru

In the case of cinnamon, the urge to find old spices in the New World had led to disaster. But the quest for the balsam of Mecca, which had already become practically unobtainable in medieval Europe, led to an early success story in applied ethnobotany.

When the Spanish began to fight their way south-eastwards from Mexico through Central America, they observed how the Pipil, the Aztec people of Sonsonate and San Salvador, used a certain balsam to help arrow wounds to heal. It came from a Salvadorean variety of a tree species found in several parts of tropical America, *Myroxylon balsamum* var. *pereirae*. The balsam was extracted from between the inner and outer bark of the tree by incision, which gave a high-quality, concentrated resin.

Spanish soldiers tried the effect for themselves, and their physicians quickly realized that this balsam of Peru ('Peru' is a very vague term here) would be an excellent substitute for the almost-lost balsam of Mecca. However, it came in much too small a quantity for the Spanish trade.

And so the Pipil began to produce more balsam of Peru by boiling the wood and skimming off the oily resin. When in 1565 Nicolás Monardes of Seville began his progressive survey of New World drugs, this thin product was all that he could get. The 'marvellous liquor' must be kept in silver bottles, he wrote – it would evaporate though tin or glass. 'Taken in the morning on an empty stomach it cures shortness of breath, and licking a few drops on the palm of the hand will cure a persistent stomach ache.' By the time Monardes wrote his *Second Part*, in 1571, a precious consignment of the more concentrated original balsam, the product of incision, had reached Spain: 'one drop of this is worth more than two gallons of the other'. An English writer of 1684 talks of 'its amicable and peculiar faculty in strengthening the Nerves'. Until the 1930s balsam of Peru was used in small quantities in wound dressings; it is still an ingredient in some patent medicines.

But the source of this wonder drug is very restricted. The *Encyclopaedia Britannica*, in the nineteenth century, confirmed the fact: 'The tree from which it is obtained grows naturally nowhere else in the world except in a limited part of the Salvadorian seaboard known as the Balsam coast,' centring on the cities of Sonsonate and San Salvador.

Monardes' *Third Part*, dated 1574, tells of an exciting new discovery, the balsam of Tolu (which is a small harbour town south of Cartagena on the north coast of Colombia). Experts can distinguish this from the balsam of Peru: it comes from other varieties of the same species, whose combined range actually extends from El Salvador to Venezuela. It, too, was already well known to the local Cenúfara people. Their traditional method of collection was to make an incision in the tree – it had to be done in hot weather, or nothing would come – and to place below it a collecting cup made of the local black beeswax. The wax, in turn, was tested by Spanish physicians.

Although not the finest variety, the *M. balsamum* trees that yield balsam of Tolu are much more plentiful, and so the European demand could be satisfied at last without compromising on quality. In the seventeenth century, balsam of Tolu was a cure for rickets, and good for the lungs. For 'shortness of breath' you could take a few drops in white wine; or, in the eighteenth and nineteenth centuries, you could suck Tolu lozenges. It is still a common ingredient in cough medicines.

In quest of spicery

By treaty between the infidels, a fleet of great ships
crosses the Indian Ocean to the Malabar coast each year
in quest of spicery.

LUÍS DE CAMÕES, *The Lusiads.*

Spices, linguists and historians

The early history of spices is hard to handle, in terms both of language and of history. The long-distance trade in them means that historians have to go beyond the usual linguistic range of their source materials. The wide distribution of loan-words naming spices means that linguists have to deal with unfamiliar language families.

It is necessary to look hard at what ancient texts say, because it is up to the historian to decide whether they are telling the truth: no one else will do the job. Early Chinese texts say that pepper was grown in Persia, and nutmeg in Vietnam – both assertions unlikely in the extreme, yet both accepted by critical historians. We have to ask whether the authors or their immediate sources are likely to have known, or whether they are more likely to have been guessing on the basis of the fact that Chinese supplies of pepper and nutmeg happened to come by way of Persia and Vietnam.

Dating the texts has to be done critically, even in unfamiliar territory. Some other books about spices are less conservative than this one: readers may have seen the Indian *Rgveda* discussed as if it were six thousand years old, and the book of *Exodus* quoted as evidence for the time of Jacob and Joseph. In reality, the details in traditional texts will only work as evidence about the period at which they were written down or otherwise fixed – the *Rgveda* something over 2,500 years ago, much of the Old Testament about the same period. By applying the rules of evidence strictly we get a more credible and coherent story, as we saw (page 32) with the mentions of spices in the story of King Solomon. These parts of the Old Testament are not very good evidence for how things were in the time of Solomon, but they give us excellent information on the spices available in the Middle East in the sixth century.

It is also necessary to look critically at what earlier historians have said. It is easy to perpetuate errors. At some time in the twentieth century, a British historian unfamiliar with foreign food was told (possibly by his mother) that spices serve to mask the flavour of rotting meat. This assertion is now made of medieval cuisine in several otherwise well-researched histories written in Britain. It is undocumented, and, in general, for ancient and medieval cuisines, it is most unlikely to be true. Spices were a luxury item, affordable only by those who could afford very good food. No recipe or household text recommends them to mask bad flavours. On the contrary, spices are called for liberally in ancient recipe books for their positive flavour, their aroma, their preservative and dietary qualities.

Finally, it is necessary to look hard at names of spices. Identifying spices in early texts is sometimes impossible. The Egyptian hieroglyphic texts have been used as evidence for the presence of cinnamon in Egypt 3,500 years ago, but the translation of the crucial word is pure guesswork. It is said that one archaeologist scented cinnamon, faintly, when unwrapping an early Egyptian mummy; otherwise, no one has demonstrated the presence of cinnamon in Egypt until about 450 BC, more than a thousand years later.

Even if names in ancient texts are the same as names used now, we have to ask whether the meaning has remained the same. Here, historians are occasionally too ready to assume a change – because it helps with the history – while ignoring the linguistic principles involved. People do often begin to use words with new senses, but there is always some reason why they do this, and linguists will not normally posit a change of meaning without giving at least a hypothetical explanation of how the change might occur. Some historians of the Greek and Roman world, by contrast with the Egyptologists, have argued that the *kinnamomon* and *kasia* of ancient texts must be different spices from modern 'cinnamon' and 'cassia' because Greek and Latin authors said they came from east Africa and southern Arabia. It is a weak argument, unless it can be explained how, in later times, the words changed their meanings to those they have today. An alternative position, preferable in this case, is that the early authors thought cinnamon and cassia came from those places because the trade routes passed that way.

Tracing the movements of spice names is important both to linguists and historians, because names tend to travel with trade. The Greeks and Romans obtained their ginger, they said, from the region now called Eritrea. Some do not believe this, though ginger certainly grows in Eritrea now. The Greek and Latin names for it, *zingiber*, *zingiberi*, come from further away – from Pali, now the classical language of southern Buddhism.[1] In Pali, ginger is called *singivera*, and that name in turn is a loan from Tamil. Both Pali and Tamil were spoken in southern India and Sri Lanka at the time when we first read of ginger reaching the Roman Empire, so we are not surprised to learn that Sri Lanka was one more place where ginger was already grown in ancient times. The story holds together if we grant that the immediate source of Eritrea's ginger plantation was southern India or Sri Lanka, and that is certainly possible. Ginger had reached Sri Lanka, clearly enough, from Sumatra or the Malay peninsula, and we already know (page 21) how it came to that region from its original habitat in southern China. Incidentally English *ginger*, French *gingembre* and other modern European names all derive by way of Latin and Greek from the Pali name *singivera*.

Spices and cultures

To each culture its own ethnobotany. Anthropologists have only begun to explore the knowledge of plants in food and medicine possessed by hundreds and thousands of peoples who still remember and rely on their own local resources. For many, the knowledge is on the way to being forgotten, and it is already too late.

This book could have listed, for hundreds of such peoples, the aromatic and spicy products that they use in cookery, in medicine and in religion to produce effects like those of the classical spices. To take a single example: Ethiopia, during its long, isolated existence as a Christian African civilization, has had its own native peppery spice, known variously in English as grains of Selim, Ethiopian pepper, habzeli, kimba pepper and xylopia. This fruit of *Xylopia aethiopica* has not been mentioned till now, because it has never entered (much) into world trade or been adopted by other cultures.

The history of spices as told in this book is, curiously enough, the opposite of all that. It is globalization. Several millennia before any international organization attempted to control the size and the sales of bananas, ginger and sugar were beginning their spread around the world. Soon afterwards, frankincense and myrrh were travelling by camel caravan across the Arabian desert to Mesopotamia, and by ship to Egypt. Meanwhile, cardamoms were being cultivated in southern India, chillies in Mexico. In a revolutionary period from 500 BC to AD 200 a great number of spices originating between western Europe and eastern Asia entered into long-distance trade. Not long after that Chinese physicians could prescribe the mastic of Chios, European physicians could recommend cloves and galanga, and an astonishing range of heady flavours was available to cooks all over the Old World. Then, in the century between 1500 and 1600, there was a rapid two-way exchange between the Old World and the New, as chilli was welcomed to Hungary and India, pepper became a fashionable flavouring in chocolate in Mexico, and the balsam of Peru took the place in European medicine left vacant by the unobtainable and legendary balsam of Mecca.

This book has not tried to tell the later, world-wide story: of how ginger reached Jamaica, cinnamon the Seychelles; how sugar, planted by Columbus, 'germinated in seven days' in the Caribbean; or of the well-named Pierre Poivre, whose almost superhuman persistence resulted in the planting of cloves and nutmeg – defying the Dutch monopoly and the envy of fellow French administrators – in Mauritius and Réunion, and then in Madagascar, Zanzibar and the West Indies. Thanks to transplantings, by

1600 oranges were on sale in Benin, sugar and fresh ginger on the banks of the Rio de la Plata; in the Azores gardens were planted with 'potato-roots' and with 'tabacco [as] now commonly knowen and used in England, wherewith their women there dye their faces reddish, to make them seeme fresh and young'.

Yet the spice trade is globalization on a human scale. It requires people, their ingenuity and their intelligence. Vanilla has to be picked at the right time, fermented correctly, stored and transported with care; it has to be treated like an individual, in a way that differs from every other product on the market. Many have tried, but no one has succeeded in synthesizing it. The origins of nutmeg, pepper, chocolate and saffron are equally individual, equally complex. The uses of spices and aromatics, highly valued as they still are, differ almost randomly from country to country. Let us hope that the spice trade will continue to set a pattern, and that our senses of taste and smell will continue to be excited variably, unpredictably and exotically.

Source texts

This is a selection of original sources quoted above which can be read in a modern translation. The selection focuses on texts concerned with geography, trade, food and traditional medicine. Original publication dates are given for these translations. Many, even of the very old ones, are still in print.

Greece and Rome

Herodotus wrote his *Histories*, the oldest surviving Greek prose text, about 440 BC. There are many translations in print. The first known gastronomic writer is Archestratus, *c.* 350 BC; surviving fragments are translated by John Wilkins and Shaun Hill (Totnes, 1994). Theophrastus' *Study of Plants* and *On Odours* date from 310 BC; they are translated by Sir Arthur Hort (*Enquiry into plants.* 2 vols. Cambridge, Mass., 1916–26). Agatharchides, *On the Erythraean Sea* dates from the second century BC. There is a translation of the fragments by S. M. Burstein (London, 1989). *Cato On Farming*, the earliest Latin prose text, is translated by Andrew Dalby (Totnes, 1998).

Strabo's *Geography* is a semi-official Roman strategic geography, written in Greek around the time of Christ; it is translated by H. L. Jones (8 vols. Cambridge, Mass., 1917–32). Dioscorides compiled his *Materia medica* a few decades later. There is only an antiquated translation by J. Goodyer (London, 1655), but it has been reprinted in the twentieth century. Celsus *On Medicine* is one of the first scientific texts written in Latin; there is a translation by W. G. Spencer (3 vols. Cambridge, Mass., 1935–8). Pliny, author of the Latin *Natural History*, died in the eruption of Vesuvius in AD 69; the work is translated by H. Rackham and others (10 vols. Cambridge, Mass., 1938–62). The *Periplus of the Erythraean Sea* was written anonymously about AD 50; the translation and commentary by L. Casson (Princeton, 1989) supersedes the one by G. W. B. Huntingford. About 200 AD Athenaeus wrote his *Deipnosophists*, a discursive social history in Greek; translation by C. B. Gulick (Cambridge, Mass., 1927–41). The Latin recipe collection, *Apicius*, is translated by B. Flower and E. Rosenbaum (London, 1961): look out for a new translation by Sally Grainger and Chris Grocock.

Medieval Europe

Anthimus *On the Observance of Foods*, written just after AD 500, is translated by Mark Grant (Totnes, 1996). Cosmas Indicopleustes compiled his *Christian Topography* around the same date; there is an English translation by E. O. Winstedt (Cambridge, 1909) and a newer French version, *Topographie chrétienne*, by Wanda Wolska-Conus (3 vols. Paris, 1968–73).

The *Travels of Sir John Mandeville* can be read in a modern English translation by C. W. R. D. Moseley (Harmondsworth, 1983). Benjamin of Tudela's travels have been translated as *The world of Benjamin of Tudela* by Sandra Benjamin (Rutherford, N. J., 1995). William of Rubruck's report can be read as *The mission of Friar William of Rubruck*, translated by Peter Jackson (London, 1990). Marco Polo's travels are translated by Ronald Latham (Harmondsworth, 1958), and two of the original texts are currently available in good paperback editions in France (*La Description du Monde*) and Italy (*Il Milione*). *Le Mesnagier de Paris* is an anonymous household manual of the fourteenth century; there is a paperback text with modern French translation by the late Georgina Brereton and others (Paris, 1994). *An Ordinance of Pottage* is a nice title for a

Middle English cookery manuscript, edited by Constance Hieatt (London, 1988). John Russell's *Boke of Nurture* was written in the fifteenth century and is edited by F. J. Furnivall under the title *Early English meals and manners* (London, 1868).

Europe and the Discoveries

Fernando Colón's *Life of Columbus* is available as *The life of the Admiral Christopher Columbus by his son Ferdinand* translated by Benjamin Keen (New Brunswick, N. J., 1958). A handy selection of texts, including Columbus' reports and Dr Chanca's letter, is in *The four voyages of Christopher Columbus*, translated by J. M. Cohen (Harmondsworth, 1969). Bernal Díaz's *History of the Conquest of New Spain* is translated by A. P. Maudslay (2 vols. London, 1908–16). *Royal Commentaries of the Incas and general history of Peru*, by Garcilaso de la Vega, el Inca, is translated by H. V. Livermore (2 vols. Austin, Texas, 1966). Luís de Camões' epic *The Lusiads* is translated by W. C. Atkinson (Harmondsworth, 1952).

A picture book apparently made by someone who sailed with Francis Drake is known as *Histoire Naturelle des Indes*; it was published under this title (New York, 1996) and in Britain under the title *The Drake manuscript in the Pierpont Morgan Library* (London, 1996). Friar Bernardino Sahagún wrote versions of his *General History of the Things of New Spain* in Spanish and at much greater length in Aztec (Nahuatl). The latter (the Florentine codex) is translated by C. E. Dibble and A. J. O. Anderson (12 vols. 2nd edn. Santa Fe, N. M., 1970–81).

Nicolás Monardes published *Dos libros. El uno trata de todas las cosas que traen de nuestras Indias Occidentales, que sirven al uso de medicina; el otro libro trata de dos medicinas maravillosas que son contra todo veneno, la piedra bezaar, y la yerva escuerçonera* in Seville in 1565. His second edition appeared in 1569, with a new supplement in 1571; his last (third) edition appeared in 1574 and was reprinted unchanged in 1580. An English translation from the 1565 edition appeared as *Ioyfull nevves out of the newe founde worlde, wherein is declared the rare and singuler vertues of diuerse and sundrie hearbes, trees, oyles, plantes, and stones, with their aplications, aswell for phisicke as chirurgerie, the saied beyng well applied bryngeth suche present remedie for all deseases, as maie seme altogether incredible, notwithstandyng by practize founde out to bee true: also the portrature of the saied hearbes, very aptly discribed; Englished by Jhon Frampton, marchaunt* (London, 1577); Frampton then enlarged this, working from the 1574 edition, and published a full revised translation in 1580. Stephen Gaselee's new version of *Frampton's Monardes* (London, 1925) combines material from the 1577 and 1580 translations. I have set out these details because they are usually stated wrongly.

García de Orta's *Coloquios dos simples e drogas he cousas medicinais da India* ('Conversations on the simples, drugs and medicinal products of India') was published in Goa in 1563. There is a translation, but not a good one, by Sir Clements Markham (London, 1913). Monardes' and Orta's work were hot news in their time and were republished in various forms in other languages. Charles de l'Ecluse (Carolus Clusius) earned the gratitude of scientific Europe by publishing excellent illustrated précis of Monardes' and Orta's information, along with work of Prosper Alpinus, Pierre Belon and others, in Latin with his own commentary. His last omnibus edition is entitled in full: Caroli Clusii *Exoticorum libri decem, quibus animalium, plantarum, aromatum, aliorumque peregrinorum fructuum historiae describuntur*: 'Ten books of exotica: the history and uses of animals, plants, aromatics and other natural products from distant lands' (Leiden, 1605). It is a beautiful book.

The Near East and India

Several ancient Near Eastern texts are quoted here on the basis of the translations gathered by J. B. Pritchard, *Ancient Near Eastern texts relating to the Old Testament* (3rd edn. Princeton, 1969).

Few of the Arabic texts quoted here are available in English translation. Many of them can be found in French in a selection by Gabriel Ferrand, *Relations de voyages et textes géographiques arabes, persans et turks relatifs à l'Extrême-Orient du VIIIe au XVIIIe siècles* (2 vols. Paris, 1913–14). H. A. R. Gibb produced an English translation of *The travels of Ibn Baṭūṭâ, AD 1325–1354*, now completed by C. F. Beckingham (4 vols. Cambridge, 1958–94). Bîrûnî's work *On India*, written in the early eleventh century, is translated as *Alberuni's India* by Eduard Sachau (2 vols. London, 1888).

The early Persian medical text by Abû Mansûr Muwaffiq ibn 'Alî, al-Harâwî, written about 970, can be found in German as *Die pharmakologischen Grundsätze*, translated by Abdul-Chaliq Achundow (Halle a. S., 1893. *Historische Studien aus dem Pharmakologischen Institute der kaiser-lichen Universität Dorpat* ed. R. Kobert, vol. 3 pp. 140–481): an obscure item, but it can be tracked down in libraries, and when I checked the Internet I found no fewer than four secondhand copies on offer.

The *Carakasaṃhitā* has appeared in English translation in India; most recently, as far as I know, at Jamnagar in 6 volumes, published in 1949.

China

In this book Chinese is written in the standard Pinyin romanization.

Part of Sima Qian's *Shijing*, including the chapter on Zhang Qian's exploration, is translated by Burton Watson: Ssu-ma Ch'ien, *Records of the Grand Historian* (2 vols. New York, 1961). Fa Xian's fourth-century narrative is translated by James Legge as *A Record of Buddhistic Kingdoms...by Fâ-hien* (Oxford, 1886). Xuanzang's seventh-century memoir can be found as *Hiuen-tsang: Si-yu-ki, Buddhist records of the western world*, translated by Samuel Beal (London, 1884). Yi Jing's late seventh-century travels are in *I-Tsing: a record of the Buddhist religion as practised in India and the Malay Archipelago* translated by J. Takakusu (Oxford, 1896).

Early Chinese poetry quoted here comes largely from two collections, both available in English. One is *Chu ci*, available as *The songs of the South* translated by David Hawkes (Harmondsworth, 1985). The other is *Wen xuan*, available as *Wen xuan, or Selections of refined literature* translated by D. R. Knechtges (Princeton, 1982–).

Ji Han's fourth-century 'Herb and tree forms of the southern parts' is translated as: Chi Han, *Nan-fang ts'ao-mu chuang: a fourth-century flora of Southeast Asia* translated by Hui-lin Li (Hong Kong, 1979). For Zhao Rugua's 'Description of barbarous peoples', written in 1225, see *Chau Ju-kua: his work on the Chinese and Arab trade in the twelfth and thirteenth centuries* translated by F. Hirth and W. W. Rockhill (St Petersburg, 1911). Zhou Daguan's *Customs of Cambodia* is in Jeannette Mirsky's book *The great Chinese travelers* (New York, 1964). Ni Zan's brief *Cloud Forest Hall collection of rules for eating and drinking* is translated by Teresa Wang and E. N. Anderson in the journal *Petits propos culinaires* no. 60 (1998) with corrections in no. 61.

Further reading

In each section items are listed in alphabetical order of author or editor, or by title if there is no author or editor. In the notes, books and articles from this list are referred to briefly by surname and date.

ON SPICES AND AROMATICS IN GENERAL

Liberty Hyde Bailey, Ethel Zoe Bailey, *Hortus third: a concise dictionary of plants cultivated in the United States and Canada*. New York: Macmillan, 1976.

Clotilde Boisvert, Annie Hubert, *L'ABCdaire des épices*. Paris: Flammarion, 1998.

I. H. Burkill, *A dictionary of the economic products of the Malay peninsula*. London: Crown Agents for the Colonies, 1935.

Alan Davidson, *The Oxford companion to food*. Oxford: Oxford University Press, 1999.

Pierre Delaveau, *Les épices: histoire, description et usage des différents épices, aromates et condiments*. Paris, 1987.

James A. Duke, *CRC handbook of medicinal herbs*. Boca Raton: CRC Press, 1985.

Stephen Facciola, *Cornucopia: a source book of edible plants*. Vista, California: Kampong, 1990.

F. Flückiger, D. Hanbury, *Pharmacographia: a history of the principal drugs of vegetable origin met with in Great Britain and British India*. London, 1879.

Food on the move: proceedings of the Oxford Symposium on Food and Cookery 1996. Totnes: Prospect Books, 1997.

Mrs M. Grieve, *A modern herbal*. London, 1931.

Nigel Groom, *The new perfume handbook*. London: Blackie Professional, 1995.

Christopher Joyce, *Earthly goods: medicine hunting in the rainforest*. Boston: Little, Brown, 1994.

Albert Y. Leung, *Encyclopedia of common natural ingredients*. New York: Wiley, 1996. 2nd edn.

Martindale: The extra pharmacopoeia. London: Pharmaceutical Press, 1993. 30th edn by J. E. F. Reynolds.

Jill Norman, *The complete book of spices*. London: Dorling Kindersley, 1990.

The encyclopaedia of herbs, spices and flavourings ed. Elizabeth Lambert Ortiz. London: Dorling Kindersley, 1992.

J. S. Pruthi, *Spices and condiments: chemistry, microbiology, technology*. London: Academic Press, 1980.

J. W. Purseglove and others, *Spices*. London: Longman, 1981.

H. Redgrove, *Spices and condiments*. London, 1933.

H. Ridley, *Spices*. London, 1912.

Spicing up the palate: proceedings of the Oxford Symposium on Food and Cookery 1992. Totnes: Prospect Books, 1993.

The wealth of India: raw materials. New Delhi: CSIR, 1948–76.

ON TIMES AND PLACES

Vimala Begley, Richard Daniel de Puma, *Rome and India: the ancient sea trade*. Madison: University of Wisconsin Press, 1991.

C. R. Boxer, *Two pioneers of tropical medicine: Garcia d'Orta and Nicolás Monardes*. London: Wellcome Historical Medical Library, 1963.

M. Cary, E. H. Warmington, *The ancient explorers*. London: Methuen, 1929.

The Periplus of the Erythraean Sea tr. L. Casson. Princeton: Princeton University Press, 1989.

Food in Chinese culture ed. K. C. Chang. New Haven, 1977.

Sophie Coe, 'Aztec cuisine' in *Petits propos culinaires* nos 19–21 (1985).

Sophie Coe, 'Inca food' in *Petits propos culinaires* nos 29, 31, 37 (1988–91).

Sophie Coe, *America's first cuisines*. Austin: University of Texas Press, 1994.

Patricia Crone, *Meccan trade and the rise of Islam*. Princeton: Princeton University Press, 1987.

Andrew Dalby, 'Alexander's culinary legacy' in *Cooks and other people: proceedings of the Oxford Symposium on Food and Cookery 1995* ed. Harlan Walker (Totnes: Prospect Books, 1996) pp. 81–93.

Ray Desmond, *The European discovery of Indian flora*. Oxford: Oxford University Press, 1992.

Prosper Alpin: Plantes d'Egypte tr. R. de Fenoyl. Cairo: Institut Français d'Archéologie Orientale, 1980.

F. N. Hepper, *Pharaoh's flowers*. London: HMSO, 1990.

Wendy Hutton, *Tropical herbs and spices of Malaysia and Singapore*. Singapore: Periplus, 1997.

B. Laufer, *Sino-Iranica: Chinese contributions to the history of civilization in ancient Iran with special reference to the history of cultivated plants and products*. Chicago: Field Museum of Natural History, 1919.

Waruno Mahdi, three papers in *Archaeology and language* ed. Roger Blench, Matthew Spriggs (London: Routledge, 1997–9).

Lise Manniche, *An ancient Egyptian herbal*. London: British Museum Press, 1989.

J. I. Miller, *The spice trade of the Roman Empire*. Oxford: Clarendon Press, 1969.

Giles Milton, *Nathaniel's nutmeg*. London: Hodder and Stoughton, 1999.

Spices in the Indian Ocean world ed. M. N. Pearson. London: Variorum, 1996.

B. E. Read, *Chinese medicinal plants from the Pen Ts'ao Kang Mu, AD 1596*. Peking, 1936.

G. Riley, 'Tainted meat' in *Spicing up the palate: proceedings of the Oxford Symposium on Food and Cookery 1992* (Totnes: Prospect Books, 1993) pp. 1–6.

Barbara Santich, '"Nondescript gallimaufries" or sophisticated spicings? A revaluation of medieval cuisine' in *Petits propos culinaires* no. 51 (1995) pp. 15–26.

E. H. Schafer, *The golden peaches of Samarkand*. Berkeley: University of California Press, 1963.

E. H. Schafer, *The vermilion bird: T'ang images of the South*. Berkeley: University of California Press, 1967.

Wolfgang Schivelbusch, *Tastes of paradise*. New York: Pantheon, 1992.

Paul Wheatley, 'Geographical notes on some commodities involved in Sung maritime trade' in *Journal of the Malayan Branch of the Royal Asiatic Society* vol. 32 no. 2 (1959, published 1961) pp. 1–140.

C. Anne Wilson, 'The Saracen connection: Arab cuisine and the mediaeval West' in *Petits propos culinaires* nos 7–8 (1981).

Henry Yule, A. C. Burnell, *Hobson-Jobson*. London: Murray, 1903. 2nd edn.

ON INDIVIDUAL SPICES AND AROMATICS

J. Andrews, *Peppers: the domesticated capsicums*. Austin, Texas: University of Texas Press, 1985.

Esther Balogh, 'Tastes in and tastes of paprika' in *Oxford Symposium on Food and Cookery 1987: taste* (London: Prospect Books, 1988) pp. 25–40.

Sophie D. Coe, Michael D. Coe, *The true history of chocolate*. London: Thames and Hudson, 1996.

R. A. Donkin, *Manna: an historical geography*. The Hague: Junk, 1980.

Clifford M. Foust, *Rhubarb, the wonder drug*. Princeton: Princeton University Press, 1992.

J. A. C. Greppin, 'The various aloes in ancient times' in *Journal of Indo-European studies* vol. 16 (1988) pp. 33–48.

Nigel Groom, *Frankincense and myrrh*. London, 1981.

Alexandra Hicks, 'Red peppercorns: what they really are' in *Petits propos culinaires* no. 10 (1982) pp. 12–19, with note in no. 12.

P. and M. Hyman, 'Long pepper: a short history' in *Petits propos culinaires* no. 6 (1980) pp. 50–2, with notes in nos 7, 8 and 12.

Robert Johnson, 'Saffron and the good life' in *Petits propos culinaires* no. 41 (1992) pp. 30–51.

Sir William Jones, 'On the spikenard of the ancients' in *Asiatic researches* (1795).

Janet Laurence, 'Cardamom' in *Spicing up the palate: proceedings of the Oxford Symposium on Food and Cookery 1992* (Totnes: Prospect Books, 1993) pp. 160–2.

Loret Lee, 'Flavour water' in *Spicing up the palate: proceedings of the Oxford Symposium on Food and Cookery 1992* (Totnes: Prospect Books, 1993) pp. 163–72.

Jenny Macarthur, 'Malagueta pepper' in *Petits propos culinaires* nos 35–6 (1990).

Rosamond Man, Robin Weir, *The compleat mustard*. London: Constable, 1987.

Sidney W. Mintz, *Sweetness and power: the place of sugar in modern history*. London: Viking, 1985.

'The Pontefract liquorice industry' in *Petits propos culinaires* no. 39 (1991) pp. 14–34.

A. S. C. Ross, *Ginger: a loan-word study*. Oxford: Blackwell, 1952.

Helen J. Saberi, Anissa Selou and others, 'A spicy mystery' in *Petits propos culinaires* nos 47–9 (1994–5), with note in no. 57. (All about Panama wood.)

E. H. Schafer, 'Rosewood, dragon's blood, and lac' in *Journal of the American Oriental Society* vol. 77 (1957) pp. 129–36.

G. R. Schoff, 'Camphor' in *Journal of the American Oriental Society* vol. 42 (1922) pp. 355–70.

G. Watson, *Theriac and Mithridatium: a study in therapeutics*. London, 1966.

Joop Witteveen, 'Rose sugar and other medieval sweets' in *Petits propos culinaires* no. 20 (1985) pp. 22–8.

Joop Witteveen, 'Of sugar and porcelain' in *Oxford Symposium on Food & Cookery 1990: feasting and fasting: proceedings* (London: Prospect Books, 1990) pp. 212–21.

Kentaro Yamada, 'A study on the introduction of an-hsi-hsiang in China and that of gum benzoin in Europe' in *Report of the Institute of World Economics* nos 5, 7 (1954–5).

Glossary of spice names
and other exotic plants mentioned in the text

Spice names marked with an asterisk are best avoided because they are ambiguous or misleading. Those in inverted commas are not in current use (or are now used with other meanings) but are still found in translations and historical writing. Place names at the end of each entry are the original or traditional sources of these products.

Acuyo: fruit of *Piper sanctum*, Central America

African bdellium: see Opopanax

African cubebs: see Ashanti pepper

agaru: see Aloeswood

Ajowan, ammi, *black cumin, 'Ethiopian cumin', omum: seed of *Trachyspermum ammi*, Near East

Alkanet: juice of *Anchusa officinalis*, Near East

Allspice, Jamaica pepper, *pimento: fruit of *Pimenta dioica*, Caribbean. See also Wild allspice

Aloe vera: juice of *Aloe barbadensis*, Arabia

Aloes: juice of *Aloe perryi*, Arabia

Aloeswood, agaru, eaglewood, gharroowood: diseased wood of *Aquilaria malaccensis* and *A. sinensis*, south-east Asia

Amber: fossilized resin, northern Europe and elsewhere. See also Ambergris; Ladanum

Ambergris, 'amber': secretion of *Physeter macrocephalus*, Indian Ocean

Ambrette, musk mallow: fruit of *Abelmoschus moschatus*, southern Asia

American ginseng: root of *Panax quinquefolius*, North America

American storax, American sweet gum: see Sweet gum

ammi: see Ajowan

'Amomum' in Classical texts: possibly Nepaul cardamom and Bengal cardamom

ancho: see Chilli

Anise: *Pimpinella anisum*, Asia Minor. See also Star anise

Annatto: juice of *Bixa orellana*, Central America

apple chilli: see Rocoto

Arabica coffee: see Coffee

Areca nut, betel nut: *Areca catechu*, south-east Asia

Asafoetida, hing: resin of *Ferula assa-foetida* and *F. foetida*, central Asia

Ashanti pepper, African cubebs, *Guinea pepper: fruit of *Piper clusii*, west Africa

Attar of roses: oil of *Rosa centifolia* (cabbage rose), *Rosa damascena* (damask rose), Near East

baies roses: see Pink peppercorns

Balm of Gilead: resin of *Populus candicans*, North America. See also Balsam of Mecca

balsam: see also Siam benzoin; Sweet gum

Balsam of Copaiba: resin of *Copaifera langsdorffii*, South America

Balsam of Mecca, 'balm of Gilead': resin of *Commiphora opobalsamum*, Arabia

Balsam of Peru: resin of *Myroxylon balsamum* var. *pereirae*, El Salvador

Balsam of Tolu: resin of *Myroxylon balsamum*, South America

Bastard cardamom: fruit of *Amomum xanthioides* and other species, south-east Asia

Batavia cinnamon: see Padang cinnamon

Bay rum tree, West Indian bay, oil of bay: *Pimenta acris*, Caribbean

bdellium: see Gum guggul; Opopanax

Bengal cardamom: fruit of *Amomum aromaticum*, eastern Himalayas

Benin pepper, *Guinea pepper, West African pepper: fruit of *Piper guineense*, Nigeria

benzoin: see Siam benzoin; Sumatra benzoin

Betel leaf: *Piper betle*, south-east Asia

betel nut: see Areca nut

bilsted: see Sweet gum

bissabol: see Opopanax

black cumin: see Ajowan; Nigella

black pepper: see Pepper

Bombay mastic, Turk terebinth: *Pistacia mutica*, Middle East

Borneo camphor: see Camphor of Baros

Brazilwood: *Haematoxylon brasiletto* and

other species, Central and South America. See also Sappan

brea: see Elemi

'Calamus', 'sweet reed', 'scented cane' in Biblical and Classical translations: possibly lemon grass or ginger-grass

Californian pepper: see Pink peppercorns

Cambodian cardamom: fruit of *Amomum krervanh*, Indochina

Cameroon cardamom: fruit of *Aframomum hanburyi*, central Africa

Camphor of Baros, Borneo camphor: crystallized resin of *Dryobalanops aromatica*, Indonesia

Camphor, Chinese camphor: crystallized resin of *Cinnamomum camphora*, China

Candy carrot: seed of *Athamanta cretensis*, Crete

cane sugar: see Sugar

Canela: *Ocotea sassafras*, Brazil; *Ocotea usambarensis*, east Africa

Canella, white cinnamon: *Canella winterana*, Caribbean

Cannabis, hemp, ganja: *Cannabis sativa*, eastern Europe

Canton rhubarb: see Rhubarb root

Carap, white crabwood: *Carapa guianensis*, Central and South America

Caraway: seed of *Carum carvi*, central Europe

Cardamom: fruit of *Elettaria cardamomum*, southern Asia. See also Bastard cardamom; Bengal cardamom; Cambodian cardamom; Cameroon cardamom; Ethiopian cardamom; Kepulaga; Madagascar cardamom; Nepaul cardamom

cassia: see Chinese cinnamon; Padang cinnamon; Saigon cinnamon

Castoreum: secretion of *Castor fiber*, Europe and Asia

Cayenne pepper: see Chilli

Cekur, kencur: root of *Kaempferia galanga*, India

'Celtic nard': probably *Valeriana celtica*, southern Europe

Ceylon cinnamon: see Cinnamon

chile pepper: see Chilli

Chilli, ancho, Cayenne pepper, chile pepper, jalapeño, paprika, *pepper, *pimento, red pepper: fruit of *Capsicum annuum*, Central America. See also Rocoto, Scotch

bonnet, Tabasco pepper, Uchu, Ulupica

China root, Chinese sarsaparilla: *Smilax pseudo-china*, eastern Asia

Chinese camphor: see Camphor

Chinese cardamom: fruit of *Amomum globosum*, China

Chinese cinnamon, cassia: bark of *Cinnamomum cassia*, *Cinnamomum chekiangense* and other species, China

Chinese parsley: see Coriander

Chinese pepper, *fagara: fruit of *Zanthoxylum armatum*, *Zanthoxylum planispinum* and other species, China

Chinese sarsaparilla: see China root

Chios balm: see Cyprus balm

Chocolate: seed of *Theobroma Cacao*, Central America. See also Nicaragua chocolate

cilantro: see Coriander

Cinnamon, Ceylon cinnamon: bark of *Cinnamomum zeylanicum*, Sri Lanka. See also Canela; Canella; Chinese cinnamon; Padang cinnamon; Saigon cinnamon

Citronella oil, nard grass: *Cymbopogon nardus* and *C. winterianus*, southern Asia

Civet: secretion of *Viverra civetta* and other species, Africa and Asia

Cloves: bud of *Syzygium aromaticum*, northern Moluccas

Coca: leaf of *Erythroxylum coca* and *E. novogranatense*, South America

Cochineal: *Dactylopus coccus*, Central America

Coffee, Arabica coffee: seed of *Coffea arabica*, north-east Africa. See also Robusta coffee

Coriander, cilantro: fruit of *Coriandrum sativum*, eastern Mediterranean

Costmary: leaf of *Tanacetum balsamina*, perhaps Near East

costus: see Putchuk

country pepper: see Scotch bonnet

Cubebs: fruit of *Piper cubeba*, Indonesia. See also Ashanti pepper

Cumin: seed of *Cuminum cyminum*, southern Europe

Cyprus balm, *Chios balm, tsikoudia: resin of *Pistacia atlantica*, Mediterranean lands

Dragon's blood: juice of *Dracaena cinnabari*, *D. schizantha* and *D. draco*, north-east Africa, Socotra and Canary Islands eaglewood: see Aloeswood

Egyptian balsam: see Zachum oil

Egyptian thorn: see Gum arabic

Elecampane: leaf of *Inula helenium*, Europe

Elemi, brea, Manila resin: *Canarium luzonicum, C. commune* and other species, Malay archipelago

Ethiopian cardamom, Korarima cardamom: fruit of *Aframomum korarima*, Ethiopia

Ethiopian cumin: see Ajowan

Ethiopian pepper: see Grains of Selim

fagara: see Chinese pepper; Japanese pepper; Sichuan pepper

false myrrh: see Opopanax

Frankincense, olibanum: resin of *Boswellia carterii, B. frereana* and *B. sacra*, Arabia and north-east Africa

galanga, galingale: see Greater galanga; Lesser galanga

Galbanum: resin of *Ferula galbaniflua*, Iran

ganja: see Cannabis

gharroowood: see Aloeswood

Giant fennel: *Ferula communis*, north Africa

gingelly: see Sesame

Ginger: root of *Zingiber officinale*, China. See also Wild ginger

Ginger-grass: root of *Cymbopogon schoenanthus*, south-west Asia

Ginseng: root of *Panax ginseng* and *P. pseudo-ginseng*, northern Asia. See also American ginseng; Sanchi ginseng

gith: see Nigella

Gorka: fruit of *Garcinia pictoria*, south-east Asia

Grains of Paradise, Guinea grains, *Guinea pepper, *Melegueta pepper: fruit of *Aframomum melegueta*, west Africa

Grains of Selim, Ethiopian pepper, habzeli, kimba pepper, xylopia: fruit of *Xylopia aethiopica*, Africa

greater cardamom: see Nepaul cardamom

Greater galanga, galanga, laos, lengkuas: root of *Alpinia galanga*, south-east Asia

Guaiacum: resin of *Guaiacum officinale*, Caribbean

guggul: see Gum guggul

Guinea grains: see Grains of Paradise

Guinea pepper: see Ashanti pepper; Benin pepper; Grains of Paradise

Gum ammoniac: juice of *Dorema ammoniacum*, Near East

Gum arabic, Egyptian thorn: *Acacia nilotica*, Red Sea shores

gum benzoin: see Siam benzoin; Sumatra benzoin

Gum guggul, bdellium: resin of *Commiphora mukul*, Sind

Gum tragacanth: resin of *Astragalus gummifer*, and other species, south-west Asia

Gumbo-limbo resin: *Bursera simaruba*, Caribbean

habañero: see Scotch bonnet

habzeli: see Grains of Selim

hemp: see Cannabis

hing: see Asafoetida

Honduras balsam: see Sweet gum

horns of abath: see Rhinoceros horn

Horseradish: root of *Armoracia rusticana*, northern Eurasia

Hypocistis: juice of *Cytinus hypocistis*, Europe

iris root: see Orris

jalapeño: see Chilli

Jamaica pepper: see Allspice

Japanese pepper, *fagara: fruit of *Zanthoxylum piperitum*, Japan

Japanese star anise, shikimi: fruit of *Illicium anisatum*, Japan

Jasmine: flower of *Jasminum officinale*, central Asia. See also Sambac

Java cinnamon: see Padang cinnamon

Java long pepper: fruit of *Piper retrofractum*, Indonesia

Juniper berry: *Juniperus communis*, and other species, Eurasia

kalamos: see '*Calamus*'

Kao-liang ginger: *Alpinia kumatake*, China

Karanda: fruit of *Carissa carandas*, India

Kava: *Piper methysticum*, Pacific islands

kencur: see Cekur

Kepulaga, round cardamom, Siam cardamom: fruit of *Amomum compactum*, Indonesia

kimba pepper: see Grains of Selim

Korarima cardamom: see Ethiopian cardamom

kuchoora: see Zerumbet

kushth: see Putchuk

Ladanum, *amber: resin of *Cistus ladaniferus*, Arabia

Lakawood: *Dalbergia parviflora*, southern Asia

laos: see Greater galanga

Lemon grass: root of *Cymbopogon citratus*, southern Asia

lengkuas: see Greater galanga

Lentisk, shina oil: *Pistacia lentiscus*, Near East

Lesser galanga, galanga: root of *Alpinia officinarum*, China

Levant storax: see Liquid storax

Licorice: root of *Glycyrrhiza glabra*, Russia. See also Wild licorice

Liquid storax, Levant storax: resin of *Liquidambar orientalis*, Near East

liquidambar: see Sweet gum; Liquid storax

locoto: see Rocoto

Long pepper: fruit of *Piper longum*, India. See also Java long pepper

mace: see Nutmeg

Madagascar cardamom: fruit of *Aframomum angustifolium*, Madagascar

malobathrum: see Tejpat

Manila resin: see Elemi

Mastic: resin of *Pistacia lentiscus* var. *chia*, Greece. See also Bombay mastic; Peruvian mastic

Mechoacan: root of *Ipomoea jalapa*, Central America

Melegueta pepper: see Grains of Paradise

Mioga ginger: shoots of *Zingiber mioga*, China

Musk: secretion of *Moschus moschiferus*, and other species, Asia

musk mallow: see Ambrette

Mustard: seed of *Brassica hirta*, *B. juncea* and *B. nigra*, Eurasia

Myrrh: resin of *Commiphora myrrha* and other species, Arabia and north-east Africa. See also Opopanax

Myrtle: fruit of *Myrtus communis*, southern Europe

nard: see spikenard; Celtic nard; Syrian nard

nard grass: see Citronella oil

Nepaul cardamom, greater cardamom: fruit of *Amomum subulatum*, Himalayas

Nicaragua chocolate, pataxte, Peru cacao: seed of *Theobroma bicolor*, Central America

Nigella, gith, *black cumin, *onion seed: seed of *Nigella sativa*, Near East

nikkel oil: see Saigon cinnamon

Nutmeg, mace: fruit of *Myristica fragrans*, Banda Islands

oil of bay: see Bay rum tree

olibanum: see Frankincense

omum: see Ajowan

onion seed: see Nigella

onycha: see Sweet hoof

opium: see Poppy seed

Opopanax, African bdellium, bissabol, false myrrh: resin of *Commiphora erythraea* and *C. kataf*, north-east Africa and Arabia

Oriental sweet gum: see Storax

Orris, iris root: *Iris germanica* var. *florentina* and other species, Europe

Padang cinnamon, Batavia cinnamon, Java cinnamon: bark of *Cinnamomum burmannii*, Indonesia

Palmarosa oil, rosha grass: root of *Cymbopogon martini*, southern Asia

Panama wood: *Quillaja saponaria*, South America

Pandanus, screwpine: leaf of *Pandanus tectorius*, southern Asia

paprika: see Chilli

pataxte: see Nicaragua chocolate

Patchouli: essential oil of *Pogostemon cablin*, south-east Asia

Pepper, black pepper, white pepper: fruit of *Piper nigrum*, India. See also Allspice; Ashanti pepper; Benin pepper; Chilli; Chinese pepper; Grains of Selim; Japanese pepper; Java long pepper; Long pepper; Melegueta pepper; Pink peppercorns; Scotch bonnet; Sichuan pepper; Tabasco pepper; Uchu

Peru cacao: see Nicaragua chocolate

Peruvian pepper, California pepper: fruit of *Schinus molle*, Peru. See also Uchu

pimento: see Allspice; Chilli

Pine kernel: seed of *Pinus pinea*, Europe

Pink peppercorns, red peppercorns, baies roses, Brazilian pepper: fruit of *Schinus terebinthifolius*, Brazil

piri-piri: see Scotch bonnet

Poppy seed, opium: *Papaver somniferum*, Europe

Putchuk, costus, kushth: root of *Saussurea lappa*, Kashmir

red pepper: see Chilli

red peppercorns: see Pink peppercorns

Red sanders: wood of *Pterocarpus santalina*, India

Rhinoceros horn, 'horns of abath': *Rhinoceros* spp., southern Asia

Rhubarb root, Canton rhubarb: *Rheum officinale*, Tibet

Robusta coffee: seed of *Coffea canephora*

rock rose: see ladanum

Rocoto, locoto, apple chilli: fruit of *Capsicum pubescens*, high Andes

rose: see Attar of roses

Rose-mallows: wood of *Altingia excelsa*, south-east Asia

rosha grass: see Palmarosa oil

round cardamom: see Kepulaga

Safflower: *Carthamus tinctorius*, Asia or Europe

Saffron: stamen of *Crocus sativus*, Near East

Sagapenum: resin of *Ferula persica*, Iran

Saigon cinnamon, cassia, nikkel oil: *Cinnamomum loureirii*, Indochina

Salep: root of *Orchis morio*, *O. latifolia* and other species, Near East

Sambac, zambac: flower of *Jasminum sambac*, south-west Asia

Sanchi ginseng: root of *Panax notoginseng*, northern Asia

Sandalwood, sanders: *Santalum album*, southern Asia

Sandarac, pounce, citronwood: *Callitris quadrivalvis*, western Mediterranean

sanders: see Red sanders; Sandalwood

Sappan, 'brazilwood': *Caesalpinia sappan*, possibly India

Sarsaparilla: root of *Smilax* spp., America. See also China root

Sassafras: bark of *Sassafras albidum*, North America. See also Canela sassafras

'Scented cane': see 'Calamus'

Scotch bonnet, country pepper, habañero, piri-piri: fruit of *Capsicum chinense*, Central and South America

screwpine: see Pandanus

Sesame, gingelly: seed of *Sesamum indicum*, east Africa or India

setwall: see Zedoary

shina oil: see Lentisk

Siam benzoin, gum benzoin, Siam balsam: resin of *Styrax tonkinense*, Indochina

Siam cardamom: see Kepulaga

Sichuan pepper, fagara, Szechwan pepper: fruit of *Zanthoxylum simulans*, China

Silphium: resin of an extinct plant cf. genus *Ferula*, north Africa

Spicewood: see Wild allspice

Spikenard: root of *Nardostachys jatamansi*, Himalayas

Star anise: fruit of *Illicium verum*, China

Storax, styrax: resin of *Styrax officinalis*, Near East. See also Liquid storax

Sugar, cane sugar: sap of *Saccharum officinarum*, Malay archipelago

Sumach: ground fruit of *Rhus coriaria*, Near East

Sumatra benzoin, gum benzoin: resin of *Styrax benzoin*, Indonesia

'Sweet reed': see 'Calamus'

Sweet flag: root of *Acorus calamus*, northern Asia

Sweet gum, liquidambar, American storax, bilsted, Honduras balsam, white Peru balsam: resin of *Liquidambar styraciflua*, North America. See also Storax

Sweet hoof, onycha: operculum of *Strombus lentiginosus*, *Eburna japonica*, and other species, Indian and Pacific Oceans

'Syrian nard': probably *Valeriana sisymbrifolia*, Near East

Szechwan pepper: see Sichuan pepper

Tabasco pepper: fruit of *Capsicum frutescens*, Central America

Tahitian vanilla: pod of *Vanilla tahitensis*, eastern Pacific

Tea: leaf of *Camellia sinensis*, southern China

Tejpat, malobathrum: leaf of *Cinnamomum tamala*, eastern Himalayas

Tellicherry bark: *Holarrhena antidysenterica*, India

Terebinth, 'turpentine': resin of *Pistacia terebinthus*, Near East. See also Bombay mastic

Tobacco: leaf of *Nicotiana tabacum*, Central America. See also Wild tobacco

tragacanth: see Gum tragacanth

tsikoudia: see Cyprus balm

Turk terebinth: see Bombay mastic

Turmeric: root of *Curcuma domestica*, southern Asia. See also Yellow zedoary

Turnsole: *Chrozophora tinctoria*, western Mediterranean lands

turpentine: see Bombay mastic; Terebinth

Uchu, Peruvian pepper: fruit of *Capsicum pendulum*, South America

Ulupica: fruit of *Capsicum cardenasii*, South America

Vanilla: fruit of *Vanilla fragrans*, Central America. See also Tahitian vanilla; West Indian vanilla

West African pepper: see Benin pepper

West Indian bay: see Bay rum tree

West Indian vanilla: fruit of *Vanilla pompona*, Caribbean

white cinnamon: see Canella

white pepper: see Pepper

white Peru balsam: see Sweet gum

Wild allspice, spicewood: *Lindera benzoin*, North America

Wild ginger: *Alpinia chinensis*, and other species, southern China

Wild licorice: *Abrus precatorius*, Japan

Wild tobacco: leaf of *Nicotiana rustica*, South America

xylopia: see Grains of Selim

Yellow zedoary, wild turmeric: *Curcuma aromatica*, eastern India

Zachum oil, Egyptian balsam: *Balanites aegyptiaca*, Near East

Zedoary, 'setwall': root of *Curcuma zedoaria*, India. See also Yellow zedoary

Zerumbet, kuchoora: root of *Zingiber zerumbet*, India

Notes

The phoenix's nest

1 Vergil, *Georgics* 1.53, 2.116–27.

2 *The Phoenix* (anonymous Latin poem) 79–88. Panchaea was a mythical island in the Indian Ocean, imagined source of myrrh.

3 *Song of Songs* 4.13–14. Calamus is probably not sweet flag (*Acorus calamus*), the traditional translation. It has been suggested that it is lemon grass (*Cymbopogon citratus*) or a related plant.

4 Guillaume de Lorris, *Roman de la Rose* 1328–44. Apples were often considered risky to eat fresh, which is why these fantasy apple trees bear pomegranates. Geoffrey Chaucer translated this text into English around 1370; he managed to fit *gingere* into the list of spices, alongside *notemigges*, *clow-gelofre* (cloves), *licoryce*, *greyn de paradys*, *canelle* (cinnamon) and *setewale* (zedoary).

5 Cosmas Indicopleustes, *Christian Topography* 2.29–30.

6 Ibn Khurdâdhbih (De Goeje p. 44). Medieval 'brazilwood' is now called sappan.

7 Mas'ûdî (Barbier de Meynard pp. 341–2).

8 Dimashqî (Ferrand pp. 370–1).

9 Monardes' own title for his enlarged edition, 1574, begins: *Primera y segunda y tercera partes de la historia medicinal de las cosas que se traen de nuestras Indias Occidentales, que sirven en medicina* ('Parts one and two and three of the medical history of the things that are imported from New Spain that are of use in medicine').

10 Theophrastus, *Study of Plants* 6.3.

11 Archestratus (Athenaeus 101c, 311a); Xenocrates (Oribasius, *Medical Collections* 2.58.114).

12 Dioscorides, *Materia Medica* 3.80.

13 Celsus, *On Medicine* 12.59.4–5. 'Syrian *laser*' is asafoetida.

14 Strabo, *Geography* 17.3.22; Pliny, *Natural History* 19.40.

15 Arrian, *Alexander's Expedition* 3.28; Strabo, *Geography* 15.2.10.

Exports from paradise

1 Milton, *Paradise Lost* 2.639–40.

2 Ibn Baṭûṭâ, *Travels* (Yerasimos, vol. 3 p. 209).

3 Dioscorides, *Materia Medica* 2.160.

4 *Apicius* 3.18.2–3.

5 *Qur'ân* 76. Translation after N. J. Dawood.

6 Ji Han, *Nanfang caomu zhuang* 5; Li Shizhen, *Bencao gangmu*; Marco Polo, French text 113, Tuscan text 112 (Latham's translation p. 140); Zhao Rugua, *Zhufan zhi* 1.4.

7 Shakespeare, *Henry V* 3.7.

8 John Russell, *Boke of Nurture* 129–32. *Maydelyne* is a mistake in copying for *Maykyne* or something similar.

9 *Le Mesnagier de Paris* 2.5.272. Ross 1952.

10 García de Orta, *Colloquies* 26.

11 Abridged from preface and p. 1 of *Olivia's book of old Maulmain recipes* (Rangoon, 1935).

12 Ji Han, *Nanfang caomu zhuang* 13.

13 Strabo, *Geography* 15.1.20.

14 Dioscorides, *Materia Medica* 2.82.5.

15 *Carakasaṃhitā*, *Sûtrasthânam* 25(2).16, 27.182–5, 27.240–5. Marco Polo, French text 174, Tuscan text 176 (Latham's translation p. 262).

16 John Russell, *Boke of Nurture* 139; Eduardus de Sande, *De Missione Legatorum Iaponensium* (Hakluyt, *Principal Navigations* vol. 2 [F] item 13).

17 *Carakasaṃhitā*, *Sûtrasthânam* 25.51.

18 *Mahâbhârata* 4.45.12. Some consider *Santalum album* native to India, though botanically this would be hard to explain.

19 *Milindapâñha* 4.6.39.

20 Vâlmîki, *Râmâyaṇa* 4.41.

21 Kaṭiyalur Uruttirankaṇṇanâr, *Paṭṭiṇappâlai* 186 (translation after K. Zvelebil); Fa Xian 39.

22 Zhao Rugua, *Zhufan zhi* 2.12.

23 'Annals of Tiglathpileser III' (Pritchard 1969 pp. 283–4).

24 *I Kings* 10.1–3, 10. Translation of the Jerusalem Bible.

25 Agatharchides, *On the Erythraean Sea* (99b Burstein; Diodorus Siculus 3.46). Like so many others, he is misled by earlier writers into believing that cinnamon and cassia grew in Arabia.

26 *Genesis* 37.25.

27 The balm of Gilead of modern herbalists is quite different – sometimes a resin from the North American tree *Populus candicans*, sometimes from other sources.

28 Josephus, *Jewish Antiquities* 8.6.6; Ezekiel 27.17.

29 Theophrastus, *Study of Plants* 9.6.

30 Pliny, *Natural History* 12.112.

31 Martial 3.63.

32 Dioscorides, *Materia Medica* 1.19.

33 Duan Chengshi, *Youyang zazu* 18.12 (translation after Laufer 1919, p. 429). The Chinese term (*a-bwut-sam* in early Chinese) derives from Aramaic *afursama*.

34 Laufer 1919, p. 432, summarizing a report by Abd al-Laṭîf.

35 Doubt remains: see, for example, Groom 1995 s.v. 'balsam of Judaea'.

36 Ezekiel 27.17–33. Versions of this text differ, but 'balsam' and 'cinnamon' (or 'cassia') are always there.

37 Sappho (44 Lobel and Page). The 'master of the lyre' is the god Apollo.

38 *Psalms* 45.8 (modern English translations omit the cassia).

39 Herodotus 3.110–11.

40 Pliny, *Natural History* 12.87–8; compare Ptolemy, *Geography* 7.2.16.

41 Ji Han, *Nanfang caomu zhuang* 35.

42 *Exodus* 30.23; *Proverbs* 7.17–18. Translation after the Jerusalem Bible. The identification of *ahâlim* as 'aloeswood', here and in *Numbers* 24.6, is very uncertain.

43 *Summary of Marvels* (Ferrand p. 153).

44 Yâqût (Ferrand pp. 223–4).

45 Buzurg ibn Shahriyar, *The Marvels of India* 132.

46 Ibn Baṭûṭâ, *Travels* (Yerasimos vol. 3 pp. 213, 255).

47 Gaspar Correia, *Legends of India*; Duarte Barbosa (Hakluyt Society translation vol. 1 p. 167).

48 Dimashqî (Ferrand p. 380).

49 John Russell, *Boke of Nurture* 133–6.

50 *Periplus Maris Erythraei* 65–6. Translation after L. Casson.

51 *Apicius* 1.29.

52 The discovery was certainly made around that date, and not in the first century AD, but who was the discoverer? See the *Periplus Maris*

Erythraei 57 (Hippalus); Strabo, *Geography* 2.98–9 (Eudoxus).

53 Jian Zhen (Mahdi 1998 p. 155).

54 Ibn Khurdâdhbih (De Goeje p. 51).

55 Cosmas Indicopleustes, *Christian Topography* 2.45–6.

56 See Jeannette Mirsky, *The great Chinese travellers* (New York, 1964).

57 Sima Qian, *Shijing* 123. Both of these products came from Shu, modern Sichuan, in south-western China.

58 Eduardus de Sande, *De Missione Legatorum Iaponensium* (Hakluyt, *Principal Navigations* vol. 2 [F] item 13).

59 Jerome, *Against Jovinian* 2.

60 Simeon Seth, *On the Properties of Foods*.

61 Ben Jonson, *Cynthia's Revels* 5.4.

62 Ya'qûbî (Ferrand p. 50).

63 Abûl Fazl Ja'far, *Book of Merchandise* (Wiedemann pp. 38–9).

64 Muwaffiq ibn 'Alî s.v. *misk*.

65 Zhou Daguan, *Customs of Cambodia*.

66 Ni Zan, *Cloud Forest Hall Rules for Eating and Drinking* 36/35. Translation after Wang and Anderson.

67 John Russell, *Boke of Nurture* 137; Richard Eden, 'A voiage made out of England unto Guinea and Benin, 1553' (Hakluyt, *Principal navigations* vol. 2 [E] item 4); Richard Eden, 'The second voiage to Guinea, 1554' (Hakluyt, *Principal navigations* vol. 2 [E] item 5).

THE SPICE ISLANDS

1 *Carakasaṃhitā, Sûtrasthânam* 5.76–7; Ying Shao cited by Schafer 1963, p. 171 note 170.

2 Pliny, *Natural History* 12.30.

3 Paul of Aegina, *Practice of Medicine* 7.3.

4 Su Gong, *Tangben caozhu*; Li Xun, *Haiyao bencao*; Schafer 1963, p. 171. It is very often said that cloves were prescribed for Chinese courtiers at imperial audiences as early as the third century BC: this thousand-year antedating seems to be based on a mistake.

5 Ibrâhîm ibn Wâṣif-Shâh, *Summary of Marvels* (Carra de Vaux p. 44).

6 Bîrûnî (Ferrand pp. 164–6).

7 Idrîsî, *Geography* (Ferrand p. 186).

8 Vinidarius, *Short Apicius*.

9 Anthimus, *Rules on Diet* 3. The *solidus* and *tremissis* were gold coins, but Anthimus treats

them here as weights: the *solidus* about 4.5 gm, the *tremissis* about 1.5 gm.

10 García de Orta, *Colloquies* 32.

11 Thomas Cogan, *Haven of Health* (1584), as quoted by P. Targett in *Petits propos culinaires* no. 24 (1986) p. 57.

12 Ji Han, *Nanfang caomu zhuang* 34. Translation after Hui-lin Li.

13 Zhao Rugua, *Zhufan zhi* 2.14. Translation after Hirth and Rockhill.

14 Pliny, *Natural History* 12.32; García de Orta, *Colloquies* 32. H. Rackham and A. C. Andrews, commenting on Pliny, tentatively identify *macir* with Tellicherry bark, *Holarrhena antidysenterica*. There is no good reason to suppose – as some do – that the unidentified spice *komakon* known to Theophrastus in the fourth century BC was nutmeg.

15 *Le Mesnagier de Paris* 2.5.272.

16 Chaucer, *Canterbury Tales: Sir Thopas* 49–54. *Cetewale* is zedoary; *clowe-gilofre* is cloves.

17 Boileau, *Le repas ridicule*.

18 Zhao Rugua, *Zhufan zhi* 2.28.

19 Corn 1999, p. 35.

20 Camões, *Lusiads* 10.132–3.

21 Ibn Khurdâdhbih (De Goeje pp. 46, 45).

22 Wheatley 1961, p. 101.

23 Zhao Rugua, *Zhufan zhi* 2.1; Dimashqî (Ferrand pp. 368–70); Marco Polo, French text 165, Tuscan text 166 (Latham's translation p. 229).

24 Mahdi 1999. The find is described as *Cinnamomum camphora* (Chinese camphor, unknown in the west until the fifteenth century) by mistake, I would guess, for *Dryobalanops aromatica*.

25 Somadeva, *Kathâsaritsâgara* 56.61.

26 Zhao Rugua, *Zhufan zhi* 1.39. Translation after Hirth and Rockhill.

27 Ibrâhîm ibn Wâṣif-Shâh, *Summary of Marvels* (Carra de Vaux p. 70).

28 Schafer 1963, pp. 167–8.

29 Ibn Baṭûṭâ (vol. 3 p. 303 Yerasimos).

30 García de Orta, *Colloquies* 9.

31 Ben Jonson, *Cynthia's Revels* 5.4.

32 Ludovico di Varthema (Corn 1999, pp. 25–7).

33 Robert Thorne (Hakluyt, *Principal Navigations* vol. 1 [B] item 57).

34 For more of the human story surrounding the trade in cloves and nutmeg, see Corn 1999 and Milton 1999.

THE AROMATIC SHORE

1 Vâlmîki, *Râmâyaṇa* 3.33.21–6. The identification of ambrette and areca nut in this text is very uncertain.

2 Mas'ûdî (Barbier de Meynard p. 307).

3 Abû Zayd (Ferrand p. 83).

4 Abû Dulaf Mis'ar (Ferrand p. 221).

5 Zhou Daguan, *Customs of Cambodia*.

6 Abû Zayd (Ferrand p. 39).

7 Abû Zayd (Ferrand p. 45); Mas'ûdî (Barbier de Meynard p. 388).

8 Abûl Fazl 'Allâmî, *Ayn-i Akbarî* 1.30.

9 Duan Chengshi, *Youyang zazu* (Schafer 1963, p. 174); Zhao Rugua, *Zhufan zhi* 2.41, citing Zhou Qufei, *Lingwai daida*. Wheatley 1961, pp. 125–30.

10 García de Orta, *Colloquies* 3.

11 Shadwell, *The virtuoso* 3.55. Maréchale and Frangipani were compound perfumes named after a French lady and an Italian lord respectively. Frangipani is now also the name of a West Indian aromatic flower (*Plumeria rubra*) and of an almond cream used in patisserie, both of them reminiscent of the historic perfume and both named after it. Recipes for Orangery and Frangipani are provided in Groom 1995 (appendix B nos 22, 34).

12 Abûl 'Abbâs al-Ṣufrî quoted by Yâqût (Ferrand p. 230).

13 *Song of Songs* 4.14; *Psalms* 45.8, both already quoted.

14 Ibn Khurdâdhbih (De Goeje pp. 47–8). The Indian kind was formerly identified by botanists as a distinct species, *Aquilaria agallocha*, but no longer.

15 Ji Han, *Nanfang caomu zhuang* 38–44.

16 Camões, *Lusiads* 10.129.

17 Feng Ang (Schafer 1967, p. 197).

18 Dioscorides, *Materia Medica* 1.22.

19 Abûl Fazl 'Allâmî, *Ayn-i Akbarî* 1.30; Abûl Fazl Ja'far, *Book of Merchandise* (Ferrand pp. 604–5).

20 Schafer 1963 p. 164.

21 *Correspondence of Charles, First Marquis Cornwallis* ed. C. Ross (London, 1859), vol. 1 p. 390.

22 Hakluyt, *Principal Navigations* vol. 2 [E] item 15.

23 Zhou Daguan, *Customs of Cambodia*.

THE CINNAMON MOUNTAINS

1 Qu Yuan, *Li sao* 25–9, 313–20. Translation of second passage by David Hawkes.

2 *Zhao yin shi* 1–4, 11–14. Translation after David Hawkes.

3 Zuo Taichong, *Shu Capital Rhapsody* 37–8, 121–37, 177–80, 242–56. Translations after David R. Knechtges. The 'Divine Husbandman' knows all about medicinal plants.

4 Ji Han, *Nanfang caomu zhuang* 10. Here I accept the arguments of Hui-lin Li in his commentary on Ji Han.

5 Ban Gu, *Western Capital Rhapsody* 178–80. Translation by David R. Knechtges.

6 E. N. and M. L. Anderson in Chang 1977, p. 332.

7 Hanshan. Translation after Schafer 1963, p. 149. Sichuan and Chinese peppers are sometimes called 'fagara' in English.

8 Yü in Chang 1977, pp. 56–7.

9 Ji Han, *Nanfang caomu zhuang* 2–3. Translation after Hui-lin Li. This is a contentious passage, since the Chinese name for jasmine is borrowed from an early Persian form such as *yâsam* or *yâsmin*. Although not found in Persian literature until the tenth century, this is known to be an old word, borrowed into Greek some time before the fifth century. Even so, it is surprising that the flowers and their Persian name should have reached China from Persia, apparently by sea, as early as the fourth century.

10 Zhao Rugua, *Zhufan zhi* 2.10.

11 Hong Chu, *Xiangpu* (Schafer 1963, p. 159).

12 Lee 1993, p. 166.

13 Aetius 11.13.116.

14 *Le Mesnagier de Paris* 2.5.272. Incidentally the botanical genus to which these two species belong, a genus of tuberous plants with juicy stems and showy flowers, is named in honour of Prosper Alpinus, the sixteenth-century hunter of spices and aromatics.

15 Marco Polo, Tuscan text 151, French text 154 (Latham's translation p. 203).

16 García de Orta, *Colloquies* 14, rearranged.

17 'The voyage of M. Anthony Ienkinson into Russia' (Hakluyt, *Principal Navigations* vol. 1 [A] item 22).

18 William of Rubruck, *Report* 39. Translation after Peter Jackson.

19 *Carakasaṃhitā, Sûtrasthânam* 25.52; Hakluyt, *Principal Navigations* vol. 1 [B] item 117. Lee 1993.

20 Eduardus de Sande, *De Missione Legatorum Iaponensium* (Hakluyt, *Principal Navigations* vol. 2 [F] item 13).

21 Li Xun and Zhen Quan (Li Shizhen, *Bencao gangmu* 12.15a). Translations after E. H. Schafer.

22 Duke 1985, p. 339.

23 I have not come across the evidence for this. The first citation of star anise in the *Oxford English dictionary* is dated 1727; the first occurrence of *badiane* in French is said in 'Le Robert' to be 1681.

24 *Recueil des Voyages* (Amsterdam, 1702–7) vol. 7 p. 512.

THE LAND OF PEPPER

1 Cosmas Indicopleustes, *Christian Topography* 11.15. 'Cloves-wood' is possibly mace.

2 Yi Jing, *Nanhai jigui neifa chuan*.

3 Qazwînî, *Book of Wonders* (Ferrand p. 307).

4 *Periplus Maris Erythraei* 47–9.

5 *Periplus Maris Erythraei* 39.

6 Idrîsî, *Geography* (Ferrand p. 197). Kârmût is possibly Assam or northern Bengal – there was no nearer source of aloeswood – but it was much more than fifteen days' journey away.

7 Anthimus, *Rules on Diet* 13.

8 Pliny, *Natural History* 12.41.

9 Buzurg ibn Shahriyar, *The Marvels of India* 54. Mansura was a lower Indus port, north-east of Hyderabad in Sind.

10 Culpeper, *The Complete Herbal*. Culpeper's 'both sorts' looks back to Pliny, quoted above.

11 *Periplus Maris Erythraei* 63.

12 Horace, *Odes* 4.12.13–23.

13 Mark 14.4–9. The same story is told in Matthew 26.6–13 and with romantic additions in John 12.1–8. There is an entirely different version in Luke 7.36–50.

14 Pliny, *Natural History* 12.42–6. Casson 1989, pp. 193, 207.

15 Apicius 7.6.8, 8.2.7.

16 *Periplus Maris Erythraei* 56, 60.

17 Zhao Rugua, *Zhufan zhi* 1.16. Similar Indian royal processions are described in other sources – for example, in Strabo's Roman *Geography* (15.1.55) of the first century BC and in Idrîsî's Arabic *Geography* (Jaubert vol. I p. 177) of the twelfth century AD.

18 *Carakasaṃhitā, Sûtrasthânam* 27.298, 26.2.8.

19 Theophrastus, *Study of Plants* 9.20.1; fragment 166 Wimmer (*Epitome of Athenaeus* 66f). 'Pepper' was apparently found (Manniche 1989) in the mummy of Ramesses II, who died six hundred years before any other record of long pepper or black pepper in the Mediterranean. Perhaps it was juniper.

20 Pliny, *Natural History* 12.28–9.

21 Pliny, *Natural History* 19.92.

22 Su Gong (Li Shizhen, *Bencao gangmu* 14.37a). Translation by E. H. Schafer.

23 Hyman and Hyman 1980.

24 *Carakasaṃhitā, Sûtrasthânam* 27.299.

25 *Râmâyaṇa* 3.35–44.

26 *Periplus Maris Erythraei* 56; Ibn Baṭûṭâ, *Travels* (Yerasimos vol. 3 p. 198). Casson 1989, pp. 220–1.

27 Tâyan-Kaṇṇanâr (*Âgam* 149.7–11); Pliny, *Natural History* 12.84.

28 Petronius, *Satyricon* 33, 36, 38, 138.

29 *Apicius* 2.2.8.

30 John Russell, *Boke of Nurture* 843–6.

31 *Voyage de Charlemagne* 392–414. *Claret* was spiced wine.

32 *The Travels of Sir John Mandeville* (Letts chapter 18).

33 García de Orta, *Colloquies* 46.

34 Paraṇar (*Puṟam* 343).

35 Ibn Baṭûṭâ, *Travels* (Yerasimos vol. 3 p. 198).

36 Zhou Daguan, *Customs of Cambodia*.

37 *Carakasaṃhitā, Sûtrasthânam* 5.76–7.

38 Aśoka, *Rock Edict II*. Translation after N. A. Nikam and R. McKeon. 'Antiochus' means Antiochus I or II, successors to Seleucus who is named below.

39 Wan Zhen, *Nanzhou yi wu zhi* (Li Shizhen, *Bencao gangmu* 14.22). Translation after Laufer 1919 p. 317.

40 *Diocletian's Price Edict* 36.60; Marco Polo, French text 154, Tuscan text 151 (Latham's translation p. 203).

41 Marco Polo, French text 185 (Latham's translation p. 273). García de Orta also had heard of sandal in Madagascar, though which species is not stated.

42 García de Orta, *Colloquies* 49; Abûl Fazl Ja'far, *Book of Merchandise* (Ferrand p. 605).

43 *An Ordinance of Pottage* 14.

44 Athenaeus, *Deipnosophists* 153d–e.

45 Ibn Baṭûṭâ, *Travels* (Yerasimos vol. 3 p. 194).

46 *Mîlindapâñha* 2.3.6; *Carakasaṃhitā, Sûtrasthânam* 26.54, 26.2.33.

47 Onesicritus (Strabo, *Geography* 15.1.30).

48 *Mîlindapâñha* 1.2.

49 Kâlidâsa, *Meghadûta*.

50 Ibn Baṭûṭâ, *Travels* (Yerasimos vol. 3 p. 224).

51 Fa Xian, *Record of Buddhistic Kingdoms* 39. Translation after J. Legge.

52 Benjamin of Tudela 90–1.

53 Culpeper, *The Complete Herbal*. 'Mesue' is the tenth-century writer Yaḥyâ ibn Mâsawayh; 'Avicenna' (ibn Sînâ) and 'Rhasis' (al-Râzî) were Arabic writers of about the same date.

54 García de Orta, *Colloquies* 57.

55 García de Orta, *Colloquies* 46.

56 Pearson 1996.

57 Camões, *Lusiads* 9.3.

58 Camões, *Lusiads* 9.14.

59 Camões, *Lusiads* 10.51.

60 Pliny, *Natural History* 12.50.

61 Cf. Miller 1969, pp. 67–9.

62 Juvenal 8.159.

63 *Geoponica* 8.22, attributed to Didymus.

64 Li She. Translation by E. H. Schafer 1967, p. 194.

65 Hutton 1997, p. 17 (the heading reads 'Cardamom, *Elettaria Cardamomum*' but the photographs are of round cardamom, *Amomum compactum*).

66 Theophrastus, *Study of Plants* 9.7.2–3; *On Odours* 25, 32.

67 Vinidarius, *Short Apicius* 6.

68 *Apicius* 1.34.

69 Pliny, *Natural History* 12.50; Ji Han, *Nanfang caomu zhuang* 4. Translation after Hui-lin Li.

70 Zhou Daguan, *Customs of Cambodia*.

71 Laurence 1993.

The rarest of spices

1 Theophrastus, *Study of Plants* 9.6–7.

2 'Calah stela' (Pritchard 1969, p. 559).

3 Herodotus, *Histories* 3.97.

4 Xenophon, *Agesilaus* 9.3; Aristoxenus of Tarentum (Athenaeus 545d).

5 Ptolemy Euergetes, *Commentaries* (Athenaeus 438e).

6 Pliny, *Natural History* 13.18.

7 Claudian, *Stilicho's Consulship* 1.54–66.

8 Theophrastus, *Study of Plants* 4.4.13; Strabo, *Geography* 15.2.3; *Periplus Maris Erythraei* 39; Ibn al-Baithâr. Yule and Burnell 1903, pp. 76, 386; Laufer 1919, p. 462; Yamada 1954–5.

9 Yule and Burnell 1903, p. 418. 'Popper-cake' is of course poppadom.

10 Dioscorides, *Materia Medica* 3.80; Galen, *Properties of Simples* 8.18.16 (Kuhn vol. 12 p. 123).

11 *Apicius* 4.4.2.

12 Su Gong, *Tangben caozhu* (Laufer 1919, p. 358).

13 *Carakasaṃhitā, Sûtrasthânam* 25.50, 27.300.

14 It is because of this exchange (which, if it took place at all, was in an Indian language) that some reference books in modern English list 'food of the gods' as an alternative name for asafoetida.

15 Herodotus, *Histories* 3.107, 112. Translation after A. de Selincourt. As we know, Herodotus was wrong about cassia and cinnamon. Nigel Groom (1995, p. 178) observes that ladanum is a main constituent of a third of modern quality perfumes, sometimes listed as ladanum, sometimes as 'amber'.

16 *The Phoenix* 1–2, 31, 79–88.

17 Agatharchides (99–103 Burstein).

18 Herodotus 3.107.

19 Theophrastus, *Study of Plants* 9.4.3–6. Heroonpolis was near modern Suez.

20 Pliny, *Natural History* 12.55–6, based on Theophrastus, *Study of Plants* 9.4.2, 7–8 and Juba. But Theophrastus did not pretend to say what was 'the view of King Antigonus'.

21 Pliny, *Natural History* 12.62. Alexander was never master of Arabia.

22 Ji Han, *Nanfang caomu zhuang* 32.

23 Pindar (fragment 107 Bowra); Cato, *On Farming* 134.

24 *Periplus Maris Erythraei* 28–9, 32.

25 Pliny, *Natural History* 12.59.

26 Marco Polo, French text 30–1 (cf. Tuscan text 30–1; Latham's translation pp. 28–9). The special significance of myrrh in this story happens to be expressed best in French (the language of the version translated here) because in middle French *mirre* ('myrrh') and *mire* ('physician') sound the same.

27 Dioscorides, *Materia Medica* 1.25.

28 Pliny, *Natural History* 12.68–71.

29 Herodotus, *Histories* 2.73.

30 Sappho (44 Lobel and Page); *Proverbs* 7.17–18; Horace, *Odes* 3.14.21–4; Theophrastus, *On Odours* 32; *Geoponica* 8.22.

31 Dioscorides, *Materia Medica* 1.64.

32 Groom 1995, p. 237; Casson 1989, pp. 124–5. The name opopanax belonged to a different plant, *Opopanax cheironium*, in the past.

33 Cosmas Indicopleustes, *Christian Topography* 2.49–50.

34 Richard Eden, 'The second voiage to Guinea, 1554' (Hakluyt, *Principal Navigations* vol. 4 [E] item 5); cf. Pliny, *Natural History* 33.116–17.

35 Abû al-Faraj, *Kitâb al-Aghânî* 16.15. Translation by R. A. Nicholson.

36 Ibn Khurdâdhbih. Translation after Reinaud's French version.

Cargoes of complacence

1 'Building Inscription of Amen-hotep III' (Pritchard 1969).

2 Theophrastus, *Study of Plants* 9.7.3. Words left untranslated cannot be identified with confidence.

3 Plutarch, *Sulla* 38; Pliny, *Natural History* 12.83, 84.

4 *Chanson de Girart de Roussillon* 203–8, 281–8.

5 *Libel of English Policie* (Hakluyt, *Principal Navigations* vol. 1 [B] item 55).

6 Theophrastus, *On Odours* 10.

7 *Geoponica* 8.31, attributed to 'Democritus'.

8 *Geoponica* 8.25.

9 *Apicius* 1.1.

10 Harûn Ibn Yahyâ. Translation after Izzedin's French version.

11 Pliny, *Natural History* 14.68.

12 Dioscorides, *Materia Medica* 5.39.

13 John Russell, *Boke of Nurture* 121–4.

14 John Partridge, *The Good Huswifes Handmaide for the Kitchin* (Corn 1999, p. 112).

15 Anaxippus (Athenaeus 403e–f).

16 Plutarch, *Symposium Questions* 8.9 (733e).

17 Horace, *Satires* 2.8.43–53.

18 Anthimus, *Rules on Diet* 13.

19 Guillaume d'Aquitaine (5 Jeanroy).

20 *Le Mesnagier de Paris* 2.5.276. Verjuice, a once-familiar ingredient, is the juice of unripe grapes.

21 Theophrastus, *Study of Plants* 3.18.5; Solon (41 Bergk; Photius, *Lexicon* s.v. *Rous*).

22 Pliny, *Natural History* 12.28.

23 Columella, *On Farming* 12.57, rearranged.

24 Celsus, *On Medicine* 5.23.3. Pliny knew a different recipe, with fifty-four ingredients, but he does not quote it.

25 Pliny, *Natural History* 19.168.

26 Petronius, *Satyricon* 31.

27 Pitton de Tournefort, *Relation d'un voyage du Levant* (Paris, 1717) vol. 1 pp. 378–9.

28 *Exodus* 30.23–5, 34–5. Translation of the Jerusalem Bible.

29 *Liang shu* 54.7b; Pliny, *Natural History* 24.24.

30 Daniel, *Pilgrimage* 4.

31 Jahângîr, *Memoirs* (H. M. Elliot, *History of India as told by its own historians* vol. 6 p. 375).

'I HAVE FOUND CINNAMON!'

1 Garcilaso de la Vega, el Inca, *Comentarios reales* 1.1.18, 2.25, 8.12, 2.25, 8.15. Translations after H. V. Livermore.

2 Sir Arthur Conan Doyle, 'A scandal in Bohemia'; 'The man with the twisted lip'.

3 Bernal Díaz, *History of the Conquest of New Spain* 91.

4 Jean-Baptiste Labat, *Voyage aux Iles*.

5 Fernando Colón, *Life of Christopher Columbus* 89.

6 Francis Pretty, 'The admirable and prosperous voyage of Thomas Candish' (Hakluyt, *Principal Navigations* vol. 3 [G] item 179).

7 Jean-Baptiste Labat, *Voyage aux Iles*.

8 This section on chocolate, largely based on Coe and Coe 1996, was first written, in a different form, for Alan Davidson's *Oxford companion to food*.

9 Bernal Díaz, *History of the Conquest of New Spain*; Christopher Columbus, *Fourth Letter*.

10 *Narrative of Some Things of New Spain* ('Anonymous Conqueror').

11 Francisco Hernández, *Obras completas* (1959) part 2 vol. 1 pp. 138–9; Coe 1985.

12 Sahagún, *General History of the Things of New Spain*, Florentine codex, book 10 (translation after Dibble and Anderson pp. 67–8).

13 Chios. This odd spelling is a Spanish version of the then-standard Italian name of the island, *Scio*.

14 Christopher Columbus, *First Letter*.

15 *Letter of Dr Chanca to the City of Seville, 1494*.

16 Christopher Columbus, *Log-Book* 19 and 21 October 1492 (Las Casas, *Historia de las Indias*). Translation by J. M. Cohen.

17 Fernando Colón *Life of Columbus* 62. Statements that the Aztecs already added allspice to their chocolate are, I think, mistaken.

18 *Histoire Naturelle des Indes* ('Drake manuscript') 28r.

19 Fernando Colón *Life of Columbus* 27.

20 Garcilaso de la Vega, el Inca, *Comentarios reales* 2.3.2.

IN QUEST OF SPICERY

1 Historians often describe Greek and Latin names for eastern products as borrowed from Sanskrit. This is usually a mistake. When Greeks and Romans were visiting India, Sanskrit was already a classical language: it was not current among traders. Often, in fact, the Sanskrit terms used in early Indian scientific books (like Sanskrit *śṛṅgavera*, 'ginger') were newly invented by learned writers on the basis of the everyday Pali or Prakrit forms.

Index

Page numbers in bold italics indicate principal references. An index of recipes follows the main index on page 183.

Illustration references

PRINTED BOOKS

Frontispiece: Prosperi Alpini *De rhapontico disputatio*. Patavii, 1612. BL (1185.k.31).

Colour plate IV*t*: Carel Allard, *Atlas maior*. 1710. BL (Maps C6c4).

Plates 1, 4, 7*t*, 7*b*, 8*t*, 8*b*, 9, 11*t*: François Valentyn, *Oud en nieuw Oost-Indien*. Dordrecht, Amsterdam, 1724. BL (455.g.3).

Plate 2*t*: Nicolás Monardes, *Dos libros*. Sevilla, 1569. BL (546.c.10).

Plates 2*b*, 3*tr*, 5*t*, 10*tl*, 10*tr*: Georgius Everhardus Rumphius, *Het Amboinsche kruid-boek*. Amsterdam, 1741–50. BL (39.h.1).

Plates 3*tl*, 19*tl*, 20*tl*, 20*tr*, 23*t*: Francisco Hernandez, *Rerum medicarum Novae Hispaniae thesaurus* ed. N. A. Recchi. Rome, 1648–51. BL (985.h.6).

Plate 3*bl*: Prosperi Alpini *De balsamo dialogus*. Venetiis, 1591. BL (546.g.2).

Plates 3*br*, 10*b*, 19*tr*, 19*b*, 20*bl*, 21: Caroli Clusii *Exoticorum libri decem*. [Leiden] 1605. BL (449.k.6 and 35.g.9.1).

Plates 6*t*, 12*t*, 12*b*, 13, 14, 15*t*: Engelbert Kaempfer, *Amoenitatum exoticarum politico-physicomedicarum fasciculi V*. Lemgoviae, 1712. BL (88.g.18).

Plates 18*b*, 20*br*: Nicolás Monardes, *Simplicium Medicamentorum...historia* tr. C. Clusius. Antverpiae, 1579. BL (988.f.2.4).

MANUSCRIPTS AND MUSEUM OBJECTS

Colour plate I*t*: Bodleian Library, Oxford, 'Codex Mendoza' (MS.Arch.Seld.A.1, f.61r).

Colour plate I*b*, plates 22, 23*b*: Pierpont Morgan Library, *Histoire naturelle des Indes* (MA3900, f.15; f.22r; f.28r), photos Art Resource, NY.

Colour plates II*t*, II*b*, plates 6*b*, 11*b*, 15*b*, 16*t*, 16*b*, 17*t*, 17*br*: BM (OA 1999.2-3.055, Maj. J. P. S. Pearson Bequest; OA F.746+; OA F.797+; OA 1999.2-3.017, Pearson Bequest; EA 37986; EA 18; GR Bronze 481; MLA 66,12-29,1; MLA 66,12-29,2).

Colour plate III*t*, plate 5*b*: Trustees of the Victoria & Albert Museum, London (IS.66-1949; M.148-1939).

Colour plates III*b*, IV*b*: Musée du Louvre, Paris (1215, photo © RMN-Jean Schormans; 26228, photo Bridgeman Art Library).

Plate 17*bl*: Worthing Museum and Art Gallery (3500).

Plates 18*t*, 24: BL (MS Add 24065, 1550; India Office Library and Records WD 2976).

t=top; *b*=below; *l*=left; *r*=right.

British Museum photographs (noted BM) © The British Museum; British Library photographs (BL) © and reproduced by permission of the British Library Board.